GERMAN/ENGLISH
BUSINESS GLOSSARY

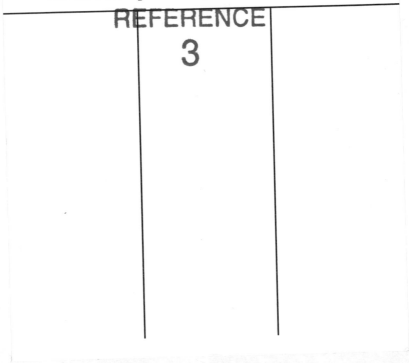

In the same series

GERMAN/ENGLISH
BUSINESS GLOSSARY

Paul Hartley
and
Gertrud Robins

London and New York

Paul Hartley is Dean of the School of International Studies and Law at Coventry University.

Gertrud Robins is Lecturer in German at the East Warwickshire College, Rugby.

First published 1997
by Routledge
11 New Fetter Lane, London EC4P 4EE

Simultaneously published in the USA and Canada
by Routledge
29 West 35th Street, New York, NY 10001

©1997 Paul Hartley and Gertrud Robins

Typeset in Rockwell and Univers by Routledge
Printed and bound in Great Britain by TJ International Ltd, Padstow, Cornwall

British Library Cataloguing in Publication Data
A catalogue record for this book is available from the British Library

Library of Congress Cataloguing in Publication Data
A catalogue record for this book is available from the Library of Congress

ISBN 0–415–16042–1

Business Glossary

Key to glossary

Grammatical abbreviations

abbr	abbreviation
adj	adjective
adv	adverb
conj	conjunction
det	determiner
n	noun
nf	feminine noun
nfpl	plural feminine noun
nm	masculine noun
nmpl	plural masculine noun
pp	past participle
pref	prefix
prep	preposition
vb	verb

Symbols

* denotes slang term
(US) term particular to USA
(GB) term particular to Great Britain

NB: Contexts are given in parentheses after term and part of speech or before multiple translations

Parts of speech are provided for all headwords and for translations where appropriate. Subterms are only supplied with parts of speech where it is considered necessary to indicate gender or to avoid ambiguity

German–English

abbauen *vb* (workforce) trim *vb*
Abdruck *nm* imprint **einen Abdruck machen** (credit card) take an imprint
abdrucken *vb* (credit card) take an imprint *vb*
abfahren *vb* leave *vb*
Abfallprodukte *nnpl* waste products *npl*
abfertigen *vb* clear sth through customs *vb*
Abfindung (-en) *nf* severance pay **großzügige Abfindung** golden parachute **hohe Abfindung** golden handshake
Abfindungszahlung (-en) *nf* severance pay *n*
Abflauen (-) *nn* abatement *n*
Abgabe (-n) *nf* toll *n*
abgabenfrei *adj* zero-rated
Abgabenordnung (-en) *nf* tax code *n*
abgemacht! *adj* it's a deal!
Abgeordnete/r *nmf* Member of parliment *n* **Abgeordnete/r des Europarlaments** Member of the European Parliament (MEP)
abhalten *vb* **eine Sitzung abhalten** hold a meeting
Abhebungen *nfpl* withdrawal of funds *n*
abhören *vb* listen to *vb* **ein Gespräch abhören** bug a call
Abkommen (-) *nn* formal agreement *n* **internationales Abkommen** international agreement *n*
Abkühlung *nf* cooling *n* **konjunkturelle Abkühlung** economic slowdown
abkürzen *vb* abbreviate *vb*
Abkürzung (-en) *nf* abbreviation *n*
Ablagesystem (-e) *nn* filing system *n*
Ablauf *nm* expiry *n*, expiration (US)
ablegen *vb* file *vb*
ablehnen *vb* (goods) reject *vb* (offer) turn down *vb* **einen Anspruch ablehnen** refuse a claim
Ablehnung (-en) *nf* refusal *n*
abonnieren *vb* subscribe *vb*
Abordnung (-en) *nf* secondment *n*
abrechnen *vb* (cheque) clear a cheque *vb*

Abrechnungszahlung (-en) *nf* clearing payment *n*
abreisen *vb* (hotel) check out *vb*
absagen *vb* (an appointment) cancel *vb*
Absatz *nm* sales *n* **den Absatz steigern** boost sales
Absatzgebiet (-e) *nn* market outlet *n*
Absatzprognose (-n) *nf* sales forecast *n*
Absatzquote (-n) *nf* sales quota *n*
Absatzschwankungen *nfpl* fluctuation in sales *n*
abschaffen *vb* abolish *vb*
Abschaffung *nf* abolition *n*
Abschätzung (-en) *nf* appraisal *n*
Abschied *nm* farewell *n*, parting *n* **von jemandem Abschied nehmen** take leave of sb
abschließen *vb* clinch *vb* **ein Geschäft abschließen** clinch/close a deal
Abschluß *nm* terminal *n*
Abschlußzahlung (-en) *nf* final settlement *n*
abschreiben *vb* (debts) write off *vb*
Abschreibung *nf* write-off *n*
Abschwung (-ünge) *nm* (economic) downturn *n*
absenden *vb* (goods) dispatch *vb*
Absender (-) *nm* consigner/or *n*, dispatcher *n*, sender *n*
absetzbar *adj* marketable *adj*
Absicherung *nf* **Absicherung von Risiken** risk management
absolut *adj* absolute *adj*
absorbieren *vb* absorb *vb*
Absprache (-n) *nf* working agreement *n*
absteigend *adj* downward *adj*
abstimmen *vb* vote *vb*
Abstimmung *nf* voting *n*
Abteilung (-en) *nf* department *n*
Abteilungsleiter (-) *nm* head of department *n*
abverkaufen *vb* sell off *vb*
abwägen *vb* weigh *vb*
Abwertung (-en) *nf* devaluation *n*
abwesend *adj* absent *adj*

Abwesenheit *nf* non-attendance *n* **häufige Abwesenheit** absenteeism *n*
abwiegen *vb* weigh *vb*
abziehbar *adj* deductible *adj*
abziehen *vb* deduct *vb*
Abzug (-üge) *nm* deduction *n*
Adresse(-n) *nf* address *nf* **Adresse unbekannt** zero address
Adressenkartei (-en) *nf* mailing list *n*
adressieren *vb* address *vb*
aggressiv *adj* high-powered *adj*
Agrar- *cpd* agrarian *adj*
Agrarerzeugnisse *nfpl* produce *n*
Agrargeschäft (-e) *nn* agribusiness *n*
Agrarsubventionen *nfpl* farming subsidies *npl*
Agronom (-e) *nm* agronomist *n*
Akkordarbeit *nf* contract labour *n*, piecework *n*
Akkreditiv (-e) *nn* letter of credit *n* **unwiderrufliches Akkreditiv** irrevocable letter of credit **widerrufliches Akkreditiv** revocable letter of credit
Akte (-n) *nf* file *n*
Aktenschrank (-änke) *nm* filing cabinet *n*
Aktie (-n) *nf* share *n* **Aktien und Obligationen** stocks and shares **Aktien im Publikumsbesitz** outstanding stock **börsennotierte Aktie** listed share, listed stock (US)
Aktienbezugsrecht (-e) *nn* share option *n*, stock option (US)
Aktienbörse (-n) *nf* stock market *n*
Aktienemission (-en) *nf* share issue *n*, stock issue (US)
Aktiengesellschaft (-en) *nf* joint stock company *n*, incorporated company (US)
Aktienhandel *nm* equity trading *n*
Aktienindex (-e) *nm* share index *n*
Aktienkaduzierung *nf* forfeit *n*
Aktienmakler (auf Provisionsbasis) (-) *nm* commission broker *n*
Aktienmarkt (-märkte) *nm* stock market *n*
Aktienrendite *nf* yield on shares *n*
Aktienzertifikat (-e) *nn* share certificate *n*, stock certificate (US)
Aktionär (-en) *nm* shareholder *n* **vorgeschobener Aktionär** nominee shareholder
Aktiva *npl* assets *n* **immaterielle Aktiva** intangible assets
Aktuar (-e) *nm* actuary *n*
aktuell *adj* up-to-date *adj*
Akzept *nn* acceptance *nm* **eingeschränktes Akzept** qualified acceptance
Akzeptbank (-en) *nf* acceptance house *n*

akzessorisch *adj* **akzessorische Sicherheit** collateral security
Alarmzeichen (-) *nn* warning sign *n*
allgemein *adj* general *adj* **allgemeine Personengesellschaft (-en)** general partnership **allgemeine Verwaltung** general management
Altersrente (-n) *nf* retirement pension *n*
Altmetall *nn* scrap metal *n*
Amortisation *nf* amortization *n*
Amortisationsfonds (-) *nm* redemption fund *n*
Amortisationsschuld (-en) *nf* redeemable bond *n*
amortisierbar *adj* redeemable *adj*
amortisieren *vb* amortize *vb*, redeem *vb*
Amortisierung *nf* redemption *n*
Amt *nn* office *n* **im Amt sein** hold office **Amt für Anlagen und Wertpapiere** SIB (Securities and Investment Board) (GB) *abbr*
amtierend *adj* office holder *n*
Amtsperiode (-n) *nf* tour of duty *n*
Amtsschimmel *nm* red tape *n*
Amtszeichen (-) *nn* (phone) dialling tone *n*, dial tone (US)
Amtszeit *nf* tenure *n*, term of office *n*
Analyse *nf* analysis **horizontale Analyse** horizontal analysis
analysieren *vb* analyze *vb*
Anbieter (-) *nm* offeror *n*
ändern *vb* amend *vb* (market) turn *vb*
Änderung (-en) *nf* amendment *n*
anerkennen *vb* validate *vb*
Anfangskapital *nn* initial capital *n*
Anfangslohn (-löhne) *nm* starting wage *n*
Anforderungen *nfpl* requirements *npl* **Ihren Anforderungen entsprechend** in accordance with your requirements
Anfrage (-n) *nf* enquiry *n*
Angabe (-en) *nf* specification *n*
angeben *vb* specify *vb*
Angebot (-e) *nn* bid *n*, tender *n* **ein Angebot einreichen** lodge a tender **endgültiges Angebot** final offer **Angebot gilt bis** offer valid until... **Angebot und Nachfrage** supply and demand **Angebot vorbehaltlich der Bestätigung** offer subject to confirmation **ein Angebot zurückziehen** withdraw an offer **festes Angebot** firm offer **höheres Angebot** higher bid **schriftliches Angebot** offer in writing **unverbindliches Angebot** tentative offer
Angebotspreis (-e) *nm* tender price *n*
Angebotsteller (-) *nm* tenderer *n*

angelernt *adj* semi-skilled *adj*
angemessen *adj* **angemessener Lohn** fair wage
angesammelt *adj* accumulated *adj*
angestellt *adj* **neu angestellt** *adj* newly-appointed *adj*
Angestellte/r *nmf* white-collar worker *n*
Angestellter sein be an employee **leitender Angestellter** executive
Ankaufskurs *nm* buying rate *n*
anklagen *vb* charge sb with sth *vb*
Ankündigung (-en) *nf* advance notice *n*
Ankurbelung *nf* boost *n*
Anlage (-n) *nf* enclosure *n*, facility *n* (machinery) plant *n*
Anlageberater (-) *nm* investment adviser *n*
Anlagenausschlachtung *nf* asset stripping *n*
Anlagenvermietung *nf* plant hire *n*
Anlagevermögen *nn* fixed capital *n*, fixed assets *npl*
anlegen *vb* (ship) dock *vb*
Anlegeplatz (-plätze) *nm* mooring *n*
Anlegerecht *nn* mooring rights *n*
Anleihe *nf* loan *n*, borrowing *n* **Anleihe ohne Zinseinschluß (-n)** flat bond **gesicherte Anleihe (-n)** debenture bond **zweckgebundene Anleihe (-n)** tied loan
Anleihegläubiger (-) *nm* bondholder *n*
Anleihekapital *nn* debenture capital *n*, debenture stock (US)
anmelden (sich) *vb* (register in an hotel) check in *vb*
Annahmeverweigerung *nf* non-acceptance *n*
annullieren *vb* cancel *vb*
Annullierung (-en) *nf* annulment *n*
anpassen *vb* adjust *vb* (adapt) tailor *vb*
Anpassung (-en) *nf* adjustment *n*
anrechenbar *adj* chargeable *adj*
Anreiz (-e) *nm* incentive *n*
Anruf (-e) *nm* telephone call *n*
Anrufbeantworter (-) *nm* Ansaphone (R) *n*, answering machine *n*
ansammeln *vb* accumulate *vb*
Anschlag (-äge) *nm* touch *n*
Anschläge *npl* **Anschläge pro Minute** wpm (words per minute)
Anschlüsse *nmpl* **Anschlüsse und unbewegliches Inventar** fixtures and fittings *npl*
Ansehen *nn* kudos *n*
Anspruch (-üche) *nm* claim *n* **Ansprüche geltend machen** put in a claim
Anstalt (-en) *nf* institution *n*

Anstieg (-e) *nm* (in earnings) rise *n*, raise (US) (in unemployment) rise *n*
anstreben *vb* tend toward *vb*
Anteil (-e) *nm* stake *n*
anteilig *adj* pro rata
Anteilseigner (-) *nm* stakeholder *n*, stockholder *n*
antiinflationär *adj* **antiinflationäre Maßnahmen** anti-inflationary measures
Antragsformular (-e) *nn* claim form *n*
Antragsteller (-) *nm* claimant *n*
Antwort (-en) *nf* answer *n*
antworten *vb* answer *vb*
Anwalt (-älte) *nm* solicitor *n*, lawyer (US)
Anweisung (-en) *nf* instruction *n* **Anweisungen befolgen** follow instructions
Anwendung *nf* use *n* **intensive Anwendung** intensive usage
Anwerbung *nf* employee recruitment *n*
Anzahlung *nf* down payment
anzapfen *vb* tap *vb*
Anzeige (-n) *nf* classified advertisement *n*
Apparat(-e) *nm* appliance *n*, telephone **am Apparat bleiben** (on telephone) hang on *vb*
Appell (-e) *nm* appeal *n*
Arbeit *nf* employment *n*, labour *n*, work *n*, workload *n* **Arbeit einstellen** (finish work) knock off* **Arbeit suchen** look for work **nach Stunden bezahlte Arbeit** hourly-paid work
arbeiten *vb* work *vb*
arbeitend *adj* **arbeitendes Unternehmen** going concern
Arbeiter (-) *nm* worker *n*, blue-collar worker *n* **manueller Arbeiter** manual worker **ungelernter Arbeiter** labourer
Arbeiterdirektor (-en) *nm* worker-director *n*
Arbeitgeber (-) *nm* employer *n*
Arbeitgeberverband (-ände) *nm* employers' federation *n*
Arbeitnehmer (-) *nm* employee *n*
Arbeitsamt (-ämter) *nn* Job centre *n*, Job shop *n*
Arbeitsanalyse (-n) *nf* Job analysis *n*
Arbeitsaufteilung *nf* division of labour *n*
Arbeitsbedingungen *nfpl* working conditions *npl*
Arbeitsbereich (-e) *nm* working area *n*
Arbeitsbeschaffung *nf* job creation *n*
Arbeitsbeziehungen *nfpl* labour relations *npl* **industrielle Arbeitsbeziehungen** industrial relations
Arbeitsfreude *nf* job satisfaction *n*

Arbeitsgemeinschaft (-en) *nf* workers' collective *n*, working party *n*
Arbeitsgenehmigung (-en) *nf* work permit *n*
Arbeitsgericht (-e) *nn* industrial tribunal *n*
Arbeitshygiene *nf* industrial health *n*
arbeitsintensiv *adj* labour-intensive *adj*
Arbeitskampf (-kämpfe) *nm* industrial action *n*, industrial dispute *n*, labour dispute *n*
Arbeitskollege (-) *nm* workmate *n*
Arbeitskosten *npl* labour costs *npl*
Arbeitskräfte *nfpl* human resources *npl*
arbeitslos *adj* jobless *adj*, redundant *adj*, unemployed *adj* **arbeitslos sein** be out of work
Arbeitslosen (die) *npl* the jobless *npl*
Arbeitslosengeld *nn* unemployment pay *n*
Arbeitslosenrate (-n) *nf* rate of unemployment *n*
Arbeitslosenunterstützung *nf* unemployment benefit *n*
Arbeitslosenversicherung *nf* unemployment insurance *n*
Arbeitslosenziffer (-n) *nf* level of unemployment *n*
Arbeitslosigkeit *nf* redundancy *n*, unemployment *n*
Arbeitsmarkt *nm* labour market *n*
Arbeitspapier (-e) *nn* working paper *n*
Arbeitsplan (-pläne) *nm* work schedule *n*
Arbeitsplatz (-plätze) *nm* workplace *n*
Arbeitsplatzverlust (-e) *nm* loss of job *n*
Arbeitsrecht (-e) *nn* employment law *n*, labour law *n*
Arbeitsstreitigkeit (-en) *nf* industrial dispute *n*
Arbeitstag (-e) *nm* working day *n*, workday (US)
Arbeitsteilung *nf* work sharing *n*
Arbeitsumwelt *nf* working environment *n*
Arbeitsunfall (-älle) *nm* industrial accident *n*
Arbeitsverhältnis (-isse) *nn* working relationship *n*
Arbeitsverhältnisse *nnpl* working conditions *npl*
Arbeitsvermittlung *nf* employment agency *n*
Arbeitsvertrag (-äge) *nm* employment contract *n*
Arbeitswoche (-n) *nf* working week *n*, workweek (US)
Arbeitswütige/r *nmf* workaholic *n*
Arbeitszeit (-en) *nf* working hours *npl* **festgesetzte Arbeitszeit** fixed hours

Arbeitszeugnis (-se) *nn* certificate of employment *n*
Arbitrage (-n) *nf* arbitrage *n*
Art *nf* (method) mode *n*
Artikel (-) *nm* item *n*
ärztlich *adj* medical *adj*
Aufenthaltserlaubnis (-isse) *nf* Green Card (US) *n*, residence permit *n*
Aufgabe (-n) *nf* task *n*
Aufgabenbereich *nm* terms of reference *n*
Aufgabenverteilung *nf* task management *n*
aufgeben *vb* abandon *vb* **ein Geschäft aufgeben** close a business **das Geschäft aufgeben** (informal) shut up shop
aufgelaufen *adj* **aufgelaufene Zinsen** accrued interest
aufgeschoben *adj* (tax) deferred *adj*
aufgliedern *vb* itemize *vb*
Aufgliederung *nf* breakdown *n* **Aufgliederung der Zahlen** (of figures) breakdown
aufhalten *vb* (delay) hold up *vb*
aufhängen *vb* (telephone) hang up *vb*
aufheben *vb* close *vb*, lift up *vb* **ein Embargo aufheben** lift an embargo **eine Sitzung aufheben** close a meeting **einen Vertrag aufheben** cancel a contract
Aufkauf (-käufe) *nm* buy-out *n*
aufkaufen *vb* buy out *vb*
auflegen *vb* (shares) float *vb*
auflösen *vb* break up *vb* **ein Konto auflösen** close an account
Auflösung (-en) *nf* breakup *n*
aufnahmefähiger Markt (Märkte) *nm* broad market *n*
aufschieben *vb* (postpone) defer *vb*, postpone *vb*
aufschreiben *vb* write down *vb*
Aufschub (-übe) *nm* deferment *n*
Aufschwung (-ünge) *nm* upswing *n*, upturn *n* **Aufschwung nehmen** boom
Aufseher (-) *nm* supervisor *n*
aufsichtsführend *adj* supervisory *adj*
Aufsichtsrat (-räte) *nm* factory board *n*, supervisory board *n*
Aufsichtsratsvorsitzende/r *nmf* (of company) president *n*
Auftrag (-äge) *nm* brief *n* **eiliger Auftrag** rush job *n*
Auftragnehmer (-) *nm* contractor *n*
Auftragsbuch (-bücher) *nn* order book *n*
aufwärts *adv* upwards *adv*
Aufwärts- *cpd* upward *adj*
Aufwärtsentwicklung *nf* upward trend *n*
Aufwendung *nf* expenditure *n*

Aufwendungen *nfpl* **betriebliche Aufwendungen** operating costs *npl*
aufwerten *vb* (currency) revalue *vb*
Aufwertung (-en) *nf* (of currency) revaluation *n*
Aufzeichnung *nf* record *n* **gemäß unseren Aufzeichnungen** according to our records
Auktionator (-en) *nm* auctioneer *n*
Ausbeute *nf* spoils *npl*
ausbilden *vb* (staff) train *vb*
Ausbildung *nf* training *n* **betriebliche Ausbildung** inhouse training
Ausbildungslehrgang (-gänge) *nm* training course *n*
Ausbildungszentrum (-en) *nn* training centre *n*
ausbreiten *vb* (payments) spread *vb*
ausdiskutieren *vb* (agreement, policy) thrash out *vb*
Außenbezirke *nmpl* outer suburbs *npl*
Außendienstleiter (-) *nm* field manager *n*
Außenhandel *nm* foreign trade *n*
Außenmarkt (-märkte) *nm* foreign market *n*
Außenstände *npl* outstanding debt *n*
außerordentlich *adj* extraordinary *adj* **außerordentliche Reservefonds** funds surplus **außerordentlicher Wert** extraordinary value **außerordentliche Versammlung** extraordinary meeting
ausführen *vb* carry out *vb*
Ausfuhrsteuer (-n) *nf* export tax *n*
Ausgaben *nfpl* expenditure *n*, spending *n*
Ausgaben reduzieren axe* expenditure
Ausgabenstruktur *nf* spending patterns *npl*
Ausgabesteuern *nfpl* expenditure taxes *n*
Ausgänge *nmpl* outgoings *npl*
ausgeben *vb* spend *vb*
ausgleichen *vb* equalize *vb*
ausländisch *adj* foreign *adj*
Auslands- *cpd* external *adj*
Auslandsabsatz *nm* export sales *n*
Auslandsbank (-en) *nf* foreign bank *n*
Auslandsgelder *nnpl* foreign currency holdings *npl*
Auslandshilfe *nf* foreign aid *n*
Auslandshilfsprogramm *nn* foreign aid programme *n*
Auslandsinvestitionen *nfpl* foreign investment *n*
Auslandskonkurrenz *nf* foreign competition *n*
Auslandskredit (-e) *nm* foreign loan *n*
Auslandsreise (-n) *nf* foreign travel *n*

Auslandsunternehmen (-) *nn* foreign company *n*
auslaufen *vb* expire *vb*
auspacken *vb* unpack *vb*
Ausprobieren *nn* trial and error *n*
ausreichen *vb* tide over *vb*
Ausrüstung *nf* (equipment) kit *n*
ausschließen *vb* exclude *vb*
Ausschlußklausel (-n) *nf* exclusion clause *n*
ausschreiben *vb* put something out for tender *vb* **einen Vertrag ausschreiben** tender for a contract
Ausschreibung *nf* tendering *n*
Ausschuß (-üsse) *nm* committee *n*
Ausschußsitzung (-en) *nf* committee meeting *n*
Aussichten (die) *nfpl* future prospects *npl*
Aussperrung (-en) *nf* (of strikers) lockout *n*
ausstatten *vb* equip *vb*
Ausstattung *nf* equipment *n*
ausstehend *adj* outstanding *adj*
ausstellen *vb* display *vb*, exhibit *vb* (cheque) draw *vb* (policy) issue *vb*
Ausstellung (-en) *nf* (of goods) display *n* show *n*, exhibition *n*
Ausstellungshalle (-n) *nf* exhibition hall *n*
Austauschrelationen *nfpl* terms of trade *npl*
Ausverkauf (-äufe) *nm* clearance sale *n*
ausverkauft *adj* out of stock *adj*
Auswanderung *nf* emigration *n*
ausweichen *vb* evade *vb*
Ausweichklausel (-n) *nf* escape clause *n*
Ausweis (-e) *nm* identity card *n*
Ausweitung *nf* expansion *n* **industrielle Ausweitung** industrial expansion
Auswirkung *nf* consequence *n*
Auswirkungen *nfpl* **die finanziellen Auswirkungen** financial effects
auszahlen *vb* disburse *vb*
Auszahlung *nf* net(t) proceeds *n*, payola (US)
Auszubildende/r *nmf* trainee *n*
Auszug (-üge) *nm* abstract *n*
autark *adj* self-sufficient *adj*
Autoindustrie (-n) *nf* automobile industry *n*, motor industry *n*
Automat (-en) *nm* vending machine *n*
automatisch *adj* automatic *adj*
Automatisierung *nf* automation *n*
autonom *adj* autonomous *adj*
Autoversicherung *nf* car insurance *n*
Bahn *nf* **per Bahn** by rail
Bahntransport *nm* rail transport *n*
Baissemarkt (-märkte) *nm* bear market *n*

Baissier (-s) *nm* (stock exchange) bear *n*
Balkendiagramm (-e) *nn* bar chart *n*
Bankangestellte/r *nmf* bank clerk *n*
Bankdarlehen (-) *nn* bank loan *n*
Bankdirektor (-en) *nm* bank manager *n*
Bankfeiertag (-e) *nm* bank holiday *n*
Bankgebühren *nfpl* bank charges *npl*
Bankguthaben (-) *nn* bank balance *n*
Bankier (-s) *nm* banker *n*
Bankkonto (-konten) *nn* bank account *n*
Bankkredit (-e) *nm* bank loan *n*
Bankkreise *nmpl* banking circles *n*
Banknetz (-e) *nn* banking network *n*
Banknote (-n) *nf* banknote *n*
bankrott *adj* bankrupt *adj* **bankrott sein** be bankrupt
Bankspesen *npl* bank charges *npl*
Banküberweisung (-en) *nf* bank transfer *n*
Bankwechsel (-) *nm* bank draft *n*
bar *adj* cash *adj* **bar zahlen** pay in cash
Barangebot (-e) *nn* cash offer *n*
Bargeld *nn* cash *n*, hard cash *n*
Barrabatt *nm* cash discount *n*
Barrengold *nn* gold bullion *n*
Barriere (-n) *nf* barrier *n*
Barscheck (-s) *nm* open cheque *n*
Barzahlung (-en) *nf* cash payment *n* **Barzahlung bei Erhalt der Ware** cash on receipt of goods **Barzahlung vor Lieferung** cash before delivery **Barzahlung bei Lieferung** cash on delivery (COD)
Basiseinkommen *nn* basic income *n*
Basiszins (-en) *nm* base rate *n*
Baufirma (-firmen) *nf* building firm *n*
Baugenehmigung (-en) *nf* building permit *n*
Bauindustrie *nf* building industry/trade *n*, construction industry *n*
Baumaterial *nn* building materials *npl*
Bausparkasse (-n) *nf* building society *n*
Baustelle (-n) *nf* building site *n*
Bauträger (-) *nm* property developer *n*
Bauunternehmer (-) *nm* builder *n*, building contractor *n*
beachtenswert *adj* noteworthy *adj*
Beamte/r *nmf* official *n*
beanspruchen *vb* (demand) claim *vb*
beanstanden *vb* complain about sth *vb*
beantworten *vb* answer *vb*
bearbeiten *vb* machine *vb*, process *vb*
beauftragen *vb* brief *vb*
Bedarf *nm* requirement *n*
Bedarfserfassung *nf* needs assessment *n*
Bedienung *nf* service *n* **inklusive Bedienung** service included

Bedienungsanleitung (-en) *nf* instruction book *n*, instruction sheet *n*
Bedingungen *nfpl* terms and conditions *npl* **günstige Bedingungen** favourable terms
bedingungslos *adj* unconditional *adj*
Bedürfnis *nn* need *n*
Bedürfnishierarchie (-n) *nf* hierarchy of needs *n*
Bedürfnisse *nnpl* **industrielle Bedürfnisse** needs of industry
beeinflußt *adj* weighted *adj*
beendigen *vb* wind up *vb*
Beendigung (-en) *nf* termination *n* **Beendigung des Dienstverhältnisses** termination of employment
befördern *vb* forward *vb*, upgrade *vb* (person) promote *vb*
Beförderung *nf* (road) haulage *n*, freight (US) (of person) promotion *n*
Befrachter (-) *nm* freighter *n*
befreit von *adj* exempt *adj*
Befreiung *nf* exemption *n*
befürworten *vb* advocate *vb*
begebbar *adj* negotiable *adj*
Beginn *nm* start-up *n*
beglaubigen *vb* witness a signature *vb*
begleichen *vb* settle a claim *n* **eine Rechnung begleichen** pay an invoice
begrenzt *adj* limited *adj* **begrenzter Markt (-märkte)** narrow market
behalten *vb* retain *vb*
Behälter (-) *nm* container *n*
Behörde (-n) *nf* (official) authority *n*
Beibehaltung *nf* retention *n*
beilegen *vb* enclose *vb* (dispute) settle *vb*
Beirat (-äte) *nm* advisory committee *n*
beitragen *vb* contribute *vb*
beitragsfrei *adj* non-contributory *adj* **beitragsfreies Programm** non-contributory scheme
bekannt *adj* well-known *adj*
bekanntgeben *vb* announce *vb* **etwas bekanntgeben** give notice of sth
bekommen *vb* obtain *vb*
belasten *vb* (account) debit *vb* **ein Konto mit etwas belasten** charge sth to an account
Belastung *nf* (of tax) imposition *n* load *n*
Belastungsanzeige (-n) *nf* debit note *n*
Belastungssaldo (-en) *nm* debit balance *n*
belegen *vb* etwas mit einem Embargo **belegen** impose an embargo
Belegschaft *nf* staff *n*, workforce *n*
Bemerkung (-en) *nf* comment *n*

Bemessungsgrundlage (-n) *nf* basis of assessment *n*
benachrichtigen *vb* notify *vb*
Benachrichtigung *nf* notification *n*
benützen *vb* use *vb*
benutzerfreundlich *adj* user-friendly *adj*
beobachten *vb* watch *vb*
Beobachtung *nf* **unter Beobachtung** under observation
beraten *vb* advise *vb*, consult *vb*
beratend *adj* advisory *adj*
Berater (-) *nm* adviser/advisor *n*, consultant *n*
Beratung *nf* consultancy firm *n*, consulting firm (US)
Beratungs- *cpd* advisory *adj*
Beratungsgebühren *nfpl* consultancy fees *npl*, consulting fees (US)
Beratungstätigkeit *nf* consultancy work *n*, consulting work (US)
berechnen *vb* calculate *vb*, charge for sth *vb* **eine Gebühr berechnen** charge a fee
Berechnung (-en) *nf* calculation *n*
Berechtigung (-en) *nf* warranty *n*
Bergbau *nm* mining *n*, mining industry *n*
Bergungsplan (-pläne) *nm* recovery scheme *n*
Bericht (-e) *nm* report *n*
Berichterstattung *nf* reporting *n* **aktuelle Berichterstattung** news coverage
berichtigen *vb* **die Zahlen berichtigen** adjust the figures
Beruf (-e) *nm* occupation *n*, profession *n* **von Beruf** by trade **die gehobenen Berufe** the professions
Berufs- *cpd* vocational *adj*
Berufsberatung *nf* careers advice *n*
Berufserfahrung *nf* employment/work history *n* work experience *n*
Berufskrankheit (-en) *nf* occupational disease *n*
Berufsleben *nn* working life *n*
Berufsrisiko (-iken) *nn* occupational hazard *n*
berufstätig *adj* working *adj*
berufstätig sein *vb* be in work *vb*
Berufsverband (-bände) *nm* functional organization *n*
Berufsvergehen (-) *nn* malpractice *n* (management) misconduct *n*
beschädigen *vb* damage *vb*
Beschaffung *nf* sourcing *n*
beschäftigen *vb* employ *vb*
beschäftigt *adj* busy *adj*

Beschäftigtenstand *nm* level of employment *n*
Bescheid *nm* information *n* **rechtzeitiger Bescheid** due warning *n*
bescheinigen *vb* certificate *vb*, certify *vb*
Bescheinigung (-en) *nf* attestation *n*, certificate *n*
Beschlagnahme *nf* appropriation *n*
beschlagnahmen *vb* impound *vb*
beschleunigen *vb* accelerate *vb*, expedite *vb*
Beschleunigung *nf* acceleration *n*
beschließen *vb* resolve to do sth *vb*
Beschluß (-üsse) *nm* (decision) resolution *n* **einen Beschluß fassen** make a resolution *vb*
beschlußfähig *adj* (meeting) quorate *adj*
beschränken *vb* restrict *vb*
beschränkend *adj* restrictive *adj*
beschränkt *adj* **beschränkte Haftung** limited liability
Beschränkung (-en) *nf* restriction *n* **Beschränkungen auferlegen** impose restrictions
Beschwerde *nf* complaint *n* **Beschwerde einlegen** make a complaint
Beschwerdeabteilung (-en) *nf* complaints department *n*
Beschwerdepunkt (-e) *nm* grievance *n*
beschweren *vb* complain *vb* **sich beschweren über** complain about sth
Besetztton (-töne) *nm* busy signal (US) *n*
besichtigen *vb* inspect *vb*
Besitz *nm* property *n*
besitzen *vb* own *vb*
Besitzer (-) *nm* owner *n* **Besitzer im eigenen Haus** owner-occupier
Bestand (-ände) *nm* supply *n*
Bestandskontrolle *nf* inventory control *n*
bestätigen *vb* warrant *vb* **den Empfang bestätigen** confirm receipt of sth
Bestätigung (-en) *nf* attestation *n*, confirmation *n*
bestechen *vb* bribe *vb*
Bestechung *nf* bribery *n*
Bestechungsgeld (-er) *nn* bribe *n*
bestehen auf *vb* insist on *vb*
Bestellformular (-e) *nn* order form *n*
Bestellnummer (-n) *nf* order number *n*
Bestellung (-en) *nf* order *nf* **eine Bestellung erteilen** place an order
Besteuerung *nf* taxation *n*
Bestseller (-) *nm* best seller *n*
Besuch (-e) *nm* visit *n*
besuchen *vb* visit *vb*
Besucher (-) *nm* visitor *n*

Beteiligung (-en) *nf* holding *n* **eine Beteiligung besitzen** have holdings **finanzielle Beteiligung** vested interests
Betracht *nm* **etwas in Betracht ziehen** take sth into account
betrachten *vb* look at *vb*, view *vb*
Betrag (-äge) *nm* amount *n* **ausstehender Betrag** outstanding amount
betragen *vb* amount to *vb*
Betreff *nm* re *prep*
betreffen *vb* (be of importance to) concern *vb*
betreiben *vb* (manage) run *vb* **ein Hotelgeschäft betreiben** run an hotel
Betreiber (-) *nm* operator *n*
Betrieb (-e) *nm* company *n*, works *n* (of business) operation *n*, running *n* **außer Betrieb** out of action **gewerkschaftspflichtiger Betrieb** closed shop **verstaatlichter Betrieb** state-owned enterprise
Betriebsausschuß (-üsse) *nm* works committee *n*
Betriebsausgaben *nfpl* operating expenditure *n*
Betriebsbilanz (-en) *nf* operating statement *n*
Betriebseinkommen *nn* operating income *n*
Betriebsergebnis *nn* operating profit *n*
Betriebskapital *nn* trading capital *n*, working capital *n*
Betriebskosten *npl* running cost *n*, operating expenses *npl*
Betriebsleiter (-) *nm* plant manager *n*
Betriebsplan (-pläne) *nm* **dreischichtiger Betriebsplan** the three-shift system
Betriebsrat (-räte) *nm* works council *n*
Betriebsschluß *nm* closure of business hours *n* **nach Betriebsschluß** after hours
Betriebsstillegung (-en) *nf* closure of a company *n*
Betriebsverlust (-e) *nm* trading loss *n*
Betriebswirtschaftslehre *nf* business studies *n*
betroffen *adj* affected *adj* **schwer betroffen** hard-hit **von etwas schwer betroffen sein** be hard hit by sth
Betrug *nm* fraud *n*
betrügen *vb* defraud *vb*
betrügerisch *adj* fraudulent *adj*
beurlauben *vb* give/grant leave *vb* **sich beurlauben lassen** take leave
Beurlaubung *nf* leave of absence *n*
Bevölkerung *nf* population *n* **arbeitende Bevölkerung** working population *n*
bewährt *adj* well-tried *adj*

Bewährung *nf* field test *n*
bewerben *vb* **sich bewerben um** apply for
Bewerber (-en) *nm* (for job) candidate *n*
Bewerbungsformular (-e) *nn* application form *n*
Bewerbungsschreiben (-) *nn* letter of application *n*
Bewertungsdurchschnitt (-e) *nm* weighted average *n*
Bewertungsindex (-en) *nm* weighted index *n*
bewirten *vb* entertain a client *vb*
bewohnen *vb* (premises) occupy *vb*
Bewohner (-) *nm* occupant *n*
bezahlt *adj* paid *adj*
bezeugen *vb* witness *vb*
Beziehungen *nfpl* relations *npl* **Beziehungen zwischen Arbeitgebern und Gewerkschaften** industrial relations
Bezug *nm* **mit Bezug auf** with reference to
bezüglich *prep* regarding *prep*
Bezugsrechtsangebot (-e) *nn* rights issue *n*
bieten *vb* (auction) bid *vb*
Bilanz *nf* (financial) balance *n* balance sheet *n*
Bilanzbuchhalter (-) *nm* chartered accountant *n*
billigen *vb* approve *vb*
Billigung *nf* approval *n*
Binnenmarkt (-märkte) *nm* home market *n*, domestic market *n*
Bitte (-n) *nf* appeal *n*, request *n*
bitten *vb* appeal *vb*, request *vb*
Blankokredit *nm* open credit *n*, unlimited credit *n*
Blankoscheck (-s) *nm* blank cheque *n*
Block (-öcke) *nm* block *n*
Blockade (-n) *nf* blockade *n*
blockieren *vb* blockade *vb*
Bodenrechtsreform (-en) *nf* land reform *n*
Bodenschätze *nmpl* natural resources *npl*
Bond-Zertifikat (-e) *nn* bond certificate *n*
Bondmarkt (-märkte) *nm* bond market *n*
Bonität *nf* credit rating *n*
Börse (-n) *nf* stock exchange *n*
Börsenaufsichtsrat *nm* SEC (Securities and Exchange Commission) (GB) *abbr*
Börsenmakler (-) *nm* floor broker *n*, stockbroker *n*
börsennotiert *npl* **börsennotierte Aktien** quoted shares, quoted stocks (US) **börsennotiertes Unternehmen (-)** quoted company **börsennotierte Wertpapiere** quoted investment
Börsentip (-s) *nm* market tip *n*

Bote (-n) *nm* messenger *n*
Botschaft (-en) *nf* embassy *n*
Boykott (-s) *nm* boycott *n*
boykottieren *vb* boycott *vb*
Branchengeheimnis (-isse) *nn* trade
secret *n*
Branchenverzeichnis (-isse) *nn* the Yellow
pages (R) (GB) *npl*
Brandversicherung *nf* fire insurance *n*
Brauch *nm* usage *n*
brauchen (dringend) *vb* be in (urgent)
need *vb*
brechen *vb* break *vb* einen Vertrag bre-
chen break an agreement
breit *adj* wide-ranging *adj*
Briefkopf (-köpfe) *nm* letterhead *n*
Briefwechsel *nm* correspondence *n*
bringen *vb* yield *vb* auf den Markt bringen
(product) bring out
britisch *adj* British *adj*
Broker (-) *nm* broker *n*
Bruch- *cpd* fractional *adj*
Bruchteil (-e) *nm* fraction *n*
brutto *adj* gross *adj*
Bruttoeinkommen *nn* gross income *n*
Bruttogewicht *nn* gross weight *n*
Bruttoinlandsprodukt *nn* GDP (Gross
Domestic Product) *abbr*
Bruttoinvestition *nf* gross investment *n*
Bruttoproduktion *nf* gross output *n*
Bruttosozialprodukt *nn* GNP (Gross Na-
tional Product) *abbr.*
Bruttospanne (-n) *nf* gross margin *n*
Bruttosumme *nf* gross amount *n*
Bruttotonnage *nf* gross tonnage *n*
Bruttoumsatz *nm* gross sales *n*
Bruttoverlust (-e) *nm* gross loss *n*
Bruttozins *nm* gross interest *n*
buchen *vb* book *vb*, reserve *vb* einen Flug
buchen book a flight im voraus buchen
book in advance
Bücher *nnpl* die Bücher the books *n* die
Bücher führen keep the books
Buchführung *nf* accountancy *n*
Buchgewinn *nm* book profit *n*
Buchhalter (-) *nm* accountant *n*, book-
keeper *n*
Buchhaltung *nf* book-keeping *n*, general
accounting *n* die doppelte Buchhaltung
(bookkeeping) double-entry
Buchhaltungsnormen *nfpl* accounting
conventions *n*
Buchhändler *nm* bookseller *n*
Buchhandlung (-en) *nf* bookshop *n*,
bookstore (US)
Buchprüfer (-) *nm* auditor *n*

Buchprüfung (-en) *nf* audit *n*, external
audit *n*
Buchwert (-e) *nm* book value *n*
Budget (-s) *nn* budget *n* im Budget
einplanen budget for
Budgetabweichung (-en) *nf* variance *n*
Bulletin (-s) *nn* news bulletin *n*
Bummelstreik (-s) *nm* (strike) go-slow *n*
Bund (Bünde) *nm* federation *n*
Bündel (-e) *nn* bundle *n*
bündeln *vb* bundle up *vb*
Bundes- *cpd* federal *adj*
Bundestagsabgeordnete/r *nmf* Member
of Parliament (MP) (in Germany)
Bundestagswahl (-en) *nf* general election
(in Germany) *n*
Büro (-s) *nn* office *n*
Büroangestellte/r *nmf* office clerk *n*
Büroarbeit *nf* clerical work *n*
Büroeinrichtung (-en) *nf* office
equipment *n*
Bürogebäude *nn* office premises *npl*
Bürokraft (-kräfte) *nf* clerical worker *n*
Bürokrat (-en) *nm* bureaucrat *n*
Bürokratie *nf* bureaucracy *n*
bürokratisch *adj* bureaucratic *adj*
Büropersonal *nn* office staff *n*
Bürotätigkeit *nf* office work *n*
Büroverwaltung *nf* office management *n*
Busbahnhof (-höfe) *nm* bus station *n*
Cashflow *nm* cash flow *n*
Charter (-s) *nm* charter *n*
Charterflug (-üge) *nm* charter flight *n*
Chef (-s) *nm* boss *n*
Chefbuchhalter (-) *nm* head accountant *n*
Chemieindustrie (-n) *nf* chemical
industry *n*
Chemieprodukt (-e) *nn* chemical product *n*
Clearingbank (-en) *nf* clearing bank *n*
Clearingstelle (-n) *nf* clearing house *n*
Computer (-) *nm* computer *n*
Computergrafik *nf* computer graphics *n*
Computerhardware *nf* computer
hardware *n*
Computernetz (-e) *nn* computer network *n*
Computerprogramm (-) *nn* computer
program *n*
Computersprache (-n) *nf* computer
language *n*
Computerterminal (-s) *nn* computer
terminal *n*
Container (-e) *nm* container *n*
Containerlager (-) *nn* container terminal *n*
Containerschiff (-e) *nn* container ship *n*
Dachsorganisation *nf* parent
organisation *n*

Dachorganisation der britischen Ge-werkschaften Trades Union Congress
Dankadresse (-n) *nf* vote of thanks *n*
Darlehen (-) *nn* loan *n* **hartes Darlehen (-)** hard loan
Datei (-en) *nf* computer file *n*
Daten *nnpl* data *npl*
Datenbank (-en) *nf* data bank *n*, database *n*
Datenerfassung *nf* data capture *n*
Datenfernübertragung *nf* teleprocessing *n*
Datenhierarchie *nf* data hierarchy *n*
Datenspeicherung *nf* information storage *n*
Datenverarbeitung *nf* data handling *n*
Datum (-en) *nn* date *n*
Datumsgrenze (-n) *nf* International Date Line *n*
Dauerauftrag (-äge) *nm* standing order *n*
Dauerbenutzer (-) *nm* heavy user *n*
Dauerbeschäftigung *nf* permanent employment *n*
Debit *nn* debit *n*
Deckungsbestätigung (-en) *nf* cover note *n*
Deckungszusage *nf* cover note *n*
Defekt (-e) *nm* fault *n*, defect *n* **schwerer Defekt (-e)** serious fault
Defizit (-e) *nn* budgetary deficit *n*, deficit *n*
Defizitwirtschaft *nf* deficit financing *n*
Deflation *nf* deflation *n*
deflationär *adj* deflationary *adj*
degradieren *vb* (employee) demote *vb*
deklarieren *vb* declare *vb* **nicht deklariert** (goods) undeclared
Delegation *nf* delegation *n*
delegieren *vb* delegate *vb*
Delegierte/r *nmf* delegate *n*
Demographie *nf* demography *n*
Design (-s) *nn* design *n*
Designer (-) *nm* (commercial) designer *n*
deutsch *adj* German *adj* **deutsche Mark** Deutschmark *n*
Devisen *nfpl* foreign exchange *n*
Devisenbeschränkungen *nfpl* exchange restrictions *npl*
Devisenbestände *nmpl* foreign exchange holdings *npl*
Devisenhandel *nm* foreign exchange dealings *npl*, foreign exchange trading (US)
Devisenhändler (-) *nm* foreign exchange dealer *n*
Devisenkontrolle *nf* exchange control *n*
Devisenmakler (-) *nm* exchange broker *n*

Devisenmarkt (-märkte) *nm* exchange market *n*, foreign exchange market *n*
Devisenverrechnungsabkommen *nn* exchange clearing agreement *n*
Diebstahl *nm* pilferage *n*
Dienst *nm* service *n* **Dienst nach Vorschrift machen** work to rule **öffentlicher Dienst** civil service
Dienstleistung *nf* service *n*
Dienstleistungsbereich (-e) *nm* tertiary sector *n*
Dienstleistungsindustrie *nf* tertiary industry *n*, service industry *n*
digital *adj* digital *adj*
direkt *adj* direct *adj* **direkte Steuer (-n)** direct tax *n*
Direktor (-en) *nm* director *n*
Direktorium (-ien) *nn* board of directors *n*
Diskette (-n) *nf* disk *n*, floppy disk *n*, magnetic disk *n*
Diskettenlaufwerk (-e) *nn* disk drive *n*
diskontieren *vb* discount *vb*
diskontiert *adj* **diskontierter Einnahmeüberschuß** discounted cash flow (DCF)
Diskontsatz (-sätze) *nm* bank rate *n*, discount rate *n*
Diversifikation *nf* diversification *n*
diversifizieren *vb* diversify *vb*
Dividende (-n) *nf* dividend *n*
Dividendenerträge *nmpl* income from dividends *n* **Dividenderträge nach Steuern** franked income
docken *vb* (ship) dock *vb*
Dokument (-e) *nn* document *n*
Dokumentenauffindung *nf* document retrieval *n*
Dollar *nm* buck* (US) *n*
Draht *nm* wire *n* **der heiße Draht** hot line
drei *adj* three *adj*
dreifach *adj* triple *adj* **dreifache Ausführung** triplicate *n*
dreißig *adj* thirty *adj* **Dreißig-Aktien-Index** Thirty-Share Index (GB) *n*
Dreiteilung (-en) *nf* three-way split *n*
dringend *adj* urgent *adj* **dringende Angelegenheit (-en)** a matter of urgency
dringlich *adv* urgently *adv*
Dringlichkeit *nf* urgency *n* **höchste Dringlichkeit** top priority
Dritte/r *nmf* third person *n*
dritte/r *adj* third *adj* **dritte Person** third party **Dritte Welt** the Third World
Drückeberger (-) *nm* shirker* *n*
drücken *vb* (spending) squeeze *vb*
Dumping *nn* dumping *n*

dunkel adj (dealings) shady* adj
durchbrechen vb make a breakthrough vb
Durchbruch (-brüche) nm breakthrough n
durchführbar adj feasible adj, workable adj
Durchführbarkeit nf feasibility n
Durchführbarkeitsstudie (-n) nf feasibility study n
durchführen vb enforce vb **einen Lohnstopp durchführen** (prices, wages) freeze
Durchreise nf transit n
Durchreisende/r nmf (transport) transit passenger n
Durchschnitt nm general average n (average) mean n
durchschnittlich adj (average) mean adj
Durchschnittskosten npl average costs
Durchschnittskosten pro Einheit average unit costs
Durchschnittslohn (-löhne) nm average wage n
durchsetzen vb (policy) enforce vb
Durchschnitt (-e) nm average n
Dynamik nf dynamics npl
dynamisch adj dynamic adj
echt adj bona fide, genuine adj
Echtzeit nf real time n
Eckzins nm basic rate n **Eckzins für Ausleihungen** minimum lending rate **Eckzins der Clearing-Banken für Ausleihungen** base lending rate
ECU (-s) nm ECU (European Currency Unit) abbr
Edelmetallbarren nm bullion n
Effektenportefeuille (-s) nn investment portfolio n
effektiv adj actual adj **effektiver Preis** real price
Effektivlohn (-löhne) nm real wages npl
EG nf European Community (EC) n
EG-Kommission nf European Commission n
ehrenamtlich adj honorary adj
Ehrenkodex (-e) nm professional code of practice n
Eigenfinanzierung nf equity financing n, self-financing n
Eigengewicht nn dead weight n
Eigenheimerwerber (-) nm home buyer n
Eigenkapital nn equity capital n
Eigenkapitalrendite nf return on equity n
Eigenmittel nnpl capital funds n
Eigenschaft nf quality n **in meiner Eigenschaft als** in my capacity as chairman
Eigentum nn ownership n
Eigentumsschaden nm damage to property n

Eigentumsurkunde (-n) nf certificate of ownership n, title deed n
Eigentumsvorbehalt nm retention of title n
Eilauftrag (äge) nm rush order n
Eildienst nm express service n
Eiltransporter nm express carrier n
Eilzustellung (-en) nf express delivery n
einberufen vb summon vb, call vb **eine Sitzung einberufen** call a meeting
einbringen vb net(t) vb (motion, paper) table vb
einchecken vb (at airport) check in vb
einfach adj single adj **einfache Fahrkarte** (rail/flight) single/one-way ticket n
Einfuhr nf imports npl
Einfuhrbeschränkungen nfpl import restrictions n
einführen vb (product) launch vb **ein Gesetz einführen** introduce legislation
Einfuhrlizenz (-en) nf import licence n
Einfuhrquote (-n) nf import quota n
Einfuhrüberschuß (-üsse) nm import surplus n
Einführungszeit (-en) nf lead time
Einfuhrzoll nm import duty n
eingebaut adj built-in adj
eingeben vb key in vb
eingefroren adj frozen adj **eingefrorene Guthaben** frozen assets **eingefrorener Kredit** frozen credits
eingeschrieben adj registered adj **eingeschriebener Brief** registered letter
eingetragen adj registered adj **eingetragene Anschrift (-en)** registered address **eingetragene Firma (-en)** registered company **eingetragenes Warenzeichen (-)** registered trademark
einhalten vb keep vb **die Regeln einhalten** observe the rules
Einheit (-en) nf unit n
Einheitstarif (-e) nm flat rate n, flat-rate tariff n
Einkauf nm shopping n
einkaufen vb buy vb **in Mengen einkaufen** buy in bulk
Einkaufszentrum (-en) nn shopping mall n, shopping centre n
Einkommen nn income n **einheitlicher Einkommensteuersatz** flat-rate income tax **Einkommen erwirtschaften** generate income
Einkommenselastizität nf income elasticity n
Einkommenserwirtschaften nn generation of income n

Einkommensteuer (-n) *nf* income tax *n*
Einkommensverlust *nm* loss of earnings *n*
Einkommenszufluß *nm* flow of income *n*
Einkünfte *npl* takings *npl* **Einkünfte aus Kapitalvermögen** unearned income
einladen *vb* invite *vb*
Einladung (-en) *nf* invitation *n*
Einlage (-n) *nf* deposit *n* **langfristige Einlage** long deposit
Einlagenkonto (-konten) *nn* deposit account *n*
einlösen *vb* cash *vb*, redeem *vb* **einen Scheck einlösen** cash a cheque
Einlösung *nf* encashment *n*
Einnahmen *nfpl* revenue *n*
Einnahmeunterdeckung *nf* negative cash flow *n*
Einreisevisum (-a) *nn* entry visa *n*
einrichten *vb* (company) set up *vb*
Einrichtungen *nfpl* amenities *npl*
Einsatzbesprechung (-en) *nf* briefing *n*
einschalten *vb* (machine) turn on *vb*
einschätzen *vb* assess *vb*
Einschätzung (-en) *nf* assessment *n*
einschlagen *vb* hit the market *vb*
Einschränkung *nf* limiting factor *n*
Einschreibpost *nf* registered mail *n*
einseitig *adj* one-sided *adj* **einseitig bindend** (contract) unilateral
Einsparungen *nfpl* savings *npl*
Einspruch (-sprüche) *nm* veto *n*
Einstandsgeld *nn* golden hello *n*
einstellen *vb* appoint sb to a position *vb*, recruit *vb*
Einstellung (-en) *nf* (to a position) appointment recruitment *n*
Einstellungskampagne (-n) *nf* recruitment campaign *n*
einstimmig *adj* unanimous *adj*
Eintragung (-en) *nf* entry *n* **letzte Eintragung** final entry
Eintritt *nm* entry *n* **Eintritt frei** free entry
einverstanden *adj* agreed *adj*
Einverständnis *nn* consent *n* **in gegenseitigem Einverständnis** by mutual agreement
Einwand (-wände) *nm* objection *n* **Einwände erheben gegen** make/raise an objection
Einweg- *cpd* non-returnable *adj*
einwerfen *vb* post *vb*
einzahlen *vb* deposit *vb*
Einzahlung (-en) *nf* deposit *n*
Einzelhandel *nm* retail trade *n* **im Einzelhandel verkaufen** sell sth retail

Einzelhandelsgeschäft (-e) *nn* retail outlet *n*
Einzelhandelskette (-n) *nf* retail chain *n*
Einzelhandelsmarkt *nm* retail market *n*
Einzelverkaufssteuer *nf* retail sales tax *n*
einziehen *vb* collect *vb* **eine Schuld einziehen** collect a debt *vb*
Einziehung *nf* collection *n* (of debt) recovery *n*
Einzugsermächtigung *nf* direct debiting *n*
Eisenbahn (-en) *nf* railway *n*, railroad (US)
Elastizität *nf* elasticity *n*
elektronisch *adj* electronic *adj* **elektronische Abwicklung von Bankgeschäften** electronic banking **elektronische Datenverarbeitung** electronic data processing **elektronische Post** email
Elektrotechnik *nf* electrical engineering *n*
Embargo (-s) *nn* embargo *n*
Empfang *nm* receipt *n* **den Empfang bestätigen** acknowledge receipt
Empfänger (-) *nm* addressee *n*, consignee *n*, recipient *n*, sendee *n*
Empfänger eines Angebots offeree
empfehlen *vb* recommend *vb*
Empfehlung (-en) *nf* recommendation *n*, reference *n*
Empfehlungsschreiben (-) *nn* letter of introduction *n*
en gros at/by wholesale
End- *cpd* terminal *adj*
Endabnehmer (-) *nm* end user *n*
Endabrechnung *nf* final accounts *n*
Endergebnis (-isse) *nn* net(t) result *n*
Enderzeugnisse *nfpl* final products *npl*
Endprämie *nf* terminal bonus *n*
Endverbraucher (-) *nm* end consumer *n*
eng *adj* tight *adj*
englisch *adj* English *adj* **englisches Pfund** sterling
Engpaß (-pässe) *nm* bottleneck *n*
Engpaßinflation *nf* bottleneck inflation *n*
enteignen *vb* expropriate *vb*
Enteignung *nf* expropriation *n*
Enteignungsausschuß (-üsse) *nm* land tribunal *n*
entladen *vb* unload *vb*
entlassen *vb* (employee) dismiss *vb* fire* *vb*, make sb redundant *vb*, sack *vb* (workers) lay off *vb*
Entlassung (-en) *nf* dismissal *n* **unberechtigte Entlassung** wrongful dismissal
entnationalisieren *vb* denationalize *vb*
entschädigen *vb* compensate for *vb*, indemnify *vb*
Entschädigung *nf* compensation *n*,

recompense *n* **Entschädigung verlangen** claim compensation **Entschädigung zahlen** pay compensation
entsprechend *adj* relevant *adj*
entwerfen *vb* (plans) draw up *vb* draw up *vb* **einen Vertrag entwerfen** draw up a contract
Entwicklungsland (-änder) *nn* developing country *n*, third-world country *n*, under-developed country *n*
Erbe (-n) *nn* inheritance *n*
erben *vb* inherit *vb*
Erbschaft (-en) *nf* legacy *n*
Erbschaftsgesetze *nnpl* inheritance laws *npl*
Erdgas *nn* natural gas *n*
Erdölindustrie *nf* oil industry *n*
erfahren 1. *adj* experienced *adj* 2. *vb* experience *vb*
erforderlich *adj* necessary *adj*
erfüllen *vb* comply with *vb* **die Bedingungen erfüllen** comply with legislation
ergänzend *adj* supplementary *adj*
Ergebnis (-sse) *nn* outcome *n*
Ergonomie *nf* ergonomics *n*
ergreifen *vb* grasp *vb*, seize *vb* **die Gelegenheit ergreifen** seize an opportunity
erhalten *vb* receive *vb*
erheben *vb* (tax) levy *vb*
erhöhen *vb* (value) enhance *vb* (prices, taxes) increase *vb* mark up *vb* (price, interest rate) raise *vb* (capital, loan) raise *vb* **Preise erhöhen** (prices) bump up *vb*
Erhöhung (-en) *nf* (prices) escalation *n* markup *n* **Erhöhung der Lebenshaltungskosten** increase in the cost of living
erholen *vb* (improve) pick up *vb*
Erholung *nf* (economic) recovery *n*
erkennen *vb* (profit) realize *vb*
erklären *vb* account for *vb*
erledigen *vb* (account) settle *vb*
Erlös *nm* proceeds *npl*
ermächtigen *vb* authorize *vb*
ermäßigen *vb* (taxes) reduce *vb*
Ermäßigung (-en) *nf* reduction *n*
ernennen *vb* appoint *vb* **ernennen (als Mitglied des/der....)** nominate sb to a board/committee
Ernennung (-en) *nf* nomination *n*
erneuerbar *adj* renewable *adj*
erneuern *vb* (policy, contract) renew *vb*
erneut *vb* **erneut zuteilen** (funds) reallocate

eröffnen *vb* open *vb* **ein Konto eröffnen** open an account
Eröffnungskurs (-e) *nm* opening price *n*
Erpressung *nf* extortion *n*
erreichen *vb* achieve *vb* **das Ziel erreichen** reach an objective
Ersatzperson (-en) *nf* (person) replacement *n*
Ersatzteil (-e) *nn* (for machine) spare part *n*
erschließen *vb* develop *vb*, open up *vb* **den Markt erschließen** open up the market
Erschließungsunternehmen (-) *nn* developer *n*
erschöpfen *vb* (reserves) exhaust *vb*
Erschöpfung *nf* depletion *n*
ersetzen *vb* replace *vb*
Ersparnisse *nfpl* savings *npl*
erst *adj* **erste Hypothek** first mortgage *n* **erste Klasse** (plane) first class *n* **aus erster Hand** first-hand
erstellen *vb* draw up *vb* **den Haushaltsplan erstellen** draw up a budget
erstklassig *adj* (investment) first-rate *adj*, gilt-edged *adj*, high-class *adj* **erstklassiger Wechsel** first-class paper **erstklassige Wertpapiere** blue-chip securities **erstklassiges Unternehmen** blue-chip company
erteilen *vb* place *vb* **einen Auftrag erteilen** place an order
Erteilung *nf* (of a patent) grant *n*
Ertrag *nm* earnings *n*, yield *n* **Ertrag des investierten Kapitals** return on investment
Ertragsfähigkeit *nf* earning capacity *n*, earning power *n*
Ertragsrückgang *nm* diminishing returns *npl*
Ertragstendenz *nf* earnings drift *n*
Erwartung (-en) *nf* expectation *n*
erweitern *vb* expand *vb* **die Kapazität erweitern** expand capacity **die Reihe erweitern** extend the range
Erweiterung *nf* expansion *n*
Erwerb *nm* acquisition *n*
erwerben *vb* acquire *vb*
Erwerbstätigkeit *nf* gainful employment *n*
Erzeugerpreis (-e) *nm* factor price *n*
eskalieren *vb* escalate *vb*
Etat *nm* **den Etat ausgleichen** balance the budget
Etikett (-e) *nn* label *n*
etikettieren *vb* label *vb*
Eurobond (-s) *nm* eurobond *n*
Eurodollar (-s) *nm* eurodollar *n*

Eurofusion (-en) *nf* euromerger *n*
Eurogeld (-er) *nn* euromoney *n*
Eurogeldmarkt (-märkte) *nm* eurocurrency market *n*
Eurokapital *nn* eurocapital *n*, eurofunds *npl*
Eurokrat (-en) *nm* eurocrat *n*
Eurokratie *nf* eurocracy *n*
Eurokredit *nm* eurocredit *n*
Euromarkt (-ärkte) *nm* euromarket *n*
europäisch *adj* european *adj* **Europäische Investitionsbank** European Investment Bank (EIB) *n* **Europäische Rechnungseinheit** European Unit of Account *n* **Europäischer Entwicklungsfonds** European Development Fund (EDF) **Europäischer Gerichtshof** European Court of Justice (ECJ) **Europäischer Regionalentwicklungsfonds** European Regional Development Fund (ERDF) **Europäischer Sozialfonds** European Social Fund (ESF) **Europäischer Wiederaufbauplan** European Recovery Plan **Europäisches Währungssystem** European Monetary System (EMS) **Europäische Währungsunion** European Monetary Union (EMU)
Europaparlament *nn* European Parliament *n*
Europarat *nm* Council of Europe *n*
Euroscheck (-s) *nm* eurocheque *n*
Euroskeptiker *nm* eurosceptic *n*
Eurowährung (-en) *nf* eurocurrency *n*
Exmittierung *nf* eviction *n*
expansiv *adj* reflationary *adj*
Expedition *nf* forwarding *n*
Experte (-n) *nm* expert *n*
Expertensystem (-e) *nn* expert system *n*
Export *nm* export *n* **unsichtbare Exporte** invisible exports
Exportabteilung (-en) *nf* export department *n*
Exportartikel *nmpl* export goods *n*
Exporteur (-e) *nm* exporter *n*
Exporthandel *nm* export trade *n*
exportieren *vb* export *vb*
Exportkredit (-e) *nm* export credit *n*
Exportkreditversicherung *nf* export credit insurance *n*
Exportlizenz *nf* export licence *n*
Exportmarketing *nn* export marketing *n*
Exportstrategie (-n) *nf* export strategy *n*
Exporttätigkeiten *nfpl* export operations *npl*
Exportüberschuß *nm* export surplus *n*
Exportzuschüsse *nmpl* export subsidies *npl*

Fabrikarbeit *nf* factory work *n*
Fach- *cpd* expert *adj*
Facharbeiter (-) *nm* skilled worker *n*
Fachgebietsleiter (-) *nm* line manager *n*
Fachgebietsleitung *nf* line management *n*
Fachmann (-leute) *nm* specialist *n*
fachsimpeln *vb* (informal) talk shop *vb*
Fachwissen *nn* expertise *n*
Factoring *nn* (of debts) factoring *n*
Fähigkeit (-en) *nf* ability *n*
Fahrkarte (-n) *nf* ticket *n*
Fahrkartenschalter (-) *nm* ticket office *n*
fahrlässig *adj* negligent *adj*
Fahrlässigkeit *nf* negligence *n* **grobe Fahrlässigkeit** gross negligence
Fahrlässigkeitsklausel (-n) *nf* negligence clause *n*
Fahrplan (-äne) *nm* timetable *n*
fair *adj* fair *adj*
Faktor (-en) *nm* (buyer of debts) factor *n*
fakturieren *vb* (debts) factor *vb*
fallen *vb* slump *vb*
fällig *adj* due *adj* **fällig werden** fall due **fällig werden** (business, economy) mature
falsch *adj* false *adj* **falsche Behandlung** mishandling
fälschen *vb* counterfeit *vb*
Fälschung *nf* counterfeit *n*, forgery *n*
Familie (-n) *nf* family *n* **Familien-Aktiengesellschaft** family corporation
Familieneinkommen *nn* family income *n*
Familiengeschäft (-e) *nn* family business *n*
Familienindustrie *nf* family industry *n*
Familienmarke *nf* family branding *n*
Fax (-e) *nn* fax *n*, telefax *n*
faxen *vb* fax *vb*
Faxgerät (-e) *nn* facsimile (fax) machine *n*
Fehlbetrag (-äge) *nm* shortfall *n*
Fehler (-) *nm* defect *n*, fault *n*, mistake *n* **versteckter Fehler** hidden defect
fehlerfrei *adj* zero defect *adj*
fehlerhaft *adj* defective *adj* **fehlerhafte Ware** faulty goods
Fehlkalkulation (-en) *nf* miscalculation *n*
Feiertag (-e) *nm* holiday *n* **öffentlicher Feiertag** bank holiday (GB)
feilbieten *vb* peddle *vb*
feilschen *vb* bargain *vb*
Feingehaltsstempel (-) *nm* hallmark *n*
Feinmechanik *nf* precision engineering *n*
Feldforschung *nf* field research *n*
Fenster (-) *nn* window *n*
Fernkopierer (-) *nm* telecopier *n*
Fernmeldewesen *nn* telecommunications *npl*

Fernschreiber (-) nm telex n
Fernsehen nn television n **im Fernsehen bringen** televise
Fertigerzeugnisse npl finished goods npl
Fertigkeit nf skill n
Fertigung nf production n **Fertigungsgemeinkosten** factory overheads
Fertigungsindustrie nf secondary sector n
Fertigungskosten npl factory costs npl
Fertigungsstraße (-n) nf production line n
Fertigwarenlager (-) nn finished stock n
fest adj firm adj **feste Belastung** fixed charges **festes Angebot** firm offer **festes Einkommen** fixed income
festmachen vb moor vb (capital) tie up vb
Festplatte (-n) nf hard disk n
Festpreis (-e) nm firm price n, fixed price n
Festsatzkredit (-e) nm fixed credit n
festsetzen vb (prices) peg vb **eine Höchstgrenze festsetzen** put a ceiling on sth **den Preis festsetzen** fix the price
feststehendes Budget nn fixed budget n
Festzins (-e) nm fixed interest n
fett adj (type) bold adj **fett gedruckt** bold type
Fettschrift nf bold type n
Fifo-Methode (-n) nf FIFO (first in first out) abbr
fiktiv adj fictitious adj **fiktiver Vermögenswert** fictitious assets
Filiale (-n) nf branch n
Filialgeschäft (-e) nn chain store n, multiple store n
Filialleiter (-) nm branch manager n
Finanzamt (-ämter) nn the Inland Revenue n, the Internal Revenue Service (IRS) (US)
Finanzberater (-) nm financial consultant n
Finanzberatung nf financial consultancy n
Finanzbericht (-e) nm financial report n
Finanzbuchhaltung nf financial accounting n
Finanzdirektor (-en) nm company treasurer n
Finanzgeschäft nn financial operation n
Finanzgesetz (-e) nn Finance Act n
Finanzhilfe nf financial aid n
finanziell adj financial adj **finanzielle Aktiva** financial assets **finanzielle Maßnahmen** financial measures **finanzieller Anreiz** financial incentive **finanzielle Schwierigkeit** financial difficulty **finanzielles Engagement** financial exposure
Finanzier (-s) nm financier n
finanzieren vb finance vb, fund vb
Finanzierung nf financing n, funding n

Finanzierungsgesellschaft (-en) nf finance company n
Finanzierungsinstitut (-e) nn credit company n
Finanzinstitut (-e) nn financial institution n
Finanzinvestition nf financial investment n
Finanzjahr (-e) nn tax year n
Finanzkontrolle nf financial control n
Finanzkrise (-n) nf financial crisis n
Finanzlage (-n) nf financial status n, financial situation n
Finanzleiter (-) nm chief financial officer n
Finanzmanagement nn financial management n
Finanzmarkt (-märkte) nm financial market n, mart n
Finanzmaßnahmen nfpl fiscal measures npl
Finanzminister (-) nm chancellor of the exchequer (GB) n
Finanzmittel nnpl financial resources npl, financial means npl
Finanzplanung nf financial planning n
Finanzpolitik nf budgetary policy n, financial policy n, monetary policy n, fiscal policy n
Finanzstrategie (-n) nf financial strategy n
Finanzstruktur nf financial structure n
Finanzüberschuß (-üsse) nm financing surplus n
Finanzverwalter (-) nm bursar n
Finanzwechsel (-) nm finance bill n
Finanzwesen nn finance n
Firma nf firm n
Firmenbesteuerung nf corporate taxation n
Firmenname (-n) nm trade name n **eingetragener Firmenname (-n)** registered trade name
Firmenschulden nfpl corporate debt n
Firmenverzeichnis (-sse) nn trade directory n
Firmenzeitschrift (-en) nf house journal/magazine n
Fixkosten npl fixed costs n
Flaute (-n) nf (economic) depression n
fleißig adj hard-working adj
flexibel adj flexible adj **flexibler Preis** flexible price **flexibler Wechselkurs** flexible exchange rate **flexibles Budget** flexible budget
Flexibilität nf (of prices) flexibility n
florieren vb thrive vb
florierend adj booming adj, prosperous adj
Fluchtkapital nn flight capital n
Flug (-üge) nm (in plane) flight n

Fluggesellschaft (-en) *nf* airline *n*
Flughafen (-häfen) *nm* airport *n*
Flughafenterminal (-s) *nm* air terminal *n*
Flugkarte (-n) *nf* ticket *n*
Fluglotse (-n) *nm* air traffic controller *n*
Flugreisen *nfpl* air travel *n*
Flußdiagramm (-e) *nn* flow chart *n*
flüssig *adj* fluid *adj* **flüssige Mittel** quick assets
Flüssigmachung *nf* **Flüssigmachung von Vermögenswerten** realization of assets
Folge (-n) *nf* consequence *n*
Fonds *nm* fund *n*
Förderer (-) *nm* sponsor *n*
Fördergebiet *nn* **wirtschaftliches Fördergebiet (-e)** entreprise zone
fordern *vb* demand *vb*
Förderung (-en) *nf* sponsorship *n*
Forderungsübernehmer (-) *nm* assignee *n*
Formalitäten *nfpl* **die Formalitäten beachten** observe formalities
formbedürftig *adj* **formbedürftiger Vertrag** formal contract
formell *adj* formal *adj*
Formular (-e) *nn* (document) form *n*
Forschung *nf* research *n* **Forschung und Entwicklung** research and development (R&D)
Forschungsteam (-s) *nn* research team *n*
Fortbildung *nf* advanced training *n*
Fortschritt (-e) *nm* progress *n*
Fortschritte machen (research, project) progress *vb*
Fotokopie (-n) *nf* photocopy *n*
fotokopieren *vb* photocopy *vb*, xerox *vb*
Fotokopiermaschine (-n) *nf* (machine) Xerox (R) *n*
Fracht (-en) *nf* cargo *n* **ohne Frachtgebühr** free of freight **palettisierte Fracht** palletized freight **per Frachtnachnahme** carriage forward
Frachtbrief (-e) *nm* forwarding note *n*
frachtfrei *adj* carriage included *adj*, carriage paid *adj*
Frachtgebühr (-en) *nf* carriage charge *n*
Frachtgut *nn* freight *n*
Frachtkosten *npl* carriage costs *npl*
Frachtschiff (-e) *nn* cargo ship *n*
Frachtverkehr *nm* freight traffic *n*
Fragebogen *nm* questionnaire *n*
fragen *vb* enquire *vb*
Franchise *nm* franchise *n*
Franchisegeber (-) *nm* franchisor *n*
Franchisenehmer (-) *nm* franchisee *n*
franchisieren *vb* franchise *vb* **franchisierter Ortshändler**

Franchising *nn* franchising *n*
frankieren *vb* frank *vb*
frankiert *adj* franked *adj*
frei *adj* complimentary *adj*, franco *adj* free
frei an Bord FOB (free on board) **freie Kapazität** idle capacity **freie Marktwirtschaft** free market economy **freier Handel** free trade **freier Markt** free market **freier Tag** day off work **freier Warenverkehr** free movement of goods **freie Stelle** vacancy **freie Wahl** freedom of choice **freie Wirtschaft** free economy **frei Hafen** free on quay, free port **frei Haus** franco domicile **frei Längsseite Schiff** FAS (free alongside ship) **frei Preis** franco price **frei Zone** franco zone
freiberuflich *adj* freelance *adj*, self-employed *adj*
Freiberufliche/r *nmf* freelance *n*, freelancer *n*
Freihandelszone (-n) *nf* free trade area *n*
freiwillig *adj* optional *adj*, voluntary *adj*, unsolicited *adj*
Freizeichnungsklausel (-n) *nf* exemption from liability clause *n* **Freizeichnungsklausel für Fahrlässigkeit** neglect clause
Fremdenverkehrsbranche *nf* the tourist trade *n*
Fremdwährung (-en) *nf* foreign currency *n*
Frequenz *nf* frequency *n*
freundlich *adj* friendly *adj*
Frührente *nf* early retirement *n* **in Frührente gehen** take early retirement
führen *vb* (stock) carry *vb* be ahead of *vb*, manage *vb*, wage *vb* (goods) keep *vb* **ein Geschäft führen** operate a business **eine Werbekampagne führen** run a campaign
führend *adj* leading *adj*, major *adj*
Führung *nf* leadership *n* **die Führung übernehmen** take the lead
Führungsaufgaben *nfpl* executive duties *n*
Führungskräfte *nfpl* executive personnel *n*
Führungsspitze (-n) *nf* top management *n*
Führungsstress *nm* executive stress *n*
Fülle *nf* abundance *n*
Fundbüro (-s) *nn* lost-property office *n*
fundiert *adj* sound *adj*, funded *adj*
fundierte *npl* **fundierte Schulden** funded debt
Funktion *nf* (role) function *n*
funktionierend *adj* working *adj*
Funktionsanalyse *nf* functional analysis *n*
für *prep* (acc) for *prep*
Für *nn* **Für und Wider** pros and cons *n*
Fusion (-en) *nf* amalgamation *n*, merger *n*
fusionieren *vb* amalgamate *vb*, merge *vb*

galoppierend *adj* galloping *adj*
gängig *adj* going *adj*
Garantie (-n) *nf* guarantee *n*, warranty *n*
unter Garantie under warranty
Garantiegeber (-) *nm* guarantor *n*
garantieren *vb* warrant *vb*
Garantieversicherung *nf* fidelity
insurance *n*
Garantievertreter (-) *nm* del credere
agent *n*
Gastarbeiter (-) *nm* guest worker *n*, mi-
grant worker *n*
Gastgeber (-) *nm* host *n*
Gastland (-länder) *nn* host country *n*
GATT *nn* GATT (General Agreement on
Tariffs and Trade)
Gauner (-) *nm* racketeer *n*
Gaunereien *npl* racketeering *n*
Gebietsplanung *nf* regional planning *n*
Gebietsvertreter (-) *nm* area
representative *n*
Gebrauch *nm* usage *n* Gebrauch machen
von make use of sth
Gebrauchsgüter *nnpl* durable goods *npl*
Gebühr (-en) *nf* fee *n*
Gedächtnis *nn* memory *n*
Gefahr (-en) *nf* hazard *n* natürliche Gefahr
natural hazard
gefährlich *adj* hazardous *adj*
Gefallen (-) *nm* favour *n*
Gefälligkeitswechsel (-) *nm* accommoda-
tion bill *n*
gefälscht *adj* phoney* *adj*
gegen *prep (acc)* against *prep* gegen
Barzahlung for cash
gegenseitig *adj* mutual *adj*, reciprocal *adj*,
mutually *adv*
gegenzeichnen *vb* countersign *vb*
Gehalt (-älter) *nn* salary *n*
Gehaltserhöhung (-en) *nf* pay rise *n*
Gehaltsliste (-n) *nf* payroll *n*
Gehaltsskala (-en) *nf* salary scale *n*
gelb *adj* yellow *adj*
Geld *nn* money *n* Geld einziehen von
recover money from sb Geld auf dem
Konto haben be in the black Geldmittel
flüssig machen tap resources Geld ver-
dienen make money Geld zurückhalten
(money) keep back heißes Geld hot
money
Geldangebot *nn* money supply *n*
Geldautomat (-en) *nm* automatic cash
dispenser *n*, cash machine *n*
Geldgeber *nm* backer *n*
Geldhändler (-) *nm* money trader *n*
Geldmarkt (-märkte) *nm* money market *n*

Gelegenheit (-en) *nf* opportunity *n*
Gelegenheitsarbeit *nf* casual work *n*
Gelegenheitsarbeiter (-) *nm* casual
worker *n*
gelernt *adj* (worker) skilled *n*
gemäß *prep* in accordance with
gemäßigt *adj* moderate *adj*
Gemeinderat (-räte) *nm* town council *n*
Gemeinkosten *npl* overhead costs *npl*
gemeinsam *adj* joint *adj*, jointly *adv*,
common *adj* Gemeinsame Agrarpolitik
CAP (Common Agricultural Policy) Ge-
meinsamer Markt Common Market
Gemeinschaftskonto (-konten) *nn* joint
account *n*
Gemeinschaftsprogramm (-e) *nn* colla-
borative venture *n*
Gemeinschaftsunternehmen (-e) *nn* collaborative venture *n*, joint venture *n*
genau *adj* accurate *adj*
Genauigkeit *nf* accuracy *n*
genehmigen *vb* license *vb*
Generalstreik (-s) *nm* general strike *n*
Generalvertreter (-) *nm* general agent *n*
Generalvertretungen *nfpl* general agen-
cies (US) *n*
Genesungsurlaub *nm* sick leave *n*
Gepäck *nn* luggage *n*
Gepäckaufbewahrung *nf* left-luggage
office *n*, left luggage *n*
Gericht *nn* court *n* vor Gericht in court
gerichtlich *adj* judicial *adj* gerichtliche
Verfügung (-en) injunction, writ gericht-
lich vorgehen take legal action
Gerichtshof (-öfe) *nm* court *n*
Gerichtsvollzieher (-) *nm* bailiff *n*
Gesamtsumme (-n) *nf* total *n*, the grand
total *n*
Gesamtumsatz *nm* total sales *npl*
Gesamtwirtschaft *nf* national economy *n*
gesamtwirtschaftlich *adj* gesamtwirtschaftliche Finanzierung funds flow
Geschäft (-e) *nn* bargain *n*, business *n*,
business transaction *n*, deal *n* (shop)
store *n* allgemeine Geschäftskosten
overheads allgemeine Geschäftsstunden
normal trading hours das Geschäft führen keep the business running unsaubere
Geschäfte sharp practice
geschäftlich *adj* regarding business etwas Geschäftliches besprechen talk
business geschäftlich tätig sein als
(name) trade as
Geschäftsadresse (-n) *nf* business
address *n*

Geschäftsanzug (-züge) *nm* business suit *n*

Geschäftsaussichten *npl* business outlook *n*

Geschäftsbank (-en) *nf* clearing bank *n*, commercial bank *n*

Geschäftsbereich (-e) *nm* (of company) division *n*

Geschäftsbeziehungen *nfpl* business connections *npl*, business relations *npl*

Geschäftsbilanz *nf* fiscal balance *n*

Geschäftsfreund (-e) *nm* business acquaintance *n*, business associate *n*

Geschäftsfreunde *nmpl* business contacts *npl*

Geschäftsführer (-) *nm* executive secretary *n*

Geschäftshai (-e) *nm* shark* *n*

Geschäftsjahr *nn* financial year *n*, fiscal year *n*, trading year *n*

Geschäftsjahresende *nn* fye (fiscal year end)

Geschäftskarte (-n) *nf* business card *n*

Geschäftsleitung *nf* business management *n*, senior management *n*

Geschäftsräume *npl* business premises *npl*

Geschäftsreise (-n) *nf* business trip *n*

Geschäftsreisen *npl* business travel *n*

Geschäftsreisende/r *nmf* commercial traveller, commercial traveler (US)

Geschäftsschluß *nm* closing time *n*

Geschäftssinn *nm* business acumen *n*

Geschäftssitzung (-en) *nf* business meeting *n*

Geschäftsstunden *nfpl* business hours *npl*, office hours *npl*

Geschäftswert *nm* value of (a) business *n*

Geschäftszeichen (-) *nn* reference number *n*

Geschäftszentrum (-en) *nn* business centre *n*

geschlossen *adj* closed *adj* **geschlossene Sitzung** closed session/meeting

Geschworene/r *nmf* juror *n*

Geschworenen (die) *npl* jury *n*

Gesellschaft (-en) *nf* company *n* **Gesellschaft mit beschränkter Haftung** limited company **Gesellschaft mit beschränkter Haftung (in privater Hand)** private limited company **Gesellschaft mit Haftungsbeschränkung** limited company **Gesellschaft mit unbeschränkter Haftung** unlimited company

Gesellschafter (-) *nm* partner **stiller Gesellschafter** sleeping partner

Gesellschaftsrecht *nn* company law *n*

Gesetz (-e) *nn* law *n* **Gesetz des abnehmenden Ertrags** law of diminishing returns **Gesetze erlassen** legislate

Gesetzgebung *nf* legislation *n*

gesetzlich *adj* legal *adj* **gesetzliches Zahlungsmittel (-)** legal tender

gesichert *adj* secured *adj*

Gespräch (-e) *nn* talk *n* **Gespräch mit Voranmeldung (-e)** person-to-person call

Gesundheitsgefahr (-en) *nf* health hazard *n*

Gesundheitsministerium (-ien) *nn* Ministry of Health *n*

Gesundheitsweswen *nn* health care industry *n*

gewähren *vb* grant *vb* **einen Rabatt gewähren** grant a rebate

Gewerbe *nn* trade *n*

Gewerbeaufsichtssbeamte/r *nmf* factory inspector *n*

Gewerkschaft (-en) *nf* trade union *n*, union *n*

gewerkschaftsgebunden *adj* **gewerkschaftsgebundene Firma** closed shop

Gewerkschaftsmitglieder *npl* (trade unions) organized labour *n*

Gewerkschaftsmitgliedschaft *nf* union membership *n*

Gewerkschaftsverteter (-) *nm* shop steward *n*, union representative *n*

Gewicht *nn* weight *n*

gewichtig *adj* weighty *adj*

Gewinn *nm* gain *n*, profit *n* **einen Gewinn machen** make a profit **Gewinne reinvestieren** (profits) plough back *vb*, plow back (US) **Gewinn je Stammaktie** earnings yield **Gewinn und Verlust** profit and loss **Gewinn- und Verlustrechnung** profit and loss account **unerwarteter Gewinn** windfall profit

Gewinnbeteiligung *nf* gain sharing *n*, profit-sharing scheme *n*, a share in the profits *n*

gewinnen *vb* gain *vb*, win *vb* **an Wert gewinnen** gain in value

Gewinnschwelle (-n) *nf* break-even point *n*

Gewinnspanne (-n) *nf* profit margin *n*, return on sales *n*

Gewohnheitsrecht *nn* common law *n*

gewöhnlich *adj* ordinary *adj* **gewöhnliche Sitzung** ordinary general meeting

gezielt *adj* targeted *adj* **gezielte Aktion** targeted campaign *n*

Girokonto (-konten) *nn* current account *n*

Gläubiger (-) *nm* creditor *n*
Gläubigerquorum (-a) *nn* quorum of creditors *n*
gleich *adj* equal *adj* gleicher Lohn equal pay
Gleichgewicht *nn* equilibrium *n*
gleitend *adj* sliding *adj* gleitende Arbeitszeit flexitime *n*, flextime (US) gleitender (Lohn) Tarif sliding scale
global *adj* global *adj* globale Risikoversicherung all-risks insurance
Globallsierung *nf* globalization *n*
Glücksfall (-fälle) *nm* a stroke of luck *n* unerwarteter Glücksfall windfall
Gold *nn* gold *n*
Goldmarkt (-märkte) *nm* gold market *n*
Goldmünze (-n) *nf* gold coin *n*
Goldreserven *nfpl* gold reserves *npl*
Goldstandard *nm* gold standard *n*
Gönner (-e) *nm* benefactor *n*
graduleren *vb* graduate *vb*
Graduierte/r *nmf* (of university) graduate *n*
Greenwich Mean Time *nf* Greenwich Mean Time (GMT)
Grenz- *cpd* marginal *adj*
Grenze (-n) *nf* frontier *n*, limit *n*
Grenzertrag *nm* marginal revenue *n*
Grenzkosten *npl* marginal cost *n*
Grenznutzen *nm* final utility *n*, marginal utility *n*
groß *adj* large *adj*, big *adj* groß angelegt large-scale
Großbritannien *nn* Britain *n*
Größe (-n) *nf* size *n*
Großgedrucktes *nn* large type *n*
Großhandel *nm* wholesale *n*, wholesale trade *n* im Großhandel at/by wholesale im Großhandel verkaufen sell sth wholesale
Großhandelsmarkt (-märkte) *nm* wholesale market *n*
Großhandelspreis (-e) *nm* trade price *n*, wholesale price *n*
Großhändler (-) *nm* wholesaler *n*
Großindustrie *nf* big business *n*
Großindustrielle/r *nmf* tycoon *n*
Großrechner (-) *nm* mainframe computer *n*
Großzügigkeit *nf* generosity *n*
grün *adj* green *adj* grüne Währung green currency grünes Pfund green pound
Grundausbildung *nf* basic training *n*
Grundbesitzer (-) *nm* landowner *n*
Grundbuch *nn* land register *n*
Gründe *npl* rationale *n*
gründen *vb* establish *vb* ein Geschäft

gründen set up in business ein Unternehmen gründen found a company
Gründer (-) *nm* founder *n*
Grundkapital *nn* registered capital *n*
Grundkentnisse *nfpl* working knowledge *n*
Grundsteuer (-n) *nf* land tax *n*
Grundstoff (-e) *nm* basic commodity *n*
Grundstoffindustrie *nf* primary sector *n*
Grundstückskauf *nm* land purchase *n*
Gründung *nf* establishment *n* (of company) formation *n*
Gruppenreise *nf* group travel *n*
Gruppenversicherung *nf* group insurance *n*
Gulden (-) *nm* guilder *n*
gültig *adj* valid *adj*
Gültigkeit *nf* validity *n*
gut *adj* good *adj* gut beraten well-advised *adj*
gutbezahlt *adj* well-paid *adj*
Güter *npl* goods *n*, freight *n* leicht verderbliche Güter perishable goods
Güterverkehr *nm* goods transport *n*
Güterzug (-üge) *nm* goods train *n*, freight train (US)
Gütezeichen (-) *nn* kite mark (GB) *n*
gutgläubig *adj* trusting *adj*
Guthaben (-) *nn* balance in hand *n*
Gutschein (-e) *nm* voucher *n*
gutschreiben *vb* credit *vb* einem Konto gutschreiben credit sth to an account
Gutschrift(sanzeige) (-n) *nf* credit note *n*, advice note *n*
habgierig *adj* acquisitive *adj*
Hafen (Häfen) *nm* (for berthing) dock *n*, port *n*, harbour *n* ab Hafen ex-quay, ex-wharf
Hafenanlagen *nfpl* harbour facilities *npl*
Hafenbehörden *nfpl* harbour authorities *npl*
Hafengebühren *nfpl* harbour fees *npl*
Hafengeld *nn* harbour dues *npl*
haftbar *adj* liable *adj* haftbar machen für hold sb liable
Haftpflichtversicherung *nf* third party insurance *n*
Haftung *nf* liability *n* beschränkte Haftung limited liability unbeschränkte Haftung unlimited liability volle Haftung full liability
halb *adj* half *adj* halber Preis half-price
halbieren *vb* halve *vb*
Halbjahr (-e) *nn* half-year *n*
Halblohn *nm* half-pay *n*
Halbpension *nf* half-board *n*

Hälfte (-n) *nf* half *n* **um die Hälfte reduzieren** reduce sth by half
haltbar *adj* durable *adj*
halten *vb* comply *vb*, maintain *vb* **sich an die Regeln halten** comply with the rules
Hand (Hände) *nf* hand *n*
Handbuch (-bücher) *nn* handbook *n*
Händedruck (-ücke) *nm* handshake *n*
Handel *nm* commerce *n*, dealing *n*, trade *n* **der bilaterale Handel** bilateral trade **günstige Handelsbilanz** favourable balance of trade
handeln *vb* trade *vb* (deal) handle *vb* **handeln mit** trade with sb
Handels- *cpd* mercantile *adj*
Handelsabkommen (-) *nn* trade agreement *n*, commercial treaty *n*
Handelsbank (-en) *nf* merchant bank *n*
Handelsbeschränkungen *nfpl* trade restrictions *npl*
Handelsbezeichnung (-en) *nf* trade name *n*
Handelsbilanz (-en) *nf* balance of trade, trade balance **ungünstige Handelsbilanz** adverse balance of trade
Handelsbilanzdefizit (-e) *nn* trade gap *n*
Handelsembargo (-s) *nn* trade embargo *n*
Handelserweiterung *nf* expansion of trade *n*
handelsgerichtlich *adj* **handelsgerichtlich eingetragene Gesellschaft** registered company
Handelsgesellschaft (-en) *nf* trading partnership *n*
Handelsgespräche *nnpl* trade talks *npl*
Handelskammer (-n) *nf* Chamber of Commerce *n*
Handelskreise *nmpl* the commercial world *n*
Handelsmarine *nf* merchant marine *n*, merchant navy *n*
Handelsministerium *nn* Board of Trade *n*
Handelsnation (-en) *nf* trading nation *n*
Handelsnormen *nfpl* trading standards *npl*
Handelsnormenausschuß *nm* Trading Standards Office (US)
Handelspartner (-) *nm* trading partner *n*
Handelsrecht *nn* business law *n*
Handelssanktionen *nfpl* trade sanctions *npl*
Handelsschiff (-e) *nn* merchant ship *n*
Handelsschranke (-n) *nf* trade barrier *n*
Handelsspanne (-n) *nf* trading margin *n*
Handelsüberschuß (-üsse) *nm* trade surplus *n*

Handelsvertreter (-) *nm* sales representative *n*
Handelsvertretung (-en) *nf* agency **unabhängige Handelsvertretung** free agent
Handelsvolumen *nn* trading volume *n*
Handelsziffern *nfpl* trade figures *npl*
handgearbeitet *adj* handmade *adj*
handgeschrieben *adj* handwritten *adj*
Händler (-) *nm* dealer *n*, distributor *n*, merchandiser *n*, trader *n*
Handzettel (-) *nm* broadsheet *n*
hart *adj* hard *adj* **harte Währung** hard currency
Haupt- *cpd* main *adj*
Hauptbuch (-bücher) *nn* factory ledger *n*, ledger *n*
Hauptbucheintragung *nf* ledger entry *n*
Hauptbuchhalter *nm* chief accountant *n*
Hauptgewinn (-) *nm* jackpot *n*
Hauptkassierer *nm* chief cashier *n*
Hauptlieferant (-en) *nm* main supplier *n*
Hauptniederlassung (-en) *nf* registered office *n*
Hauptperson (-en) *nf* key person *n*
Hauptprodukt (-e) *nn* leading product *n*
Hauptprodukte *nnpl* staple commodities *npl*
Hauptsitz *nm* headquarters *n*
Hauptverwaltung (-en) *nf* (HO) head office *n*, main office *n*
Hauptzahlungsagent (-en) *nm* fiscal agent *n*
Hausbesitzer (-) *nm* home owner **nicht ortsansässiger Hausbesitzer** absentee landlord
Haushalt (-e) *nm* household *n*
Haushaltsausgaben *nfpl* household expenditure *n*
Haushaltsüberschuß (-üsse) *nm* budget surplus *n*
Haushaltsumfrage (-n) *nf* household survey *n*
Haushaltswaren *nfpl* domestic goods *npl*, household goods *npl*, housewares (US) *npl*
Hausinhaber (-) *nm* householder *n*
Hauspreise *nmpl* house prices *npl*
Haussemarkt (-märkte) *nm* bull market *n*
Haussier (-s) *nm* (stock exchange) bull *n*
Haussteuer (-n) *nf* house duty (US) *n*
Haustelefon (-e) *nn* house telephone *n*
Haustürverkauf *nm* door-to-door selling *n*
Hausverkauf (-äufe) *nm* house sale *n*
Heimarbeit *nf* home/out work *n* **Heimarbeit am Computer** teleworking
Heimat *nf* home country *n*

Heimatanschrift (-en) *nf* home address *n*
herabsetzen *vb* (prices) bring down *vb*
(price) knock down *vb* (price, interest rate)
lower *vb* (price) mark down *vb*
Herabsetzung *nf* markdown *n*
herausbringen *vb* (product) bring out *vb*
herausstellen *vb* (end) turn out *vb*
hergestellt *adj* made *adj* **in Frankreich
hergestellt** made in France
Herkunftsland (-länder) *nn* country of
origin *n*
herrenlos *adj* abandoned *adj* **herrenlose
Güter** abandoned goods
herstellen *vb* manufacture *vb*
Hersteller (-) *nm* manufacturer *n*
Herstellung *nf* manufacture *n*
Herstellungsfehler (-) *nm* faulty
workmanship *n*
Herstellungspreis (-e) *nm* cost price *n*
Hierarchie (-n) *nf* (corporate) hierarchy *n*
Hilfs- *cpd* auxiliary *adj*
Hilfsarbeiter (-) *nm* unskilled worker *n*
Hilfsfonds *nm* emergency fund *n*
Hilfskasse *nf* Friendly Society *n*
hinsichtlich *prep (gen)* in respect of... *prep*
Hinweis (-e) *nm* indication *n* (suggestion)
tip *n*
hinweisen *vb* **hinweisen auf** indicate *vb*
hoch *adj* high *adj* **hoch im Kurs** at a
premium
Hochfinanz *nf* high finance *n*
Hochsaison (-en) *nf* high season *n*
highest *adj*
höchst *adj* highest *adj* **höchster Verwaltungsbeamter** company secretary
Höchstpreis (-e) *nm* maximum price *n*,
threshold price *n*
Höchstpreise *nmpl* top prices *npl*
Hochtechnologie *nf* high technology *n*
hochwertig *adj* high-grade *adj*
Höhepunkt (-e) *nm* zenith *n*
höher *adj* senior *adj* **höhere Position**
seniority *n*
Holding-Gesellschaft (-en) *nf* holding
company *n*
Home-Shopping *nn* home shopping *n*
horten *vb* hoard *vb*
Hotel (-s) *nn* hotel *n* **Hotel mit 5 Sternen**
five-star hotel
Hotelindustrie *nf* hotel industry/trade *n*
Hotelkette (-n) *nf* hotel chain *n*
Hotelunterkunft *nf* hotel
accommodation *n*
Hotelverwaltung *nf* hotel management *n*
Hypothek (-en) *nf* home loan *n*, mortage *n*

Hypothekendarlehen (-) *nn* mortgage
loan *n*
Hypothekengläubiger (-) *nm* mortgagee *n*
Hypothekenschuldner (-) *nm* mortgagor *n*
Hypothekenvertrag (-äge) *nm* mortgage
deed *n*
Hypothese (-n) *nf* hypothesis *n*
illegal *adj* illegal *adj*
Immobilien *npl* real estate
Immobiliengesellschaft (-en) *nf* property
company *n*, estate agency *n*
Immobilienmakler (-) *nm* estate agent,
realtor (US), real estate agent (US)
Immobilienmarkt *nm* property market
(GB) / real estate market (US) *n*
Import *nm* import *n*, importation *n* **un-
sichtbare Importe** invisible imports
Importabteilung (-en) *nf* import
department *n*
Importagent (-en) *nm* import agent *n*
Importamt (-ämter) *nn* import office *n*
Importartikel *nmpl* import goods *npl*
Importeur (-e) *nm* importer *n*
importieren *vb* import *vb*
Importkontrolle (-n) *nf* import control *n*
Importland (-länder) *nn* importing
country *n*
Importschranke (-n) *nf* import barrier *n*
Inanspruchnahme *nf* takeup *n*
Index (-e) *nm* index *n*
indirekt *adj* indirect *adj* **indirekte Kosten**
indirect cost, indirect expenses **Indirekte
Steuer** indirect tax
Indossament *nn* endorsement *n*
industrialisieren *vb* Industrialise *vb* **neu
industrialisiert** newly-industrialised
Industrie (-n) *nf* industry *n*
Industriegebiet (-e) *nn* industrial region *n*
Industriegelände (-en) *nn* trading estate *n*
Industriegewerkschaft (-en) *nf* industrial
union *n*
Industriekapazität *nf* industrial capacity *n*
industriell *adj* industrial *adj*
Industriemüll *nm* industrial waste *n*
Industriesiedlung (-en) *nf* trading estate *n*
Industriestaat (-en) *nm* advanced
country *n*
ineffizient *adj* inefficient *adj*
Inflation *nf* inflation *n* **galoppierende In-
flation** galloping inflation **übermäßige
Inflation** hyperinflation
inflationär *adj* inflationary *adj*
Inflationslücke (-n) *nf* inflationary gap *n*
Inflationsrate (-n) *nf* rate of inflation *n*,
level of inflation *n*

Inflationssicherung *nf* hedge against inflation *n*
Inflationsspirale (-n) *nf* inflationary spiral *n*
Information (-en) *nf* information *n* **konkrete Information** hard news/information
Informationsbearbeitung *nf* information processing *n*
Informationsbüro (-s) *nn* information office *n*
Informationsschalter (-) *nm* information desk *n*
Informationssysteme *npl* information systems *npl*
Informationstechnik (IT) *nf* information technology *n*
Informationstechnologie (IT) (-n) *nf* information technology (IT) *n*
Informationswiedergewinnung *nf* information retrieval *n*
informieren *vb* inform *vb*
Infrastruktur (-en) *nf* infrastructure *n*
Inhaber (-) *nm* bearer *n*, holder *n*, occupier *n*, proprietor *n*
Inhaberaktie (-n) *nf* bearer share *n*
Inhaberscheck (-s) *nm* bearer cheque *n*
Inhaberschuldverschreibung (-en) *nf* bearer bond *n*
Inkasso *nn* collection *n*
Inkassoagentur (-en) *nf* collecting agency *n*
Inkrafttreten *nn* entry into force *n*
Inland *nn* inland *adj*
inländisch *adj* domestic *adj*
Inlandsabatz *nm* home sales *n*
Inlandsindustrie (-n) *nf* home industry *n*
Inlandspolitik *nf* domestic policy *n*
Inlandsverkäufe *nmpl* home sales *npl*
inoffiziell *adj* unofficial *adj*
Insider (-) *nm* insider *n*
Insidergeschäfte *nnpl* insider dealing *n*, insider trading (US)
Insiderhandel *nm* insider dealing *n*, insider trading (US)
Inspektor (-en) *nm* inspector *n*
Instabilität *nf* instability *n*
Installation *nf* installation *n*
installieren *vb* instal(l) *vb*
Institut (-e) *nn* institute *n* **Institut für Wirtschaftsforschung** National Bureau of Economic Research (US)
instruieren *vb* brief *vb*
Integration *nf* integration **horizontale Intergration** horizontal integration **wirtschaftliche Integration** economic integration

intensiv *adj* intensive *adj*
Interimsschein (-e) *nm* scrip *n*
international *adj* international *adj* **internationale Konkurrenz** international competition
intervenieren *vb* intervene *vb*
Intervention (-en) *nf* intervention *n* **staatliche Intervention** state intervention
Inventar (-e) *nn* inventory *n*
Inventur *nf* stocktaking *n*
investieren *vb* (money) invest *vb*
Investition (-en) *nf* investment *n*
Investitionsausgaben *nfpl* capital expenditure *n*
Investitionsgüterleasing *nn* equipment leasing *n*
Investitionskapital *nn* invested capital *n*
Investitionsmangel *nm* lack of investment *n*
Investitionsplan (-pläne) *nm* capital budget *n*
Investitionsprogramm (-e) *nn* investment programme *n*, investment program (US)
Investitionsrate (-n) *nf* rate of investment *n*
Investitionsstrategie (-n) *nf* investment strategy *n*
Investmentfonds *nm* investment fund *n* **offener Investmentfonds** mutual funds (US)
Investor (-en) *nm* investor *n*
Jahr (-e) *nn* year *n*
Jahresabschluß (-üsse) *nm* financial statement *n*
Jahresbericht (-e) *nm* annual report *n*
Jahreseinkommen *nn* yearly income *n*
Jahreshauptversammlung *nf* AGM (Annual General Meeting) *abbr*
Jahresschlußinventar (-e) *nn* year-end inventory *n*
Jahreszeit (-en) *nf* season *n*
jahreszeitlich *adj* seasonal *adj* **jahreszeitlich bedingt** seasonal *adj*
jährlich *adj* yearly *adj*
Jobber (-) *nm* jobber *n*
Journalismus *nm* journalism *n*
jung *adj* young *adj* **junge Wirtschaft (-en)** young economy
Junk *nm* junk *n* **Junk Bond** junk bond
Kabine (-n) *nf* (phone) kiosk *n*
Kaduzierung *nf* forfeit *n*, fortfeiture *n*
Kai (-s) *nm* quay *n*
Kaigebühren *npl* quayage *n*
Kampagne (-n) *nf* campaign *n* **eine Kampagne führen** wage a campaign

Kandidat (-en) *nm* (for job) candidate *n* nominee *n*

Kapital *nn* capital *n*, funds *n* **begrenztes Kapital** limited capital **Kapital aufbringen** raise capital **langfristiges Kapital** long capital **voll eingezahltes Kapital** paid-up capital

Kapitalanlagegesellschaft *nf* investment trust *n*, unit trust *n*

Kapitalaufnahme *nf* **Kapitalaufnahme durch Emission von Aktien** flotation *n*

Kapitalausfuhr *nf* capital exports *npl*, export of capital *n*

Kapitalbeteiligung *nf* equity interests *npl*

Kapitalbildung *nf* capital formation *n*

Kapitalgewinn (-e) *nm* capital gain *n*

Kapitalgewinnsteuer (-n) *nf* capital gains tax *n*

Kapitalgüter *nnpl* capital goods *npl*

Kapitalhandel *nm* equity transaction *n*

kapitalintensiv *adj* capital-intensive *adj*

kapitalisieren *vb* capitalize *vb*

Kapitalismus *nm* capitalism *n*

Kapitalist (-en) *nm* capitalist *n*

Kapitalkosten *npl* capital cost *n*, capital outlay *n*

Kapitalmarkt (-märkte) *nm* capital market *n*

Kapitalsteigerung *nf* expansion of capital *n*

Kapitaltransferierung *nf* capital transfer *n*

Kapitalumschlag *nm* capital turnover *n*

Kapitalverkehrssteuer (-n) *nf* transfer tax *n*

Kapitalverlust (-e) *nm* capital loss *n*

Kapitalvermögen *nn* capital assets *npl*

Kapitalverzinsung *nf* return on capital *n*

Kapitalzuwachssteuer (-n) *nf* capital gains tax *n*

Karenzzeit *nf* cooling-off period *n*, period of grace *n*

karitativ *adj* charitable *adj* **karitative Organisation** charitable trust, charity

Karriere (-n) *nf* career *n*

Kartell (-e) *nn* cartel *n*

Kassageschäft (-e) *nn* cash sale *n*, cash transaction *n*

Kassakurs (-e) *nm* spot rate *n*

Kassapreis (-e) *nm* spot price *n*

Kasse (-n) *nf* box office *n*, cash desk *n*, ticket office *n* **Kasse machen** cash up

Kassengeschäft (-e) *nn* cash transaction *n*

Kassenleistungen *nfpl* health benefits *npl*

kassieren *vb* cash up *vb*

Kassierer/in *nm/nf* cashier *n*

Kauf (-äufe) *nm* purchase *n* **Kauf und Verkauf** buying and selling

Kaufbedingungen *nfpl* conditions of purchase *npl*

kaufen *vb* purchase *vb* **aus zweiter Hand kaufen** buy sth second hand **im Großhandel kaufen** buy sth wholesale **auf Kredit kaufen** buy sth on credit

Käufer (-) *nm* buyer *n*, vendee *n*

Käufermarkt (-märkte) *nm* buyer's market

Kaufhaus (-äuser) *nn* department store *n*

Kaufkraft *nf* buying power *n*, purchasing power *n*

kaufmännisch *adj* commercial *adj*

Kaufoption *nf* option to buy *n*

Kaufpreis (-e) *nm* buying price *n*, purchase price *n*

Kaution *nf* bail *n*, caution money *n*

Kautionsverpflichtung (-e) *nf* fidelity bond *n*, fiduciary bond *n*

kennenlernen *vb* make the acquaintance of sb *vb*

kenntnisreich *adj* knowledgeable *adj*

Kettenladen (-läden) *nm* chain store *n*

Kindergeld *nn* family allowance *n*

Klage (-en) *nf* legal action **gegen jemanden Klage erheben** take legal action

Klammer (-n) *nf* bracket *n*

Klausel (-n) *nf* (in contract) clause *n*

Kleiderbranche *nf* (informal) the rag trade *n*

klein *adj* small *adj* **kleine Spanne (-n)** narrow margin

Kleinanzeigen *nfpl* small ads *npl*

Kleinfehler (-) *nm* minor fault *n*

Kleingedrucktes *nn* small type *n*

Kleingeld *nn* (coins) loose/small change *n*

klimatisiert *adj* air-conditioned *adj*

Knappheit (-en) *nf* scarcity *n*

Kohlengrube (-n) *nf* coal mine *n*

Kollege (-n) *nm* colleague *n*

Kollektiv (-e) *nn* collective *n*

Kolloquium (-ien) *nn* colloquium *n*

Kommanditgesellschaft (-en) *nf* limited partnership *n*

kommerziell *adj* commercial *adj*

Kommunalanleihen *nfpl* municipal bonds *npl*

Kommunalsteuern *nfpl* (tax) rates *npl*

Kommunikation *nf* communication *n*

Kommunikationsnetz (-e) *nn* communication network *n*

komparativ *adj* comparative *adj* **komparativer Vorteil** comparative advantage

kompatibel *adj* compatible *adj*

komplex *adj* complex *adj*

kompliziert *adj* complex *adj*

Kompromiß (-sse) *nm* compromise *n* **ei-**

nen Kompromiß schließen reach a compromise
Komputer nm computer n einen Komputer laden boot a computer
Konferenz (-en) nf conference n
Konglomerat (-e) nn conglomerate n
Kongreß (-sse) nm congress n
Konjunkturpolitik nf policy to prevent economic fluctuation n expansive Konjunkturpolitik reflation
Konjunkturverlauf nm economic trend n
Konjunkturzyklus (-klen) nm trade cycle n
Konkurrent (-en) nm competing company n, competitor n
Konkurrenz nf competition n harte Konkurrenz tough competition Konkurrenz auf dem Markt market competition
Konkurrenzfähigkeit nf competitiveness n
konkurrieren (mit) vb compete vb, compete with a rival vb
konkurrierend adj competing adj konkurrierende Gesellschaft competing company
Konkurs nm bankruptcy n in Konkurs gehen go to the wall Konkurs melden go out of business
Konkursbeschluß (-üsse) nm winding-up order
Konkursverwalter (-) nm (bankruptcy) receiver n, administrator (US)
Konnossement (-s) nn bill of lading, export bill of lading
Konservenfabrik nf packing house (US) n
Konsignatar (-e) nm consignee n
Konsignationsware (-n) nf goods on consignment n
konsolidieren vb consolidate vb
konsolidiert adj consolidated adj konsolidierte Bilanz consolidated figures konsolidierte Zahlen consolidated figures
Konsortium (-ien) nn consortium n
konstruieren vb design vb
Konsul (-n) nm consul n
Konsulat (-e) nn consulate n
konsultieren vb consult vb
Konsumdenken nn consumerism n
Konsument (-en) nm consumer n
Konsumforschung nf consumer research n
Konsumkredit nm consumer credit n
Konsumnachfrage nf consumer demand n
Konsumtendenzen nfpl consumer trends npl
Konsumtrends nmpl consumer trends npl

Konsumumfrage (-n) nf consumer survey n
Kontainerdepot (-s) nn container depot n
Kontakte knüpfen (business, society) network vb
kontaktieren vb contact vb
Kontenfälschung nf falsification of accounts n
Konto nn account n ein Konto eröffnen open an account ein Konto überziehen overdraw on an account neues Konto (-ten) new account
Kontoauszug (-üge) nm statement of account n, bank statement n
Kontonummer nf account number n
Kontostand (-ände) nm bank balance n
Kontrahent/in (-en/-innen) nm/nf covenantor n
Kontrollabschnitt (-e) nm counterfoil n
konvertierbar adj convertible adj konvertierbare Währung convertible currency
Konzession (-en) nf franchise n
konzessional adj konzessionale Bank chartered bank
Konzessionsinhaber (-) nm licensee n
Kopf nm head n pro Kopf per head
Kopie (-n) nf copy n
kopieren vb (photocopy) copy vb
Kopierer (-) nm (photocopier) copier n
Kopiergerät (-e) nn photocopier n
Körperschaft (-en) nf corporation n
Körperschaftssteuer (-n) nf corporation tax n
korporativ adj corporate adj
korrekt adj aboveboard adj
Korrespondenz nf correspondence n
Korruption nf corruption n
Kosten npl cost n, expense n Kosten-Nutzen-Analyse (-n) nf cost-benefit analysis laufende Kosten npl running costs
Kostenaufstellung nf cost breakdown n
Kostendegression nf economies of scale n
Kosteneinsparung nf cost trimming n
Kostenkontrolle (-n) nf expense control n
kostenlos adj complimentary adj, free of charge adj
Kostensenkung nf cost-cutting n
Kraftverkehrspedition (-en) nf haulage contractor n
Kraftverkehrunternehmen (-) nn haulage company n, freight company (US)
krank adj sick adj
Krankengeld (-er) nn sickness benefit n
Krankenurlaub nm sick leave n

Krankenversicherung *nf* health insurance *n*, medical insurance *n*
Krankheit (-en) *nf* sickness *n*
Kredit *nm* credit *n*, loan *n* **gesicherter Kredit** secured loan **Kredit aufnehmen** obtain credit **Kredit beantragen** request a loan **Kredit gewähren** extend credit, grant a loan **auf Kredit liefern** supply sth on trust **langfristiger Kredit** long credit **offener Kredit** open note (US)
Kreditanstalt *nf* credit institution *n*
Kreditaufnahme *nf* borrowing *n*
Kreditauskunft (-ünfte) *nf* credit reference *n*
Kreditauskunftei (-en) *nf* credit agency *n*
Kreditbeschränkung (-en) *nf* credit squeeze *n*
Kreditgeber (-) *nm* lender *n*
Kreditkarte (-n) *nf* bank card *n*, credit card *n*
Kreditkonditionen *nfpl* credit terms *npl*
Kreditkonto (-konten) *nn* charge account *n*
Kreditkontrolle *nf* credit control *n*
Kreditlinie (-n) *nf* credit limit *n*
Kreditvertrag (-äge) *nm* loan agreement *n*
kreditwürdig *adj* creditworthy *adj*
Kreditwürdigkeit *nf* creditworthiness *n*
Kreditwürdigkeitsprüfung *nf* credit enquiry *n*
Kreisdiagramm (-e) *nn* pie chart *n*
Krieg (-e) *nm* war *n*
Krisenpolitik *nf* brinkmanship *n*
kritisieren *vb* find fault with *vb*
Krone (-n) *nf* (Swedish) krona *n* (Danish, Norwegian) krone *n*
Kubikmeter *nm/nn* cubic metre *n*, meter (US)
Kühlhaus (-häuser) *nn* cold storage plant *n*
Kunde (-n) *nm* client *n*, customer *n* **Kunden gewinnen** win customers
Kundenbeziehungen *nfpl* customer relations *npl*
Kundendienst *nm* after-sales service *n*
Kundenkreditkarte (-n) *nf* charge card *n*
Kundentreue *nf* customer loyalty *n*
kündigen *vb* foreclose *vb*, call in *vb* **ein Darlehen kündigen** demand the repayment of a loan
Kündigung *nf* advance notice **ungerechtfertigte Kündigung (-en)** unfair dismissal *n*
Kündigungsfrist (-en) *nf* notice period, term of notice
Kundschaft *nf* clientele *n*, patronage *n*
künstlich *adj* man-made *adj*
Kupon (-s) *nm* coupon *n*
Kurier (-e) *nm* courier *n*

Kurierdienst *nm* courrier source *n* **per Kurierdienst** by courier service
Kurs *nm* price *n* **letzter Kurs** market price
Kurse *nmpl* stock exchange prices *npl*
Kursgewinn *nm* profit *n* **nicht realisierter Kursgewinn (-e)** paper profit
Kursivdruck *nm* italic type *n*
Kursrisiko (-iken) *nn* exchange risk *n*
Kursverfall *nm* (on stock market) collapse *n*
Kursverlust *nm* loss *n* **nicht realisierter Kursverlust (-e)** paper loss
kurz *adj* short *adj* **kurz arbeiten** be on short time
kürzen *vb* (reduce) cut *vb* (investment) trim *vb*
kurzfristig *adj* at short notice *adj*, short term *adj*
Kurzstrecken- *cpd* short-haul *adj*
Kürzung *nf* trimming *n*
Kurzwaren *nfpl* dry goods *npl*
Ladekosten *npl* handling charges *npl*
laden *vb* load *vb*
Laden (-äden) *nm* shop *n*
Ladenkette (-n) *nf* chain of shops *n*
Ladenpreis (-e) *nm* retail price *n*
Laderaum *nm* stowage *n*
Ladeschein (-e) *nm* bill of lading *n*
Ladung (-en) *nf* load *n* (of vehicle) payload *n*
Lager (-) *nn* (goods) stock *n*, inventory (US) **ab Lager** ex store/warehouse **auf Lager** in stock **auf Lager haben** hold sth in reserve
Lagerhaltung *nf* warehousing *n*
Lagerhaus (-häuser) *nn* warehouse *n*
Lagerkapazität *nf* storage capacity *n*
Lagerkontrolle *nf* stock control *n*, inventory control (US)
Lagerverlust (-e) *nm* stock shrinkage *n*
Lagervermögen *nn* storage capacity *n*
Lagerwirtschaft *nf* stock control *n*
Land (-änder) *nn* country *n* **Land der Dritten Welt** third-world country
Länderblock (-s) *nm* group of countries *n*
landesweit *adj* nationwide *adj*
Landtagswahl (-en) *nf* local election *n*
Landvermesser (-) *nm* chartered surveyor *n*
Landwirtschaft *nf* agriculture *n*, farming *n*
langfristig *adj* long-term *adj* **langfristige Verbindlichkeiten** fixed liabilities
Langstrecken- *cpd* long-distance *adj*, long-haul *adj*, long-range *adj*
Lastenausgleich *nm* equalization of burdens *n*
Lastkraftwagen (-) *nm* heavy goods vehicle *n*

Leasinggeber (-) *nm* lessor *n*
Leasingnehmer (-) *nm* lessee *n*
Lebenshaltungskosten *npl* cost of living *n*
Lebenshaltungskostenindex (-e) *nm* cost of living index *n*
Lebenslauf (-äufe) *nm* curriculum vitae (CV) *n*, resumé (US)
Lebensstandard (-s) *nm* standard of living *n*
Lebensunterhalt *nm* sich seinen Lebensunterhalt verdienen make a living *vb*
Lebensversicherung *nf* endowment insurance *n* life assurance/insurance
Lebensversicherungspolice (-n) *nf* endowment policy *n*
leer *adj* vacant *adj*
Lehre *nf* apprenticeship *n*
Lehrling (-e) *nm* apprentice *n*
leichtverdient *adj* **leichtverdientes Geld** easy-money policy
leihen *vb* borrow *vb*, lend *vb*
Leistung (-en) *nf* accomplishment *n*, achievement *n* (behaviour) performance *n*
Leistungsbewertung *nf* performance appraisal *n*
leistungsfähig *adj* efficient *adj*
Leistungsfähigkeit *nf* efficiency *n*, viability *n*
Leistungsprämie (-n) *nf* performance-related bonus *n*
Leistungszulage (-n) *nf* merit payment *n*
leiten *vb* (department) head *vb* manage *vb*
Leitungsausschuß (-üsse) *nm* executive committee *n*
Leitungspyramide *nf* executive hierarchy *n*
Lernkurve *nf* experience curve *n*
Lieferant (-en) *nm* supplier *n*
Liefergebühren *nfpl* delivery charges *npl*
liefern *vb* (goods) deliver *vb* supply *vb*
Lieferschein (-e) *nm* delivery note *n*
Liefertermin (-e) *nm* delivery date *n*
Lieferung (-en) *nf* delivery *n*, supply *n*
Lieferung bis Morgen overnight delivery **Lieferung frei Bestimmungsort** free delivery **Lieferung frei Haus** home delivery **Lieferung gratis** free delivery **Lieferung ist im Preis enthalten** price includes delivery
Lieferzeit (-en) *nf* delivery time *n*
Lifo-Methode (-n) *nf* LIFO (last in first out) *abbr*
Linie line *nf* **harte Linie** hard-line
Liquidation (-en) *nf* breakup *n*, liquidation *n*, winding-up *n* **in freiwillige**

Liquidation treten go into voluntary liquidation
Liquidationsmaßnahmen *nfpl* winding-up arrangements *npl*
Liquidationswert *nm* liquidation value *n*
liquide *adj* liquid *adj* **liquide Mittel** liquid assets **liquides Kapital** liquid capital
liquidieren *vb* liquidate *vb*
Liquidität *nf* liquidity *n*
Liste (-n) *nf* list *n*
Listenpreis (-e) *nm* list price *n*
Lizenz (-en) *nf* licence *n*, permit *n*
Lizenzgeber (-) *nm* licensor *n*
Lizenzgebühr (-en) *nf* licence fee *n*
Lizenzinhaber (-) *nm* licence holder *n*
Lockartikel (-) *nm* loss leader *n*
Logistik *nf* logistics *npl*
Lohn (-öhne) *nm* (salary, wages) pay *n* wage *n*
Lohnanspruch (-sprüche) *nm* wage(s) claim *n*
Lohnbegrenzung *nf* wage restraint **freiwillige Lohnbegrenzung** voluntary wage restraint *n*
Lohnerhöhung (-en) *nf* wage increase *n*, wage rise *n*
Lohnetat *nm* wage(s) bill *n*
Lohnforderung (-en) *nf* wage claim *n*, wage demand *n*
Lohnliste (-n) *nf* payroll *n*
Lohnnebenleistungsn *nfpl* fringe benefits *npl*
Lohnpolitik *nf* wage policy *n*
Lohnsteigerungen *nfpl* wage increase *n* **Verhinderung von Lohnsteigerungen** wage restraint
Lohnstopp (-s) *nm* wage(s) freeze *n*
Lohntarif (-e) *nm* wage scale *n*
Lohntüte (-n) *nf* wage packet *n*, salary package (US)
Lohnverhandlungen *nfpl* wage negotiations *npl*
Lohnvertrag (-äge) *nm* wage agreement *n*
Lohnzuschlag (-äge) *nm* double time *n*
Lombardsatz *nm* Lombard Rate *n*
lösen *vb* (sort out) resolve *vb*
Lösen *nn* severance *n*
Luftfahrtindustrie (-n) *nf* aerospace industry *n*
Luftfracht *nf* air freight *n*
Luftpost *nf* airmail *n*
Lufttransport *nm* air transport *n*
Luftverkehr *nm* air traffic *n*
lukrativ *adj* lucrative *adj*
Luxusartikel *nmpl* luxury goods *npl*
Luxussteuer (-n) *nf* luxury tax *n*

Macht *nf* power *n*
Magnat (-en) *nm* magnate *n*
Magnetband (-bänder) *nn* (DP) magnetic tape *n*
magnetisch *adj* magnetic *adj*
Mahnung (-en) *nf* reminder *n* **letzte Mahnung** final demand, final notice
Makler (-) *nm* broker *n*
Maklerfirma (-firmen) *nf* brokerage firm *n*
Maklergeschäft *nn* brokerage *n*
Makrowirtschaft(slehre) *nf* macroeconomics *npl*
Management *nn* management *n* **Management-Ausbildung** management training **mittleres Management** middle management
Manager (-) *nm* (general) manager *n* **mittlerer Manager (-)** middle manager
Mangel (-ängel) *nm* deficiency *n*, lack *n*, shortage *n*
mangelhaft *adj* deficient *adj*
Mangelrüge (-n) *nf* complaint *n*
Marke (-n) *nf* brand *n*
Marken- *cpd* proprietary *adj*
Markenartikel *nm* proprietary brand *n*
Markenimage (-s) *nn* brand image *n*
Markenführer (-) *nm* brand leader *n*
Markenname (-n) *nm* brand name *n*
Marketing *nn* marketing *n* **Marketing-Mix** marketing mix
Marketingabteilung (-en) *nf* marketing department *n*
Markt (Märkte) *nm* market *n* **fallender Markt** falling market **fester Markt** firm market **freier Markt** open market **Gemeinsamer Markt** Common Market **auf den Markt bringen** (product) introduce *vb* **einen Markt erschließen** tap a market **Markt für Staatspapiere** gilt-edged market **Markt für Termingeschäfte** futures exchange **ruhiger Markt** quiet market **schwarzer Markt** black market **umsatzloser Markt** flat market
Marktakzeptanz *nf* market acceptance *n*
Marktanalyse (-n) *nf* market analysis *n*
Marktanteil (-e) *nm* market share *n*
Markteindringen *nn* market penetration *n*
Marktforschung *nf* information management *n*, market research *n*
Marktforschungsfragebogen (-) *nm* market research questionnaire *n*
Marktforschungsstudie (-n) *nf* market research survey *n*
Marktführer (-) *nm* market leader *n*
Marktgelegenheit (-en) *nf* market opportunity *n*

Marktkräfte *nf* market forces *npl*
Marktpreis *nm* market price *n* **angemessener Marktpreis (-e)** fair market value
Marktsegmentierung *nf* market segmentation *n*
Markttrend (-s) *nm* market tendencies *npl*, market trend *n*
Marktwachstum *nn* market growth *n*
Marktwert (-e) *nm* market price *n*, market value *n* **ohne Marktwert** of no commercial value
Marktwirtschaft (-en) *nf* market economy *n* **freie Marktwirtschaft (-en)** (system) free market economy
Maschine (-n) *nf* machine *n*
Maschinenbau *nm* engineering *n*, mechanical engineering *n*
Maschinerie *nf* machinery *n*
Maße *nmpl* weights *npl* **Maße und Gewichte** weights and measures
mäßigen *vb* moderate *vb*
Mäßigung *nf* moderation *n*
maßlos *adj* exorbitant *adj*
Maßnahme (-n) *nf* measure *n* **finanzielle Maßnahme (-n)** financial measure
Massen- *cpd* bulk *adj*
Massenabsatz *nm* mass marketing *n*
Massenarbeitslosigkeit *nf* mass unemployment *n*
Massenfertigung *nf* mass production *n*
Massengüter *nnpl* bulk goods *npl*
Massengutfrachter *nm* bulk carrier *n*
Massengutladung *nf* bulk cargo *n*
Massenmedien *npl* mass media *npl*
Material *nn* materials *npl*
Mathematik *nf* arithmetic *n*
Matrix (-izen) *nf* matrix *n*
Mauer (-n) *nf* wall *n*
maximieren *vb* maximise *vb*
mechanisch *adj* mechanical *adj*
Medien *npl* media *npl*
mehrfach *adj* multiple *adj*
Mehrgewicht *nn* excess weight *n*
Mehrgewinn *nm* extra profit *n*
Mehrgewinnsteuer *nf* excess profit(s) tax *n*
Mehrheit (-en) *nf* majority *n* **arbeitsfähige Mehrheit** working majority
Mehrheitsbeteiligung *nf* majority holding *n* **Mehrheitsbeteiligung/Minderheitsbeteiligung** majority/minority holding
Mehrkosten *npl* extra cost *n*
Mehrwertsteuer (-n) *nf* VAT *abbr*, value-added tax *n*, sales tax (US)

mehrwertsteuerfrei *adj* zero-rated for VAT *adj*
Meile (-n) *nf* mile *n*
Meilenzahl *nf* mileage *n*
Mengenrabatt *nm* quantity discount *n*, volume discount *n*
merken *vb* take notice *vb*
Meßbrief (-e) *nm* bill of tonnage *n*
Messe (-n) *nf* trade fair *n*
messen *vb* measure *vb*
Metall (-e) *nn* metal *n*
Meter (-) *nm/nn* metre *n*, meter (US)
metrisch *adj* metric *adj*
Metropole (-n) *nf* metropolis *n*
Miete (-n) *nf* rent *n*, rental *n*
mieten *vb* (person) hire *vb* (house, office) rent *vb*
Mieter (-) *nm* tenant *n*
Mietkosten *npl* hire charges *npl*
Mietvertrag (-äge) *nm* hire contract *n*
Mikrochip (-s) *nn* microchip *n*
Mikrocomputer (-) *nm* microcomputer *n*
Mikrofiche (-s) *nm* microfiche *n*
Mikroprozessor (-en) *nm* microprocessor *n*
Million (-en) *nf* million *n*
Millionär (-en) *nm* millionaire *n*
Minderheit (-en) *nf* minority *n*
Minderheitsbeteiligung (-en) *nf* minority holding *n*
minderwertig *adj* shoddy* *adj*
Mindestlohn (-löhne) *nm* minimum wage *n* **indexgekoppelter Mindestlohn** index-linked minimum wage
Mindestzins (-en) *nm* minimum lending rate *n*
Mine (-n) *nf* mine *n*
Mineral (-ien) *nn* mineral *n*
minimal *adj* minimal *adj*
Minister (-) *nm* minister *n*
Ministerium (-ien) *nn* ministry *n*
mißbrauchen *vb* abuse *vb*
Mischkonzern (-e) *nm* conglomerate *n*
Mischwirtschaft (-en) *nf* mixed economy *n*
Mißmanagement *nn* mismanagement *n*
Mißtrauensantrag (-äge) *nm* vote of no confidence *n*
Mitarbeiter (-) *nm* workmate *n* **Mitarbeiter im Außendienst** field personnel
Mitbesitz *nm* joint ownership *n*
Mitbestimmung *nf* industrial democracy *n*, worker participation *n*
Mitglied (-er) *nn* member *n* **Mitglied auf Lebenszeit** life member
Mitinhaber (-) *nm* joint holder *n*

Mitteilung (-en) *nf* memo *n*, memorandum *n*, message *n*
Mitteilungsblatt (-blätter) *nn* newsletter *n*
Mittel *nnpl* means *npl*, resources *npl*
Mittel aufbringen raise money
mittelfristig *adj* medium term *adj*
Mitunterzeichner (-) *nm* cosignatory *n*
Mitverkäufer *nm* joint vendor *n*
Modell (-e) *nn* (person) model *n* working model *n*
Modellvertrag (-äge) *nm* standard agreement *n*
Modem (-s) *nm* modem *n*
modern *adj* modern *adj*
modernisieren *vb* modernize *vb*
Modernisierung *nf* modernization *n*
Modul (-n) *nm* module *n*
möglichst *adv* **möglichst bald** at your earliest convenience
monatlich *adj* monthly *adj*
monetär *adj* monetary *adj*
Monetarismus *nm* monetarism *n*
Monopol (-e) *nn* monopoly *n*
Monopolkommission *nf* Monopolies and Mergers Commission *n*
Montageband (-bänder) *nn* assembly line *n*
Montanunion *nf* ECSC (European Coal and Steel Community) *abbr*
Moral *nf* morale *n* **die Moral heben** boost morale
multilateral *adj* multilateral *adj*
multinational *adj* multinational *adj*
mündlich *adj* verbal *adj* **mündliche Absprache** gentleman's agreement, verbal agreement
Münzanstalt (-en) *nf* mint *n*
Muster (-) *nn* sample *n*
Musterfall (-fälle) *nm* test case *n*
Muttergesellschaft (-en) *nf* parent company *n*
Nachbestellung (-en) *nf* repeat order *n*
Nachfrage *nf* demand *n* **die Nachfrage ankurbeln** boost demand
Nachfrageboom (-s) *nm* boom in demand *n*
Nachfragenelastizität *nf* elasticity of demand *n*
nachkommen comply with *vb* **den Anordnungen nachkommen** comply with legislation **seinen Verpflichtungen nachkommen** meet one's obligations
nachlässig *adj* hit-or-miss *adj*
Nachlässigkeit *nf* (laxity) slackness *n*
Nachnahme *nf*, **per Nachnahme** COD (cash on delivery) *abbr*

Nachricht (-en) *nf* bulletin *n*
Nachrichten *nfpl* news *n* **finanzielle Nachrichten** financial news **gute Nachrichten** good news **schlechte Nachrichten** bad news
Nachrichtenagentur (-en) *nf* news agency *n*, newsdealer (US)
Nachrichtensendung (-en) *nf* bulletin *n*
nachschicken *vb* (mail) redirect *vb*
Nachwuchsführungskraft (-äfte) *nf* trainee manager
Nachzahlung *nf* back pay *n*
Name *nm* name *n* **im Namen** in the name of **mit Namen** by name
Namensaktie (-n) *nf* registered share *n*
Namensschuldverschreibung (-en) *nf* registered bond *n*
Nation (-en) *nf* nation *n*
Nebenkosten *npl* incidental expenses *npl*
Nebenleistung (-en) *nf* (informal) perk *n* (formal) perquisite *n*
Nebenmarkt (-märkte) *nm* fringe market *n*, secondary market *n*
Nebenprodukt (-e) *nn* by-product *n*, spin-off *n*
Nebensaison (-s) *nf* low season *n*
negieren *vb* negative (US) *vb*, negate *vb*
Nennwert (-e) *nm* nominal value *n*, nominal price *n*, face value *n*
netto *adj* net(t) *adj*
Nettoauftragseingang (-änge) *nm* net(t) sales *npl*
Nettobetrag (-äge) *nm* net(t) amount *n*
Nettoeinkommen *nn* disposable income *n*, net(t) income *n*
Nettoersparnisse *nfpl* net(t) saving *n*
Nettogewicht *nn* net(t) weight *n*
Nettoinvestition *nf* net(t) investment *n*
Nettokosten *npl* net(t) cost *n*
Nettolohn (-öhne) *nm* net(t) wage *n*
Nettopreis (-e) *nm* net(t) price *n*
Nettotonnage *nf* net(t) tonnage *n*
Nettoverdienst *nm* net(t) earnings *npl*
Nettoverlust (-e) *nm* clear loss *n*, net(t) loss *n*
Nettovermögen *nn* net(t) assets *npl*
Nettozinsen *nmpl* net(t) interest *n*
Neugeschäft *nn* new business *n*
neutral *adj* neutral *adj*
nicht *adv* not *adv* **nicht einstimmige Abstimmung** split division **nicht erwerbswirtschaftlich** non-profitmaking **nicht übertragbar** non-transferable **nicht wandelbar** non-convertible
Nichtabschluß (-üsse) *nm* non-completion *n*

nichtbegebbar *adj* non-negotiable *adj*
nichtdiskriminierend *adj* non-discriminatory *adj*
Nichteingreifen *nn* non-intervention *n*
Nichtlieferung *nf* non-delivery *n*
Nichtzahlung *nf* non-payment *n*
niedrig *adj* (price) low *adj* **niedrigster Preis** bottom price, knockdown price
Nominalbetrag (-äge) *nm* nominal amount *n*
Nominalinflation *nf* nominal inflation *n*
Nominalvermögen *nn* nominal assets *npl*
nominell *adj* nominal *adj*
Nominierung (-en) *nf* nomination *n*
Norm (-en) *nf* norm *n*
Notar (-e) *nm* notary *n*
Notenausgabe *nf* issue *n* **ungedeckte Notenausgabe** fiduciary issue
Notenbank (-en) *nf* bank of issue *n*, issuing bank *n*
Notfall (-fälle) *nm* emergency *n*
Notizen *npl* notes *npl* **Notizen machen** take notes
Notwendigkeit *nf* (goods) necessity *n*
Null *nf* nil *n*, zero *n* **null und nichtig** null and void
Nullgewinn (-e) *nm* nil profit *n*
Nullwachstum *nn* zero growth *n*
nutzbar *adj* (materials) reclaimable *adj*
Nutzen *nm* utility *n*
nützen *vb* benefit *vb*
Nutzfahrzeug (-e) *nn* commercial vehicle *n*
obenerwähnt *adj* above-mentioned *adj*
Obligation (-en) *nf* bond *n*
Obligationär (-e) *nm* bondholder *n*
Obligationsanleihe (-n) *nf* debenture loan *n*
obligatorisch *adj* obligatory *adj*
offen *adj* open *adj* **offener Kredit** unsecured credit
öffentlich *adj* public *adj* **öffentlicher Verkehr** public transport **öffentlicher Zuschuß** state subsidy **öffentliches Geld** public money
Öffentlichkeitsarbeit *nf* public relations *npl*
Öffnungszeiten *nfpl* opening times *npl*
Offshore-Gesellschaft (-en) *nf* offshore company *n*
Ökonometrie *nf* econometrics *npl*
Öldollar *nm* petrodollar *n*
Ölfeld (-er) *nn* oilfield *n*
Oligopolie (-n) *nf* oligopoly *n*
Ölindustrie *nf* petroleum industry *n*
ölproduzierend *adj* oil-producing *adj* **ölproduzierender Staat** oil state

Option (-en) *nf* option *n*
Optionsklausel (-n) *nf* option clause *n*
Optionsmarkt (-märkte) *nm* options market *n*
Organisation (-en) *nf* organization *n*
organisieren *vb* arrange (a conference) *vb*, organize *vb*
örtlich *adj* local *adj*
Ortsnetzkennzahl (-en) *nf* (telephone) code *n*
Output *nm* output *n*
Pachtbesitz *nm* leasehold *n*
Pächter (-) *nm* leaseholder *n*
packen *vb* pack *vb*
Paket (-e) *nn* bundle *n*, package *n*, packet *n*
Palette (-n) *nf* pallet *n*, (product) range *n*
palettisiert *adj* palletized *adj*
Pannendienst (-e) *nm* breakdown service *n*
Papier *nn* paper *n* **Papier mit Briefkopf** headed notepaper
Papiergeld *nn* paper money *n* **Papiergeld ohne Deckung** fiat money
Papierwährung (-en) *nf* paper currency *n*
Parität *nf* parity *n*
Partie (-n) *nf* (at auction) lot *n*
Partner *nm* associate *n*, partner *n*
Passagier (-e) *nm* passenger *n*
Patent (-e) *nn* patent *n*
patentrechtlich *adj* **patentrechtlich geschützt** patented *adj*
Patt *nn* stalemate *n*
Pauschalentschädigung *nf* lump sum settlement *n*
Pauschalreise (-n) *nf* package tour *n*
Pause *nf* break *n* **Pause machen** take a break
Pendant *nn* opposite number *n*
Pendelverkehr *nm* shuttle *n*
Pensionsplan (-pläne) *nm* pension scheme *n*
Personal *nn* human resources *npl*, personnel *n*
Personalabteilung (-en) *nf* personnel department *n*
Personalausbildung *nf* employee training *n*
Personalbestand *nm* manpower *n*
Personalbeziehungen *npl* human relations *npl*
Personalcomputer (-) *nm* personal computer (PC) *n*
Personalkredit (-e) *nm* personal loan *n*
Personalmanagement *nn* human resource management (HRM) *n*

Personengesellschaft (-en) *nf* partnership *n*
Personenzug (-üge) *nm* passenger train *n*
persönlich *adj* personal *adj*
Pfund *nn* (weight) pound *n* **Pfund Sterling (-)** pound sterling *n*
Pfundguthaben (-) *nn* sterling balance *n*
Pharmazieindustrie *nf* pharmaceutical industry *n*
Pilotanlage (-n) *nf* pilot plant *n*
Pilotprojekt *nn* pilot scheme *n*
Pipeline (-s) *nf* pipeline *n*
Piraterie *nf* (at sea) piracy *n*
Plakat (-e) *nn* (advertising) poster *n*
Plan (-äne) *nm* plan *n* **Pläne machen** make plans **vorläufiger Plan** tentative plan
planen *vb* plan *vb*, schedule *vb*
plangemäß *adv* according to plan
Planung *nf* planning *n* **langfristige Planung** long-term planning
Planwirtschaft (-en) *nf* planned economy *n*
Plastikindustrie *nf* plastics industry *n*
platzen *vb* (cheque) bounce* *vb*
Plebiszit (-e) *nn* referendum *n*
Plenar- *cpd* (assembly, session) plenary *adj*
Politik *nf* politics *npl*
politisch *adj* political *adj*
Portefeuille (-n) *nn* portfolio *n*
Posfach (-fächer) *nn* PO box *n*
Postamt (-ämter) *nn* post office *n*
Postbezirk (-e) *nm* postal zone *n*
Postdienste *nmpl* postal services *npl*
Postfach (-fächer) *nn* box number *n*
Postgebühr *nf* postal charge/rate *n* **Postgebühr bar bezahlt** Freepost (R) (GB)
postlagernd *adj* poste restante, general delivery (US)
Postleitzahl (-en) *nf* post code *n*, zip code (US)
prägen *vb* mint *vb*
praktisch *adj* handy *adj*
Prämie (-n) *nf* bonus *n*, premium *n*
Praxis *nf* usage *n*
Preis (-e) *nm* price *n* **fester Preis** hard price **günstiger Preis** favourable price **Preis ab Werk** factory price **Preise niedrig halten** keep down prices **Preise treiben** profiteer
Preisangabe (-n) *nf* (price) quotation *n*
Preisbildungspolitik *nf* pricing policy *n*
Preisbindung *nf* fair trade *n*
Preisbindungsabkommen (-) *nn* fair-trade agreement *n*
Preisentwicklung (-en) *nf* price trend *n*

Preiserhöhung nf price increase n
Preisetikett (-e) nn price ticket n
Preisindex (-e) nm price index n
Preiskampf (-kämpfe) nm price war n
Preisniveau (-s) nn level of prices n
Preisobergrenze nf (on prices) ceiling n
Preispolitik nf pricing policy n
Preissturz (-ürze) nm slump n
preiswert adj good value adj **preiswert kaufen** get value for one's money
Pressekonferenz (-en) nf press conference n
Pressezar (-en) nm press baron n
Primawechsel (-) nm first bill of exchange n
Priorität nf priority n
Privatbereich (-e) nm private sector n
Privateigentum nn private property n
Privateinkommen nn private income n
privatisieren vb privatize vb
Privatisierung nf privatization n
Privatunternehmen (-) nn private enterprise n
pro prep per prep **pro Jahr** per annum **pro Kopf** per capita
Probe nf sampling n **auf Probe** on approval **die Probe bestehen** stand the test **auf die Probe stellen** put sth to the test
Probeangebot (-e) nn trial offer n
Probezeit nf trial period
probieren vb sample vb, try out vb
Produkt (-e) nn product n **neues Produkt (-e)** new product
Produkteinführung (-en) nf product launch n
Produktion nf output n, production n **Produktion pro Stunde** per hour output **die Produktion steigern** boost production
Produktionseinheit (-en) nf unit of production n
Produktionselastizität nf elasticity of production n
Produktionsfaktor (-en) nm factor of production n
Produktionskapazität nf manufacturing capacity n
Produktionskartell (-e) nn quota agreement n
Produktionskontrolle (-n) nf production control n
Produktionsmethode (-n) nf production method n
Produktionsziel (-e) nn production target n
produktiv adj productive adj
Produktivität nf productivity n

Produktivitätssteigerung nf productivity gains npl
Produktmix nm product mix n
Produzent (-en) nm producer n
produzieren vb produce vb
profitieren vb benefit vb
Prognose (-n) nf forecast n
Programm (-e) nn (DP) program n
Programmfehler (-n) nm (listening device) bug n
Programmieren nn (DP) programming n
Programmierer (-) nm (DP) programmer n
Projekt (-e) nn project n **ein Projekt streichen** kill a project
prolongieren vb (to next month) carry over vb
Prospekt (-e) nm brochure n, prospectus n
Protektionismus nm protectionism n
protektionistisch adj protectionist adj
protestieren vb object vb
Protokoll nn (meeting) the minutes npl
Provision nf commission n **Provision berechnen** charge commission
Provisionsgebühr (-en) nf commission fee n
Provisionsvertreter (-) nm commission agent n
provisorisch adj temporary adj
Prozent nn per cent
Prozentsatz (-ätze) nm percentage n **Prozentsatz des Gewinns** percentage of profit
Prozeß (-sse) nm lawsuit n **einen Prozeß führen** litigate vb
prüfen vb check vb, examine vb, inspect vb, make a check on sth vb
Prüfer examiner n **innerbetrieblicher Prüfer (-)** internal auditor
Prüfung (-en) nf examination n
Publikumsgesellschaft (-en) nf public company n
Publizität nf publicity n
Punkt (-e) nm point n
Quadratmeter (-) nm/nn square metre, meter (US)
Qualifikation nf qualification n, academic qualification n, educational qualification n **berufliche Qualifikation** professional qualification **erforderliche Qualifikationen** necessary qualifications
qualifiziert adj qualified adj **qualifizierte Arbeitskräfte** qualified personnel
Qualität nf quality n **(von) guter Qualität** well-made adj **(von) minderer Qualität** (goods) inferior adj **(von) niedriger Qualität** (product) down-market

qualitativ *adj* qualitative *adj*
Qualitätsbericht (-e) *nm* quality report *n*
Qualitätsgarantie (-n) *nf* quality guarantee *n*
Qualitätskontrolle (-n) *nf* quality control *n*
Qualitätsnorm (-en) *nf* quality standard *n*
Quantität *nf* quantity *n*
quantitativ *adj* quantitative *adj*
Quantitätstheorie *nf* quantity theory *n*
Quantitätstheorie des Geldes quantity theory of money
Quasi- *cpd* quasi *adj* **Quasi-Einkommen** quasi-income **Quasi-Vertrag** quasi-contract
Quelle (-n) *nf* source *n*
Quittung *nf* receipt *n* **eine Quittung geben** issue a receipt
Quorum (-a) *nn* quorum *n*
Quote (-n) *nf* quota *n*
Quotenauswahlverfahren *nn* quota sampling *n*
Quotenkauf *nm* quota buying *n*
Quotensystem (-e) *nn* quota system *n*
R-Gespräch (-e) *nn* reverse-charge call *n*, collect call (US) **ein R-Gespräch machen** (call) transfer
Rabatt (-e) *nm* discount *n*, rebate *n* **mit Rabatt** at a discount
Ramsch *nm* **im Ramsch verkaufen** sell sth in bulk
Rand- *cpd* peripheral *adj*
Rang (-änge) *nm* tier *n* **von hohem Rang** high-ranking
Rate (-n) *nf* instalment *n*, installment (US)
Ratenzahlungen *nfpl* staged payments *npl*
Rathaus (-häuser) *nn* town hall *n*
ratifizieren *vb* ratify *vb*
Ratifizierung *nf* ratification *n*
rationalisieren *vb* rationalize *vb*
Rationalisierung *nf* rationalization *n*
Rationalisierungsmaßnahmen *nfpl* rationalization measures *npl*
Ratschlag (-äge) *nm* advice *n*
Raum (-äume) *nm* room *n*
Räumlichkeiten *nfpl* premises *npl*
Räumungsverkauf (-äufe) *nm* closing-down sale *n*, closing-out sale (US)
Reallohn (-löhne) *nm* real wage *n*
Realwert (-e) *nm* real value *n*
Rechenfehler (-) *nm* miscalculation *n*
rechenkundig *adj* numerate *adj*
Rechenzentrum *nn* computer centre *n*, computer center (US)
Rechnen *nn* numeracy *n*
Rechner (-) *nm* calculator *n*
rechnergestützt *adj* computer-aided *adj*

rechnergestützte Fertigung computer-aided manufacture (CAM) **rechnergestütztes Konstruieren** computer-aided design (CAD) **rechnergestütztes Lernen** computer-aided learning (CAL)
Rechnung (-en) *nf* bill *n*, invoice *n*, tally *n* **eine Rechnung ausstellen** issue an invoice **die Rechnung begleichen** pay a bill, settle an account **in Rechnung stellen** (invoice (informal)) bill
Rechnungsabschnitt (-e) *nm* accounting period *n*
Rechnungsduplikat (-e) *nn* duplicate invoice *n*
Recht (-e) *nn* right *n* **alleiniges Recht** sole rights **erworbene Rechte** vested rights **internationales Recht** international law **öffentliches Recht** public law **das Recht auf etwas** the right to sth
Rechtsanwalt (-älte) *nm* barrister *n*, lawyer (US)
Rechtskosten (-) *npl* legal charges *npl*
Rechtsmittelinstanz *nf* Court of Appeal *n*, Court of Appeals (US)
Rechtsstreit (-e) *nm* litigation *n*
rechtsverbindlich *adj* legally binding *adj*
recycelbar *adj* recyclable *adj*
reduzieren *vb* (prices) bring down *vb*, reduce *vb*
Referenz (-en) *nf* referee *n*, testimonial *n*
Reform (-en) *nf* reform *n*
regieren *vb* govern *vb*
Regierung (-en) *nf* government *n*
Regierungsabteilung (-en) *nf* government department *n*
Regierungsapparat *nm* machinery of government *n*
Regierungsausschuß (-üsse) *nm* government body *n*
Regierungschef (-s) *nm* head of government *n*
Regierungspolitik *nf* government policy *n*
Regierungssektor (-en) *nm* government sector *n*
Regierungsunternehmen (-) *nn* government enterprise *n*
Regierungszuschuß (-üsse) *nm* government subsidy *n*
regional *adj* regional *adj* **regionale Subvention** regional grant
Regionalbüro (-s) *nn* regional office *n*
Regionalleiter (-) *nm* area manager *n*
regulär *adj* regular *adj*
Regulierung (-en) *nf* adjustment *n*
Reichtum *nm* wealth *n*
Reihe (-n) *nf* (of products) range *n*

Reihenfertigung *nf* flow line production *n*, flow production *n*
Reingewinn *nm* net(t) profit *n*
Reinverlust (-e) *nm* net(t) loss *n*
Relsebüro (-s) *nn* travel agency *n*
Reisegepäckversicherung *nf* luggage insurance *n*
Reisekosten *npl* travelling expenses *npl*, travel expenses (US)
Reiseleiter (-e) *nm* courier *n*
Reisen *nn* travelling *n*, traveling (US)
Reisende/r *nmf* traveller *n*, traveler (US)
Reisescheck (-s) *nm* traveller's cheque *n*, traveler's check (US)
Reisespesen *npl* travelling expenses *npl*, travel expenses (US)
Reiseversicherung *nf* travel insurance *n*
Reißwolf (-ölfe) *nm* shredder *n*
Reklamationsabteilung (-en) *nf* claims department *n*
Reklamationsverfahren (-) *nn* claims procedure *n*
Rendite *nf* rate of return *n*
Renditekurve (-n) *nf* yield curve *n*
renovieren *vb* refurbish *vb*
Renovierung (-en) *nf* refurbishment *n*
Rentabilität *nf* profitability *n*
Rente (-n) *nf* annuity *n*, pension *n* **gehaltsabhängige Rente** earnings-related pension
Rentenfonds *nm* pension fund *n*
Reparaturkosten *npl* costs of repair *npl*
reparieren *vb* repair *vb*
Repatriierung (-en) *nf* repatriation *n*
Reservewährung (-en) *nf* reserve currency *n*
reservieren *vb* reserve *vb* **ein Hotelzimmer reservieren** book a hotel room
Reservierung (-en) *nf* (reservation) booking *n* reservation *n*
restlich *adj* residual *adj*
Restschuld (-en) *nf* unpaid balance *n*
retten *vb* salvage *vb*
revidieren *vb* revise *vb*
Revision *nf* revision *n* **innerbetriebliche Revision** internal audit
Rezession (-en) *nf* recession *n*
Richtpreis (-e) *nm* bench mark price *n*
richtungsweisend *adj* pointing the way **richtungsweisend sein** set a trend
Riesengeschäft *nn* **Riesengeschäft machen** make a fortune
riesengroß *adj* king-size(d) *adj*
Riesentanker (-) *nm* supertanker *n*
Risiko (-iken) *nn* risk *n* **finanzielles Risiko**

financial risk **vom Käufer übernommenes Risiko** at the buyer's risk
Risikoanalyse (-n) *nf* risk analysis *n*
Risikoeinschätzung (-en) *nf* risk assessment *n*
Risikokapital *nn* risk capital *n*
risikoreich *adj* high-risk *adj*
roh *adj* (unprocessed) raw *adj*
Roheisen *nn* pig iron *n*
Rohstoff (-e) *nm* primary product *n* **Rohstoffe** raw materials
Rolltreppe (-n) *nf* escalator *n*
rot *adj* red *adj*
Route (-n) *nf* itinerary *n*
rückdatieren *vb* backdate *vb*
Rückerstattung (-en) *nf* refund *n*
Rückfahrkarte (-n) *nf* return ticket *n*, round-trip ticket (US)
Rückgabe *nf* return *n*
rückgabepflichtig *adj* (deposit) returnable *adj*
Rückgang (-änge) *nm* (economic) decline *n* decrease *n*, shrinkage *n*
rückgängig *adj* declining *adj* **rückgängig machen** (offer) revoke
Rückgängigmachung (-en) *nf* cancellation *n*
Rückgriffsrecht *nn* right of recourse *n*
Rücklage reserve *n* **die freie Rücklage** earned surplus
Rückmeldung *nf* feedback *n* **negative Rückmeldung** negative feedback **Rückmeldung geben** give feedback
Rückstand arrears *n* **im Rückstand** in arrears **Rückstände** backlog **in Rückstand kommen** fall/get into arrears
Rücktritt (-e) *nm* resignation *n* **seinen Rücktritt erklären** hand in one's resignation
rückvergütbar *adj* refundable *adj*
rückvergüten *vb* reimburse *vb*
Rückvergütung (-en) *nf* reimbursement *n*
rückversichern *vb* reinsure *vb*
Rückversicherung *nf* fronting *n*, reinsurance *n*
Rückzahlung (-en) *nf* (of loan) repayment *n* **ohne Rückzahlung** ex repayment
Ruf *nm* reputation *n*
rufen *vb* call for *vb*
Ruhestand *nm* retirement *n* **in den Ruhestand treten** retire
ruinös *adj* ruinous *adj* **ruinöse Konkurrenz** cut-throat competition
rund *adj* round *adj*
Rundfahrt (-en) *nf* round trip *n*
Rundschreiben *nn* (letter) circular *n*

Sachanlage (-n) *nf* tangible asset *n*
Sache (-en) *nf* thing *n*, object *n* **bewegliche Sachen** *nfpl* chattels *npl*
Sanktion *nf* sanction *nf* **wirtschaftliche Sanktion (-en)** economic sanction
Schaden (-äden) *nm* damage *n* **beträchtlichen Schaden verursachen** cause extensive damage
Schadenersatz *nm* indemnity *n* **nomineller Schadenersatz** nominal damages **Schadenersatz beanspruchen** (legal) claim damages
Schadenersatzansprüche *nmpl* **Schadenersatzansprüche geltend machen** claim for damages *vb*
schadenersatzpflichtig *adj* liable for damages *adj*
Schadenersatzversicherung *nf* indemnity insurance *n*
Schadensfreiheitsrabatt *nm* no-claims bonus *n*
Schadhaftigkeit *nf* spoilage *n*
schaffen *vb* accomplish *vb*
Schalterbeamte/r teller *n*
Schalterstunden *nfpl* banking hours *npl*
scharf *adj* (competition) keen *adj* sharp *adj*
Schatzanweisung (-en) *nf* Treasury bill *n*, treasurer check (US)
schätzen *vb* estimate *vb*
Schätzkosten *npl* estimate of costs *n*
Schätzung (-en) *nf* estimate *n*
Schauraum (-räume) *nm* showroom *n*
Scheck (-s) *nm* cheque *n*, check (US) **begebbarer Scheck** negotiable cheque **gekreuzter Scheck** crossed cheque **geplatzter Scheck** dud cheque **per Scheck zahlen** pay by cheque **einen Scheck ausstellen** make out a cheque **einen Scheck an den Austeller zurückgeben** return a cheque to drawer **einen Scheck einlösen** cash a cheque **Scheck in Höhe von** a cheque for the amount of **einen Scheck platzen lassen** bounce* a cheque **einen Scheck rückdatieren** backdate a cheque **einen Scheck sperren** stop a cheque **einen Scheck unterschreiben** sign a cheque **unbezahlter Scheck** unpaid cheque
Scheckbuch (-ücher) *nn* cheque book *n*, checkbook (US)
Scheckheft (-e) *nn* cheque book *n*
Scheckkarte (-n) *nf* cheque card *n*
Scheinkauf (-äufe) *nm* fictitious purchase *n*
Scheinverkauf *nm* fictitious sale *n*
Schicht (-en) *nf* shift *n*

Schichtarbeit *nf* shift work *n*
Schiedsgerichtsverfahren (-) *nn* industrial arbitration *n*
Schiedsspruch (-üche) *nm* arbitrage *n*
Schiene (-n) *nf* track *n*
Schienenverkehr *nm* rail traffic *n*
Schiff (-e) *nn* ship *n* **ab Schiff** ex ship
Schiffahrtslinie (-n) *nf* shipping line *n*
Schiffbau *nm* shipbuilding *n*
Schiffskörper (-) *nm* hull *n*
Schiffskörperversicherung *nf* hull insurance *n*
Schiffsmakler (-) *nm* shipping broker *n*
Schiffsmaschinenbau *nm* marine engineering *n*
Schiffsverkehr *nm* sea traffic *n*
Schiffswerft (-en) *nf* shipyard *n*
Schlagzeile *nf* headline *n* **Schlagzeilen machen** hit the headlines
Schlange (-n) *nf* queue *n*
Schleuderpreis (-e) *nm* giveaway price *n*
Schleudersitz *nm* hot seat *n*
Schlichter (-) *nm* arbitrator *n*
Schlichtung *nf* arbitration *n*
schließen close *vb*, shut *vb* **den Laden schließen** (informal) shut up shop
Schließfach (-fächer) *nn* left-luggage locker *n*
Schlußbilanz (-en) *nf* final balance *n*
Schlußkurs (-e) *nm* closing price *n*
Schlußrechnung (-en) *nf* final invoice *n*
Schlüsselfrage (-n) *nf* key question *n*
Schlüsselindustrie (-n) *nf* key industry *n*
Schlüsselkraft (-kräfte) *nf* key person *n*
Schlüsselwährung (-en) *nf* key currency *n*
Schmiergeld *nn* backhander* *n* (bribe) sweetener* *n*
schmuggeln *vb* smuggle *vb*
Schnelldienst *nm* express agency *n*
Schnelldreher *npl* fast-selling goods *npl*
Schnellspur *nf* fast track *n*
Schnittstelle (-n) *nf* interface *n*
Schranke (-n) *nf* barrier *n*
Schreibarbeiten *npl* paperwork *n*
Schreibfehler (-) *nm* clerical error *n*
Schreibmaschine (-n) *nf* typewriter *n*
Schrott *nm* scrap metal *n* **zu Schrott fahren** (vehicle) write off
schrumpfen *vb* shrink *vb*
Schuld (-en) *nf* debt *n* **in Schuld geraten** get into debt
Schuldanerkenntnis (-sse) *nn* **schriftliches Schuldanerkenntnis** acknowledgement of debt
schulden *vb* owe *vb*
Schuldendienst (-e) *nm* debt service *n*

Schuldeneinziehung *nf* debt collection *n*
Schuldenerlaß *nm* quittance *n*
Schuldner (-) *nm* debtor *n*
Schuldschein *nm* promissary note *n* **un-gesicherter Schuldschein** (-e) unsecured bond
Schuldverschreibung (-en) *nf* bond *n* **gesicherte Schuldverschreibung** debenture
Schutzklausel (-n) *nf* n, hedge clause (US)
Schwangerschaftsurlaub (-e) *nm* maternity leave *n*
schwanken *vb* fluctuate *vb*
Schwankung (-en) *nf* fluctuation *n*
schwarz *adj* black *adj* **schwarz arbeiten** moonlight*
Schwarzhandel *nm* black economy *n*
Schwarzmarkt (-märkte) *nm* black economy *n*, black market *n*
Schwerindustrie *nf* heavy industry *n*
Schwestergesellschaft (-en) *nf* affiliated company *n*, sister company *n*
Schwindel (-) *nm* swindle* *n*
Schwindelgeschäft (-e) *nn* racket *n*
Schwindelunternehmen (-) *nn* phoney* company *n*
Schwindler (-) *nm* swindler* *n*
See- *cpd* marine *adj*
Seemeile (-n) *nf* nautical mile *n*
Seeversicherung *nf* marine insurance *n*
Sekretär/in (-en/-innen) *nm/nf* secretary *n*
Sektor (-en) *nm* sector *n*
sekundär *adj* secondary *adj*
Selbstabholung *nf* **Selbstabholung gegen Kasse** cash and carry
Selbsteinschätzung *nf* self-assessment *n*
Selbstkosten *npl* original cost *n*
Selbstverwaltung *nf* self-management *n*
senden *vb* broadcast *vb*, send *vb*, transmit *vb* **per Eilboten senden** send by courier *vb*
Sendung (-en) *nf* (of goods) batch *n* broadcast *n*, consignment *n*
senkrecht *adj* vertical *adj*
Seriennummer (-n) *nf* serial number *n*
Serienverarbeitung *nf* (DP) batch processing *n*
sicher *adj* safe *adj*, secure *adj*
Sicherheit *nf* safety *n*, security *n* **als Sicherheit halten** hold sth as security
Sicherheitsbeauftragte/r *nmf* safety officer *n*
Sicherheitsmaßnahme (-n) *nf* safety measure *n*
Sicherungsgegenstand *nm* collateral *n*
Sicht *nf* sight *n*
sichtbar *adj* visible *adj*

Sichtfernsprecher (-) *nm* visual telephone *n*
Sichtgerät (-e) *nn* visual display unit (VDU) *n*
Sichtwechsel (-) *nm* sight draft *n*
Siegel (-) *nn* seal *n*
Simulant (-en) *nm* malingerer *n*
Sitz *nm* seat *n* **den Sitz verlegen** relocate
Sitzstreik *nm* (strike) sit-in *n*
Sitzung (-en) *nf* meeting *n*
Sitzungsperiode (-n) *nf* negotiating session *n*
Sitzungssaal (-äle) *nm* board room *n*
Skala (-en) *nf* scale *n*
Slogan (-s) *nm* slogan *n*
sofortig *adj* immediate *adj* **sofortige Bezahlung** spot cash
Software *nf* software *n*
Softwarepaket (-e) *nn* software package *n*
Solawechsel (-) *nm* promissory note *n*
solide *adj* well-made *adj*
Sonderangebot (-e) *nn* bargain offer *n*, clearance offer *n*
Sonderdividende *nf* **Sonderdividende am Schluß des Jahres** (-n) year-end dividend
Sonderrücklagen *nf* excess reserves *npl*
Sonderzahlung (-en) *nf* ex gratia payment *n*
Sonderziehungsrechte *npl* SDRs (special drawing rights) *abbr*
Sorte (-n) *nf* kind *n*
Sortiment (-e) *nn* product line *n*
Sozialhilfeleistung *nf* welfare benefits *npl*
Sozialversicherung *nf* National Insurance (NI) (GB), Social Security (GB)
Sozialversicherungsbeiträge *npl* social security contributions *npl*
sozialwirtschaftlich *adj* socio-economic *adj* **sozialwirtschaftliche Begriffe** socio-economic categories
sozioökonomisch *adj* socio-economic *adj*
spalten *vb* split *vb*
Sparkasse (-n) *nf* savings bank *n*
Sparkonto (-konten) *nn* savings account *n*
Sparte (-n) *nf* line of business *n*
Spediteur (-e) *nm* carrier *n*, forwarder *n*, forwarding agent *n*, freight forwarder *n*, agent, transport agent (US)
Spedition *nf* forwarding agent *n*, road haulage *n*, road haulage company *n* **per Spedition** by road
Speicher (-) *nm* (DP) memory *n*
Speicherkapazität *nf* memory capacity *n*
Spekulant (-en) *nm* speculator *n*
Spekulationskapital *nn* venture capital *n*
spekulieren *vb* speculate *vb*

sperren *vb* block *vb*
Sperrkonto (-konten) *nn* blocked
account *n*
Sperrzone (-n) *nf* exclusion zone *n*
Spesen *npl* business expenses *npl*
Spesenkonto (-s) *nn* expense account *n*
spezialisieren *vb* specialize *vb*
Spezialität (-en) *nf* speciality *n*
Spielraum *nm* room for manoeuvre *n*
Spitze (-n) *nf* peak *n* **an der Spitze von** at
the head of
Spitzen- *cpd* high-level *adj*, top-level *adj*
Spitzennachfrage *nf* peak demand *n*
Spitzenqualität *nf* top-of-the-range *adj*
Spitzentechnologie (-n) *nf* advanced
technology *n*
Spitzenzeit (-en) *nf* peak period *n*
Spitzenzeiten *npl*, busy hours (US)
Spotmarkt (-märkte) *nm* spot market *n*
Spottpreis (-e) *nm* bargain price *n*
Sprache (-n) *nf* language *n* **offizielle
Sprache** working language
Sprachexperte (-n) *nm* language
specialist *n*
Sprecher (-) *nm* spokesperson *n*
Spur (-en) *nf* track *n*
Staatsangehörigkeit *nf* nationality *n*
Staatsanleihe (-n) *nf* government bond *n*,
government loan *n* **Staatsanleihen** pub-
lic funds
Staatsausgaben *nfpl* state expenditure *n*
Staatsdienst *nm* civil service *n*, public
service *n*
Staatspapier (-e) *nn* gilt-edged security *n*,
government security *n*
Staatsschuld *nf* national debt *n*
Staatswirtschaft *nf* (system) national
economy *n*
stabil *adj* (economy) stable *adj*
Stabilität *nf* stability *n* **finanzielle Sta-
bilität** financial stability
Stadt (-ädte) *nf* town *n*
Stadtausbreitung *nf* urban sprawl *n*
Stadterneuerung *nf* urban renewal *n*
städtisch *adj* urban *adj*
Stadtmitte (-n) *nf* town centre *n*
Stadtplanung *nf* town planning *n*
staffeln *vb* (holidays) stagger *vb*
Stagnierung *nf* stagnation *n*
Stahl (-e) *nm* steel *n*
Stahlindustrie (-n) *nf* steel industry *n*
Stammaktie (-n) *nf* equity share *n*, ordin-
ary share *n*, ordinary stock (US)
Stammkunde (-n) *nm* regular customer *n*
Standard- *cpd* standard *adj*
standhalten *vb* withstand *vb*

Standort (-e) *nm* location *n*
Startkapital *nn* start-up capital *n*
Statistik *nf* statistics *npl*
Status quo *nm* status quo *n*
Statut (-en) *nn* statute *n*
steigen *vb* rise *vb*
steigern *vb* increase *vb* **die Produktion
steigern** increase output
Steigerung *nf* (in bank rate) rise *n*
Stelle (-n) *nf* (job) post *n*
Stellenangebot (-e) *nn* job offer *n*
Stellenbeschreibung (-en) *nf* job
description *n*
Stellenbesetzung *nf* staffing *n*
Stellenrotation *nf* job rotation *n*
Stellenvermittlung (-en) *nf* employment
agency *n*
Stellung position *nf* **befristete Stellung
(-en)** temporary employment
stellvertretend *adj* deputy *adj* **stellvertretender Leiter** assistant manager **stellvertretender Direktor** deputy director
Stellvertreter (-) *nm* deputy *n*
stempeln *vb* stamp *vb* **den Arbeitsbeginn
stempeln** clock in **das Arbeitsende
stempeln** clock out
Sterlinggebiet *nn* sterling area *n*
Steuer (-n) *nf* tax *n* **nach Abzug der
Steuern** after tax **vor Abzug der Steuern**
before tax **indirekte Steuer** indirect tax
örtliche Steuern local taxes **eine Steuer
auferlegen** impose a tax **Steuern einheben** levy taxes **Steuern im Preis enthal-
ten** taxes are included
Steuerbeleg (-e) *nm* fiscal receipt *n*
Steuerbetrug *nm* tax avoidance *n*
Steuereinkommen *nn* taxable income *n*
Steuerforderung *nf* tax claim *n*
steuerfrei *adj* free of tax *adj*, tax-
exempt *adj*, tax-free *adj*, zero-rated
(taxation) *adj*
Steuerfreijahre *nnpl* tax holiday *n*
Steuerhinterziehung *nf* tax evasion *n*
Steuerjahr (-e) *nn* fiscal year *n*, tax year *n*
Steuerklasse (-n) *nf* tax bracket *n*
Steuerklassifizierung *nf* fiscal zoning *n*
steuerlich *adj* tax *adj* **steuerlich absetzbar**
tax-deductible **steuerliche Belastung** fis-
cal charges
Steuerpflicht (-en) *nf* tax liability *n*
steuerpflichtig *adj* liable for tax *adj*
Steuersatz (-sätze) *nm* tax rate *n*
Steuerschwelle (-n) *nf* tax threshold *n*
Steuersenkung (-en) *nf* tax cut *n*
Steuervergünstigung (-en) *nf* tax
allowance *n*

Steuerzahler nm taxpayer n
Steuerzuschlag (-äge) nm surtax n
stichhaltig adj (fig) watertight adj
Stichprobe nf random selection n
Stichtag (-e) nm target date n
Stichwort (-wörter) nn (computer) keyword n
Stiftung (-en) nf endowment n **eine Stiftung errichten** set up a trust
still adj silent adj **stiller Teilhaber** silent partner
Stillegung (-en) nf closure n, shutdown n (strike) stoppage n
stillschweigend adj tacit adj
Stimme (-n) nf vote n
Stimmrecht nn voting right n
Stopp (-s nm (on prices, wages) freeze n
stoppen vb (inflation) halt vb
stören vb bug vb
stornieren vb cancel vb **einen Vertrag stornieren** cancel a contract
Stornierung (-en) nf cancellation n
Stornierungsoption nf option to cancel n
Stornogebühr (-en) nf cancellation charge n
Stoßzeit (-en) nf rush hour n
Strafgericht nn criminal court n
Strafrecht nn criminal law n
strapazierfähig adj heavy-duty adj
Straße (-n) nf road n
Straßengüterverkehr nm road transport n
Straßentransport nm road transport n
Straßenverkehr nm road traffic n
Strategie (-n) nf strategy n
strategisch adj strategic adj
Streik (-s) nm strike n **offizieller Streik** official strike **wilder Streik** unofficial strike, wildcat strike
Streikabstimmung (-en) nf strike ballot n
Streikbrecher (-) nm scab* n, strikebreaker n
streiken vb strike vb
Streikende/r nmf striker n
Streikmaßnahmen nfpl strike action n
Streikposten (-) nm (strike) picket n
Streit (-e) nm dispute n
streitende Partei (-en) nf litigant n
Strichcode (-s) nm bar code n
Stückkosten npl unit cost n
Stückpreis (-e) nm unit price n
stufenweise adj in stages adj
Stunde (-n) nf hour nf **pro Stunde** adj per hour adj **Stunde Null** zero hour
Stundenlohn (-öhne) nm hourly rate n
Stundenlohnarbeiter npl hourly workers npl

Stundenplan (-äne) nm timetable n
stündlich adj hourly adj
Subunternehmer (-) nm subcontractor n
Subvention (-en) nf subsidy n
subventionieren vb subsidize vb
Supermacht (-mächte) nf superpower n **wirtschaftliche Supermacht** economic superpower
Supermarkt (-märkte) nm supermarket n
Syndikat (-e) nn syndicate n
Synergie (-n) nf synergy n
Synthese (-n) nf synthesis n
synthetisch adj synthetic adj
System (-e) nn system n
Systemanalyse nf systems analysis n
Systemanalytiker (-) nm systems analyst n
tabellarisch adj tabulated adj **tabellarische Datenaufstellung** tabulated data
tabellarisieren vb (data) tabulate vb
Tabelle (-n) nf chart n
Tabellenkalkulation nf spreadsheet n
Tagebuch (-bücher) nn journal n
Tageskurs (-e) nm transfer price n
Tagesordnung (-en) nf agenda n
Tageszeitung (-en) nf daily newspaper n
Tagewerk nn day's work n
Tagungsbericht (-e) nm conference proceedings npl
Tagungsort (-e) nm conference venue n
Taktik nf tactic n
Tarif (-e) nm tariff n
Tarifabbau nm elimination of tariffs n
Tarifabkommen (-) nn collective agreement n, wage(s) agreement n, wage(s) settlement n
Tarifverhandlung (-en) nf collective bargaining n
Tarifzone (-n) nf wage zone n
Tastatur (-en) nf keyboard n
Tatsachen nfpl the hard facts npl **die anerkannten Tatsachen** known facts npl
tatsächlich adj actual adj
Tausch (-e) nm swap n
tauschen vb barter vb, swap vb
Tauschhandel nm barter n, barter transaction n
Tauschhandelsabkommen (-) nn barter agreement n
Team (-s) nn team n
Techniker (-) nm technician n
technisch adj technical **technischer Direktor** technical director
Technologie (-n) nf technology n **neue Technologie** new technology
Technologietransfer nm technology transfer n

Teil (-e) *nn* (of a machine) part *n*
teilen *vb* share *vb*, split *vb*
Teillieferung (-en) *nf* part shipment *n*, short delivery *n*
Teilzahlung (-en) *nf* part payment *n*, token payment *n*
Teilzahlungskauf *nm* hire purchase *n*
Teilzeit- *cpd* part-time *adj*
Telefon (-e) *nn* telephone *n*
Telefonbankdienst (-e) *nm* telebanking *n*
Telefonbuch (-bücher) *nn* telephone directory *n*
Telefongebühr *nf* call charge *n* **Telefongebühr bar bezahlt** Freefone (R) (GB) *n*
Telefonist (-en) *nm* switchboard operator *n*
Telefonnummer (-n) *nf* telephone number *n*
Telefonverkauf *nm* telesales *npl*
Telefonzelle (-n) *nf* telephone box *n*, telephone booth (US)
Telefonzentrale (-n) *nf* switchboard *n*
Tendenz (-en) *nf* tendency *n*
tendieren *vb* tend *vb*
Termin (-e) *nm* (to meet) appointment *n* (meeting) engagement *n* **zum festgesetzten Termin** at term **einen Termin einhalten** keep an appointment **einen Termin vereinbaren** make an appointment
Terminal (-s) *nm* computer terminal *n*
Terminalmarkt (-märkte) *nm* terminal market *n*
Termingeschäft (-e) *nn* forward transaction *n*
Termingeschäfte *npl* futures *nnpl*
Terminhandel *nm* futures trading *n*
Terminierung *nf* timing *n*
Terminkontrakt (-e) *nm* forward contract *n*, futures contract *n*
Terminkontraktmarketing *nn* futures marketing *n*
Terminkontraktmarkt (-märkte) *nm* futures market *n*
Terminkontraktpreis (-e) *nm* futures price *n*
Terminlieferung *nf* future delivery *n*
Terminmarkt (-märkte) *nm* forward market *n*
Terminsicherung *nf* forward cover *n*
Terminware *nf* future goods *npl*
Testament (-e) *nn* will *n* **gerichtliche Testamentsbestätigung** probate *n*
Testdaten *nnpl* test data *npl*
Testmarkt (-märkte) *nm* test-market *vb*
teuer *adj* high-priced *adj*
Textil (-ien) *nn* textile *n*

Textilidustrie (-n) *nf* textile industry *n*
Textverarbeitung *nf* word processing *n*
Textverarbeitungsgerät (-e) *nn* word processor *n*
theoretisch *adj* in theory *adj*
Tiefbau *nm* civil engineering *n*
tilgen *vb* wipe out *vb* **eine Schuld tilgen** pay off a debt
tippen *vb* type *vb*
Tippfehler (-) *nm* typing error *n*
Titel (-) *nm* (to goods) title *n*
Tochtergesellschaft (-en) *nf* subsidiary company *n*, susidiary *n* **hundertprozentige Tochtergesellschaft** wholly-owned subsidiary
Tonnage *nf* tonnage *n*
Tonne (-n) *nf* ton *n* **metrische Tonne** metric ton
total *adj* total *adj*
Totalschaden *nm* write-off *n*
Tourismus *nm* tourism *n*
Tourist (-en) *nm* tourist *n*
tragbar *adj* portable *adj* **tragbarer Computer** portable computer
Träger (-n) *nm* bracket *n*
Transaktion (-en) *nf* transaction *n*
Transaktionsverwaltung *nf* transaction management *n*
Transfer (-s) *nm* transfer *n*
Transfertechnik *nf* transfer technology *n*
Transitgüter *nnpl* goods in process *npl*, transit goods *npl*
Transitlager (-) *nn* bonded warehouse *n*
Transitraum (-räume) *nm* (transport) transfer lounge *n*
Transitschäden *nmpl* damage to goods in transit *n*
Transitschalter (-) *nm* (transport) transfer desk *n*
Transitwaren *nf* goods in progress *npl*
Transport *nm* transport *n*
Transportunternehmen (-) *nn* haulier *n*
Tratte (-n) *nf* (financial) draft *n*
Trauschein (-e) *nm* marriage certificate *n*
treffen *vb* meet *vb*
Trend (-s) *nm* trend *n*
Trendanalyse (-n) *nf* trend analysis *n*
Treuhänder (-) *nm* trustee *n*
treuhänderisch *adj* **treuhänderisch verwalten** hold sth in trust
Treuhandmittel *nnpl* trust fund *n*
Treuhandschaft *nf* trusteeship *n*
Treuhandvermögen (-) *nn* trust estate *n*
Treuhandvertrag (-äge) *nm* trust agreement *n*
Trinkgeld (-er) *nn* gratuity *n*

Trust (-s) nm trust company n
Typist/in (-en/-innen) nm/nf typist n
U.A.w.g. (Um Antwort wird gebeten)
abbr RSVP (répondez s'il vous plaît) abbr
über pari above par
Überangebot nn oversupply vb
überarbeitet adj overworked adj
Überbevölkerung nf overpopulation n
überbewerten vb overvalue vb
überbieten vb outbid vb
Überbrückungskredit (-e) nm bridging
loan, bridge loan (US)
übereinstimmen vb concur vb, tally vb
übereinstimmen mit tally with
überfällig adj overdue adj
Übergewicht nn excess luggage n, excess
weight n
Überheizen nn (of economy) overheating n
überholt adj out of date adj
Überkapazität nf excess capacity n
überladen vb overload vb
Übernachfrageinflation nf excess demand inflation n
Übernahme (-n) nf buy-out n, takeover n
Übernahmeangebot (-e) nn tender offer n
Übernahmezahlung (-en) nf transfer
payments npl
übernehmen vb take charge of sth (com-
pany) take over vb
Überproduktion nf overproduction n
überproduzieren vb overproduce vb
überreichen vb hand over vb
überschreiben vb (ownership) transfer vb
überschreiten vb exceed vb
Überschrift (-en) nf heading n
Überschuß (-üsse) nm surplus n
Überschußwaren nfpl surplus stock n
Überschußwaren aufnehmen absorb surplus stock
Übersee- cpd overseas adj
Überseegebiet (-e) nn overseas territory n
Überseehandel nm overseas trade n
Überseemarkt (-märkte) nm overseas
market n
übersehen vb overlook vb
überstaatlich adj transnational adj
Überstunden nfpl overtime n
übertragbar adj transferable adj
übertragen vb carry forward vb,
transcribe vb
Übertragungsurkunde (-n) nf (law) deed n
überverkaufen vb oversell vb
überverkauft adj oversold adj
Überwachungsausschuß (-üsse) nm
watchdog committee n

Überweisung (-en) nf remittance n **bargeldlose Überweisung** credit transfer
Überweisungsanzeige (-n) nf remittance
advice n
überzahlen vb overpay vb
Überzahlung nf overpayment n
überzeichnet adj oversubscribed adj
überziehen vb overdraw vb
Überziehung nf overdraft n
Überziehungskredit (-e) nm bank
overdraft n **einen Überziehungskredit
beantragen** request an overdraft
überzogenes Konto nn overdrawn account
umfassend adj comprehensive adj
Umfrage (-n) nf field investigation n
umgehen handle vb **umgehen mit** handle
Umkehr nf turnabout n
umkehren vb reverse vb
umladen vb transship vb
Umlauf nm circulation **im Umlauf** in
circulation
Umlaufkapital nn floating assets n
Umsatz (-ätze) nm turnover n **Umsatz des
Anlagevermögens** fixed asset turnover
Umsätze nmpl **hohe(n) Umsätze** heavy
trading
Umsatzquote (-n) nf turnover ratio n
Umsatzrate (-n) nf turnover rate n
Umsatzsteuer (-n) nf turnover tax n
Umschichten nn (of funds) reallocation n
Umschreibungsgebühr (-en) nf transfer
duty n
umschulden vb reschedule a debt vb
Umschuldungsanleihe nf funding
bonds npl
umschulen vb retrain vb
Umschulung nf retraining n
Umschulungsprogramm (-e) nn retraining programme n
Umsiedlung (-en) nf relocation n
Umstand (-ände) nm circumstance n **unter keinen Umständen** under no
circumstances **nicht in unserer Hand
liegende Umstände** circumstances beyond our control **unvorhergesehene
Umstände** unforeseen circumstances
umsteigen vb (transport) transfer vb
Umstellung nf rearrangement n **Umstellung auf das metrische Maßsystem**
metrication n
umstrukturieren vb restructure vb
Umtausch exchange n **günstiger Umtausch** favourable exchange
unabgefertigt adj (customs) uncleared adj

Unannehmlichkeit (-en) *nf* inconvenience *n*
unbedeutend *adj* minor *adj*
unbeschränkt *adj* unlimited *adj*
unbeständig *adj* (prices) volatile *adj*
unbestätigt *adj* unconfirmed *adj*
unbezahlt *adj* unpaid *adj*
undatiert *adj* not dated *adj*
uneinbringlich *adj* **uneinbringliche Schuld** bad debt
unerwartet *adj* unexpected *adj*, without warning *adj*
unfachmännisch *adj* unprofessional *adj*
Unfall (-älle) *nm* accident *n*
ungefähr *adj* approximate *adj*, approximately *adv*
ungelegen *adj* inconvenient *adj*
ungelernt *adj* unskilled *adj*
ungenau *adj* hit-or-miss *adj*
ungenutzt *adj* idle *adj* **ungenutzt sein** go to waste
ungesichert *adj* unsecured *adj*
ungültig *adj* void *adj* **ungültiger Scheck** bad cheque
Unkosten costs *npl*, expenses *npl* **laufende Unkosten** standing charges
Unkostensatz (-sätze) *nm* expenditure rate *n*
unnötig *adj* non-essential *adj*
unpopulär *adj* undersubscribed *adj*
unprofitabel *adj* unprofitable *adj*
unrechtmäßig *adj* wrongful *adj*
unter under *prep* **unter Null** below zero **unter pari** below par
unterbeschäftigt *adj* underemployed *adj*
unterbewerten *vb* undervalue *vb*
unterbezahlen *vb* underpay *vb*
unterbieten *vb* undercut *vb*
untergeordnet *adj* junior *adj*
Untergeordnete/r *nmf* subordinate *n*
Unterhalt *nf* maintenance *n* (of machine) operation *n*
Unterhaltskosten *npl* maintenance costs *npl*
unterkapitalisiert *adj* undercapitalized *adj*
Unterkunft (-ünfte) *nf* accommodation *n*
Unterkunftszuschuß (-üsse) *nm* accommodation allowance *n*
Unternehmen (-) *nn* company *n*, concern, organization *n*, undertaking *n* (project) enterprise *n* **multinationales Unternehmen (-)** multinational corporation
Unternehmensimage (-s) *nn* corporate image *n*
Unternehmensberater (-) *nm* business consultant *n*, management consultant *n*

Unternehmensführung *nf* management *n* **zielgesteuerte Unternehmensführung** management by objectives
Unternehmensinvestitionen *nfpl* corporate investment *n*
Unternehmenspolitik *nf* company policy *n*
Unternehmensspitze *nf* top management *n*
Unternehmer (-) *nm* entrepreneur *n*
unternehmerisch *adj* entrepreneurial *adj*
unterschlagen *vb* embezzle *vb*
Unterschlagung *nf* embezzlement *n*
unterschreiben *vb* sign *vb*
Unterschrift (-en) *nf* signature *n*
unterstützen *vb* support *vb* **eine Initiatve finanziell unterstützen** back a venture
Unterstützung *nf* backing *n* **Unterstützung finden** win support
unterwegs *adv* in transit *adv*
unterzeichnen *vb* (cheque) endorse *vb* sign *vb* **einen Vertrag unterzeichnen** sign a contract
Unterzeichner (-) *nm* signatory *n*, underwriter *n* **die Unterzeichner** the signatories to the contract
unverkäuflich *adj* unmarketable *adj*, unsaleable *adj*
unverkauft *adj* unsold *adj*
unverzüglich *adj* without delay *adj*, prompt *adj*
unwiderruflich *adj* irrevocable *adj*
unzureichend *adj* inadequate *adj*, unsatisfactory *adj*
Urheberrecht (-e) *nn* copyright law *n*
Urkunde (-n) *nf* record *n* **eine Urkunde nicht herausgeben** withhold a document
Urlaub *nm* furlough (US) *n*, leave *n* **bezahlter Urlaub** paid holiday **auf Urlaub** on holiday, on vacation (US) **Urlaub machen** furlough (US) *vb* **Urlaub nehmen** take a break
Urlaubsgeld *nn* holiday pay *n*
Ursprung (-ünge) *nm* (of a product) origin *n*
Ursprungsangabe (-n) *nf* statement of origin *n*
Ursprungszeugnis (-sse) *nn* certificate of origin *n*
Verabredung (-en) *nf* (agreement) arrangement *n*
Veralten *nn* obsolescence *n*
veraltet *adj* out of date *adj*, obsolete *adj*
veränderlich *adj* variable *adj* **veränderliche Kosten** variable costs **veränderlicher**

Kurs variable rate **veränderlicher Markt** fluid market
veranstalten vb organize vb **eine Konferenz veranstalten** arrange a conference
verantwortlich adj accountable adj, responsible adj **jemanden für verantwortlich halten** hold sb responsible **verantwortlich sein** be in charge
Verantwortlichkeit (-en) nf accountability n
Verantwortung responsibility n **gemeinsame Verantwortung** joint responsibility **die Verantwortung übernehmen** take responsibility for sth
verarbeitend adj processing adj **verarbeitende Industrie (-n)** secondary industry
Veräußerungsgewinne nmpl capital gains npl
Verband (-bände) nm union n
verbessern vb improve vb
verbinden vb connect vb **könnten Sie mich bitte mit X verbinden?** (telephone) could you connect me to... vb **verbinden mit** (phone) put sb through (to sb)
verbindlich adj binding adj
Verbindlichkeiten nfpl current liabilities npl, accounts payable npl **langfristige Verbindlichkeiten** fixed liability
verbleibend adj (sum) remaining adj
verboten adj out of bounds adj
Verbraucher (-) nm consumer n
Verbraucherakzeptanz nf consumer acceptance n
Verbrauchererwartungen nfpl consumer expectations npl
Verbrauchergesellschaft (-en) nf consumer society n
Verbrauchergroßmarkt (-märkte) nm hypermarket n
Verbraucherzufriedenheit nf consumer satisfaction n
Verbrauchsdatum nn best-before date n
Verbrauchsgewohnheiten nfpl consumer habits npl
Verbrauchssteuer (-n) nf excise duty n
verderblich adj corrupting adj **leicht verderblich** perishable adj
verdienen vb earn vb
Verdiener (-) nm wage earner n
Verdienstausfall (-fälle) nm loss of earnings n
verdient adj earned adj **schwer verdient** hard-earned
verdünnen vb water down vb
Verein (-e) nm guild n

Vereinbarung nf understanding n
vereinheitlichen vb standardize vb
Vereinheitlichung nf standardization n
Vereinigung nf unification n
vereint adj united adj
Vereinte Nationen npl **die Vereinten Nationen** the United Nations
Verfahren (-) nn process n
Verfall nm expiration n
Verfallstag (-e) nm expiry date n, expiration (US)
Verfalltag (-e) nm termination date n
verfälscht adj weighted adj
Verfälschung nf falsification n
verfassen vb draw up vb **einen Bericht verfassen** draw up a report
verfügbar adj available adj **nicht verfügbar** not available
verfügen vb order vb, decree vb
Verfügung vb **eine Verfügung herausgeben** issue a writ
Vergehen (-) nn offence n, offense (US)
vergrößern vb enlarge vb
vergüten vb remunerate vb
Vergütung (-en) nf remuneration n **Vergütung für leitende Angestellte** executive compensation
Verhaltenskodex (-e) nm professional code of practice n
Verhältnis (-sse) nn ratio n
verhandeln (über) vb negotiate vb
Verhandlung (-en) nf negotiation n **durch Verhandlung** by negotiation **unter Verhandlung** under negotiation **Verhandlungen beginnen** begin negotiations
Verhandlungsführer (-) nm negotiator n
Verhandlungsgeschick nn negotiating skills npl
Verhandlungspaket (-e) nn package deal n
Verkauf (-aufe) nm sale n **Verkauf aufgrund einer Ausschreibung** sale by tender
verkaufen vb market vb, sell vb, sell up vb **auf Kredit verkaufen** sell sth on credit **zu verkaufen** for sale
Verkäufer (-) nm salesperson n, seller n, shop assistant n, vendor n
Verkäufermarkt nm seller's market
Verkaufsbedingungen nfpl conditions of sale npl
Verkaufsfläche (-n) nf shop floor n
Verkaufsgebiet (-e) nn trading area n
Verkaufsgespräch (-e) nn sales talk n
Verkaufskampagne (-n) nf sales campaign n
Verkaufskapital nn vendor capital n

Verkaufskonferenz (-en) *nf* sales conference *n*
Verkaufsleitung *nf* sales management *n*
Verkaufsmethode (-n) *nf* sales technique *n* **aggressive Verkaufsmethode** hard sell
Verkaufsmethoden *nfpl* selling tactics *npl*
Verkaufspotential *nn* sales potential *n*
Verkaufspunkt (-e) *nm* point of sale *n*
Verkaufsschlager (-) *nm* best seller *n* **Verkaufsschlager sein** be in hot demand
Verkaufssteigerung *nf* sales growth *n*
Verkaufsstelle (-n) *nf* sales outlet *n*, ticket agency *n*
Verkaufstaktik *nf* **aggresive Verkaufstaktik** hard sell **weiche Verkaufstaktik** soft sell
Verkaufsurkunde (-n) *nf* bill of sale *n*, deed of sale *n*
Verkaufsziel (-e) *nn* sales target *n*
Verkaufsziffern *nfpl* sales figures *npl*
Verkehrsbetrieb (-e) *nm* transport company *n*
Verkehrsministerium (-ien) *nn* Ministry of Transport *n*
verkümmern *vb* go to waste *vb*
Verladung *nf* shipping *n*
Verlag (-e) *nm* publishing house *n*
Verlagswesen *nn* publishing *n*
verlangen *vb* call for *vb*
verlängern *vb* extend *vb* **einen Vertrag verlängern** extend a contract
Verlängerung (-en) *nf* (of contract) extension *n*
verlangsamen *vb* slow down *vb*
Verlangsamung *nf* slowdown *n*
verläßlich *adj* reliable *adj*
verletzen *vb* contravene *vb*
Verletzung (-en) *nf* contravention *n*
Verleumdung *nf* slander *n* **schriftliche Verleumdung** libel *n*
verlieren *vb* forfeit *vb* (custom) lose *vb* **an Wert verlieren** depreciate
Verlust (-e) *nm* loss *n* **finanzieller Verlust** financial loss **uneinbringlicher Verlust** irrecoverable loss *n* **Verluste haben** be in the red **Verluste minimieren** minimise losses
Verlustquote (-n) *nf* wastage rate *n*
vermachen *vb* bequeath *vb*, bequest *n*
vermehren *vb* multiply *vb*
vermeiden *vb* avoid *vb*
vermieten *vb* lease *vb* (property) let *vb* **zu vermieten** for hire
vermindert *adj* reduced *adj*
vermitteln *vb* arbitrate *vb*, mediate *vb*
vermittelnd *adj* intermediary *adj*

Vermittler (-) *nm* mediator *n*
Vermittlung *nf* mediation *n*
Vermögen (-) *nn* asset *n*, wealth *n* **verstecktes Vermögen** hidden assets
Vermögenssteuer (-n) *nf* wealth tax *n*
Vernachlässigung *nf* neglect *n*
vernünftig *adj* (price) reasonable *adj*
Verpachtung *nf* lease *n* **Verpachtung von Steuern** farming of taxes
verpacken pack *vb* **in eine(r) Kiste verpacken** box sth up
Verpackung *nf* packaging *n*
verpflichten *vb* commit *vb*
verpflichtet *adj* indebted *adj* **verpflichtet sein** be obliged to do sth
Verpflichtung (-en) *nf* commitment *n*, covenant *n*, obligation *n* **gemeinsame Verpflichtung** joint obligation
verrechnet *adj* (cheque) cleared *adj* miscalculated *adj* **noch nicht verrechnet** (cheque) uncleared
versagen *vb* (negotiations) fail *vb* (attempts) fail *vb*
Versagen *nn* failure *n*
Versand *nm* (consignment) shipment *n* transportation *n*
Versandanzeige (-n) *nf* dispatch note *n*
versandbereit *adj* ready for despatch *adj*
Versanddatum (-en) *nn* date of dispatch *n*
Versandgebühren *nfpl* forwarding charges *npl*
Versandhandel *nm* mail order *n*
Versandhaus (-häuser) *nn* mail-order house *n*
verschieben *vb* (to next period) hold over *vb*
Verschleiß *nm* wastage *n* **geplanter Verschleiß** built-in obsolescence, planned obsolescence
verschleudern *vb* undersell *vb*
verschulden *vb* to be the cause of sth, to get into debt *vb*
Verschulden *nn* fault *n* **mitwirkendes Verschulden** contributory negligence
verschwenden *vb* squander *vb*, waste *vb*
verschwenderisch *adj* spendthrift *adj*
Verschwendung *nf* waste *n*
Versehen (-) *nn* oversight *n* **aus Versehen** due to an oversight
versichern *vb* insure *vb*
Versicherte/r *nmf* policy holder *n*
Versicherung *nf*, cover insurance *n*, insurance *n*, c.i.f. (cost insurance and freight) *abbr* **eine Versicherung abschließen** take out insurance

Versicherungsagent (-en) *nm* underwriter *n*
Versicherungsanspruch (-sprüche) *nm* claim *n* **einen Versicherungsanspruch regulieren** adjust a claim
versicherungsfähig *adj* insurable *adj* **nicht versicherungsfähig** uninsurable *adj*
Versicherungsfonds (-) *nm* insurance fund *n*
Versicherungsgesellschaft (-en) *nf* insurance company *n*
Versicherungsmakler (-) *nm* insurance broker *n*
Versicherungspolice (-n) *nf* insurance certificate *n*, insurance policy *n*
Versicherungsprämie (-n) *nf* insurance premium *n*
Versicherungsträger (-) *nm* insurance underwriter *n*
Versicherungsvertrag (-äge) *nm* insurance contract *n*
Versicherungsvertreter (-) *nm* insurance agent *n*, insurance representative *n*, insurance salesperson *n*
versiegeln *vb* seal *vb*
versorgen *vb* (supply) provide *vb*
Versorgung *nf* (stipulation) provision *n*
Versorgungsbetrieb (-e) *nm* public utility *n*
Versprechen (-) *nn* pledge *n*
versprechen *vb* give one's word *vb*
verstaatlichen *vb* nationalize *vb*
Verstaatlichung *nf* nationalization *n*
versteigern *vb* auction *vb*, sell sth at auction *vb*
Versteigerung (-en) *nf* auction *n*
vertagen *vb* adjourn *vb*
Vertagung (-en) *nf* adjournment *n*
Verteilernetz (-e) *nn* distribution network
Verteilung *nf* distribution *n*
vertikal *adj* vertical *n*
Vertikalintegration *nf* vertical integration *n*
Vertrag (-äge) *nm* contract *n*, treaty *n* **einen Vertrag abschließen** make a treaty **Vertrag von Rom** the Treaty of Rome
Vertragsarbeit *nf* contract work *n*
Vertragsbedingungen *nfpl* the terms of the contract *npl*
Vertragsberechtigte/r *nmf* covenantee *n*
Vertragsentwurf (-ürfe) *nm* draft contract *n*
vertragsgemäß *adj* as stipulated in the contract *adj* **vertragsgemäß wird verlangt, daß...** it is a requirement of the contract that...
Vertragshändler (-) *nm* authorized dealer *n*

Vertragsparteien *nfpl* the contracting parties *npl*
Vertragspflichten *nfpl* contractual obligations *npl*
Vertragsrecht *nn* law of contract *n*
Vertragsverletzung (-en) *nf* breach *n*, breach of contract *n*
Vertrauen *nn* trust *n*
Vertrauensmißbrauch *nm* abuse of confidence *n*
vertraulich *adj* confidential *adj* **streng vertraulich** in strictest confidence **streng vertrauliche Information** classified information
vertreiben *vb* merchandise *vb*
Vertreter (-) *nm* agent *n*, representative *n*
Vertrieb *nm* distribution *n*, merchandizing *n* **Vertrieb nach dem Schneeballprinzip** pyramid selling
Vertriebsberater (-) *nm* marketing consultant *n*
Vertriebsleiter (-) *nm* marketing director *n*
Veruntreuung *nf* misappropriation *n*
verwalten *vb* administer *vb* (money) handle *vb*
Verwalter (-) *nm* administrator *n*
Verwaltung *nf* administration *n* (of business) operation *n*
Verwaltungskosten *npl* administrative costs *npl*
verwässern *vb* water down *vb*
verwässert *adj* watered *adj* **verwässertes Aktienkapital** watered capital, watered stock
verweigern *vb* refuse *vb* **die Warenannahme verweigern** refuse goods **die Zahlung verweigern** refuse payment
verwenden *vb* use *n*, utilize *vb*
Verwendung *nf* utilization *n*
verwirken *vb* forfeit *vb*
Verzeichnis (-sse) *nn* register *n*
Verzicht *nm* waiver *n*
verzichten (auf) *vb* waive *vb*
Verzichtsleistungsklausel (-n) *nf* waiver clause *n*
Verzinsung *nf* payment of interest *n* **angemessene Verzinsung** fair rate of return
verzögern delay *vb* (withstand scrutiny) hold up *vb*
Verzögerung (-en) *nf* delay *n*, holdup *n*
Verzögerungstaktik *nf* delaying tactics *npl*
Video (-s) *nn* video *n*
Videofilm (-e) *nm* video *n*
Videogeräte *nnpl* video facilities *npl*
Videorekorder (-) *nm* video *n*
Vielzweck- *cpd* multipurpose *adj*

Viertel (-) *nn* (of year) quarter *n*
Vierteljahreszinsen *nmpl* quarterly
interest *n*
vierteljährlich *adj* quarterly *adj* **viertel-jährliche Kundenkonten** quarterly trade
accounts
vierzehntäglich *adj* biweekly *adj*
visuell *adj* visual *adj*
Visum (Visa, Visen) *nn* visa *n*
Volkseinkommen *nn* national income *n*
Volksvermögen *nn* national wealth *n*
Volkswirtschaft *nf* economics *n*
voll *adj* full *adj* **voll ausgelastet sein** work
to full capacity
Vollbeschäftigung *nf* full employment *n*
vollenden *vb* complete *vb*
Vollhafter (-) *nm* general partner
Vollkaskoversicherung *nf* comprehensive insurance policy *n*, comprehensive
insurance *n*
Vollkosten *npl* full cost
Vollmacht *nf* power of attorney *n*,
warrant *n* (power) proxy *n*
vollständig *adj* wholly *adv*
Vollzeit- *cpd* full-time *adj*
Vollzeitkraft (-kräfte) *nf* full-time worker *n*
Volumen *nn* volume *n*
vorankommen *vb* make headway *vb*
Vorarbeiter (-) *nm* foreman *n*
Vorauszahlung (-en) *nf* advance
payment *n*, prepayment *n*
vorbeugen *vb* forestall *vb*
vordatieren *vb* postdate *vb*
vorenthalten *vb* withhold *vb*
Vorfahrtsrecht *nn* right of way *n*
Vorhersage *nf* forecasting *n*
vorhersagen *vb* forecast *vb*
vorhersehbar *adj* foreseeable *adj* **aus
nicht vorhersehbaren Gründen** due to
unforeseen circumstances
vorläufig *adj* interim *adj*
vorlegen *vb* present *vb* **einen Bericht
vorlegen** submit/present a report
vornehmen *vb* **eine Reservierung vornehmen** make a reservation
Vorort (-e) *nm* suburb *n*
Vorrat (-äte) *nm* stocks **einen geringen
Vorrat haben** (stocks) run low **Vorräte
abbauen** (stocks) run down
Vorratslager (-) *nn* reserve stock *n*
Vorruhestand *nm* early retirement *n*
vorschlagen *vb* nominate *vb*
Vorschrift (-en) *nf* regulation *n*
vorschriftsgemäß *adj* according to the
regulations *adj*
Vorschuß (-üsse) **1.** *nm* (on salary)

advance *n* cash advance **2.** *vb* **Vorschuß
geben** *vb* (salary) advance *vb*
Vorsicht *nf* care *n* **Vorsicht - zerbrechlich!**
handle with care
Vorsitz *nm* chairmanship **(bei einer Sitzung) Vorsitz führen** chair a meeting **den
Vorsitz übernehmen** take the chair
Vorstand (-ände) *nm* board *n*, board of
directors *n*, factory board *n*
Vorstandssitzung (-en) *nf* board meeting *n*
Vorstandsvorsitzende/r *nmf* managing
director *n*
vorstellen (sich) *vb* introduce oneself *vb*,
attend for interview *vb*
Vorstellungsgespräch (-e) *nn* interview *n*
**ein Vorstellongsgespräch mit jemandem
führen** interview someone **zum Vorstellungsgespräch einladen** invite sb to an
interview **ein Vorstellungsgespräch führen** hold an interview
Vorteil (-e) *nm* advantage *n*
vorteilhaft *adj* advantageous *adj*
vorverlegen *vb* bring forward *vb*
Vorzug (-üge) *nm* preference *n*
Vorzugs- *cpd* preferential *adj*
Vorzugszollsystem *nn* **Vorzugszollsy-
stem in EU** community preference
Wachhund (-e) *nm* (fig) watchdog *n*
Wachstum *nn* growth *n* **durch Export
bedingtes Wachstum** export-led growth
Wachstumsindex (-e) *nm* growth index *n*
Wachstumsrate (-n) *nf* growth rate *n*, rate
of expansion *n* **jährliche Wachstumsrate**
annual growth rate
Wachstumsstrategie (-n) *nf* growth
strategy *n*
Waffenhandel *nm* arms trade *n*
Wahl (-en) *nf* election *n*
Währung (-en) *nf* currency *n* **gesetzliche
Währung** legal currency **harte Währung**
hard currency **konvertierbare Währung**
convertible currency **weiche Währung**
soft currency
Währungsfonds *nm* Monetary Fund **in-
ternationaler Währungsfonds** Interna-
tional Monetary Fund (IMF)
Währungsgebiet (-e) *nn* currency zone *n*
Währungskorb *nm* basket of currencies *n*
Währungsreform (-en) *nf* currency
reform *n*
Währungsreserve (-n) *nf* currency
reserve *n*
Währungsüberweisung (-en) *nf* currency
transfer *n*
Wanze (-n) *nf* (listening device) bug *n*

Waren *nfpl* goods *npl*, wares *npl* **Waren auf Probe** goods on approval
Warenausfuhr *nf* visible exports *npl*
Warenausgangsbuch (-bücher) *nn* sales ledger *n*
Wareneinkaufsbuch (-bücher) *nn* bought ledger *n*
Warenhaus (-häuser) *nn* department store *n*
Warenkennzeichnungsgesetz (-e) *nn* Trade Descriptions Act *n*
Warentermingeschäft *nn* commodity futures *n*
Warenverkaufskonto (-konten) *nn* trading account *n*
Warenzeichen (-) *nn* trademark *n*
warnen *vb* warn *vb*
Warnstreik (-s) *nm* token strike *n*
Warnung (-en) *nf* warning *n*
Warteliste (-n) *nf* waiting list
warten *vb* (wait) hang on *vb* (on phone) to be on hold *vb*, hold on *vb*
Warten *nn* waiting *n*
Warteraum *nm* waiting room *n* **Warteraum für Transitpassagiere (-räume)** (transport) transit lounge
Wartezone (-n) *nf* hold area *n*
Wechsel (-) *nm* bill of exchange *n* (financial) draft *n* **durch Indossament übertragbarer Wechsel** negotiable bill **unbezahlter Wechsel** unpaid bill
Wechselgeld *nn* (from purchase) change *n*
Wechselkurs (-e) *nm* exchange rate *n*, rate of exchange *n* **veränderlicher Wechselkurs** floating exchange rate
Wechselkursmechanismus *nm* exchange rate mechanism (ERM) *n*
Wechselobligo *nn* bills discounted *n*
Wechselstube (-n) *nf* bureau de change *n*
Wegwerf- *cpd* (not for reuse) disposable *adj*
weit *adj* wide-ranging *adj*
weitervergeben *vb* **weitervergeben an** subcontract *vb*
Weiterverkauf *nm* resale *n*
Welle (-n) *nf* (of mergers, takeovers) wave *n*
Wellenlänge (-n) *nf* wavelength *n*
Welt *nf* world *n*
Weltausstellung (-en) *nf* world fair *n*
Weltbank *nf* World Bank *n*
Weltexporte *nmpl* world exports *npl*
Weltgerichtshof (-höfe) *nm* World Court *n*
Welthandel *nm* international trade *n*
Weltmarkt (-märkte) *nm* global market *n*
Weltunternehmen (-) *nn* international organization *n*

Weltverbrauch *nm* world consumption *n*
weltweit *adj* worldwide *adj* **weltweites Marketing** global marketing
Weltwirtschaft (-) *nf* (system) global economy *n*
wenden *vb* turn over *vb*
Werbe- *cpd* promotional *adj*
Werbeagentur (-en) *nf* advertising agency *n*
Werbeeinkommen (-) *nn* advertising revenue *n*
Werbeetat (-s) *nm* advertising budget *n*, promotional budget *n*
Werbekampagne (-n) *nf* advertising campaign *n*, promotional campaign *n*
Werbemittel (-) *nn* advertising medium *n*
werben *vb* advertise *vb* **werben für** (product) promote *vb*
Werbeplan (-pläne) *nm* plan of campaign *n*
Werbespruch (-üche) *nm* advertising jingle *n*
Werbung *nf* advertisement *n* (of product) promotion *n* **übertriebene Werbung** hype
Werft (-en) *nf* dockyard *n*
Werk *nn* works, factory *n* **ab Werk** ex factory/works
Werksleiter (-) *nm* works manager *n*
Werksplanung *nf* facility planning *n*
Werkstatt (-stätten) *nf* shop floor *n*, workshop *n*
Wert (-e) *nm* value *n*, worth *n* **im Wert steigen** (rise in value) appreciate **an Wert verlieren** lose value **an Wert zunehmen** gain value **amtlich notierte Werte** listed securities **nicht notierte Werte** unlisted securities
wert *adj* worth *adj* **wert sein** be worth
Wertpapierbörse (-n) *nf* Stock Exchange *n*
Wertpapiere *npl* commercial paper *n*, securities *npl* **mündelsichere Wertpapiere** gilt-edged securities
Wertpapiermarkt (-märkte) *nm* stock market *n*
Wertsteigerung *nf* (in value) appreciation *n*
Wertung (-en) *nf* valuation *n*
Wertverlust *nm* depreciation *n*
wertvoll *adj* valuable *adj*
Westeuropäische Union *nf* WEU (Western European Union) *abbr*
Wettbewerb *nm* competition *n* **lauterer Wettbewerb** fair competition **unlauterer Wettbewerb** unfair competition
Wettbewerbsausschluß *nm* exclusive stipulation *n*

Wettbewerbsbeschränkung nf restrictive practices npl
wettbewerbsfähig adj competitive adj
Wettbewerbsfähigkeit nf competitiveness n
Wettbewerbsfreiheit nf free competition n
Wettbewerbsmethode (-en) nf lautere **Wettbewerbsmethode** fair-trade practice
Wettbewerbsvorteil (-e) nm competitive advantage n, competitive edge n
widerrufen vb rescind vb **eine Bestellung widerrufen** cancel an order
Wiedereinfuhr nf reimportation n
wiederernennen vb reappoint vb
Wiederernennung (-en) nf reappointment n
wiedergutmachen vb make amends vb
Wiederherstellung (-en) nf reparation n
Wiederinbesitznahme (-n) nf repossession n
wiederverwerten vb recycle vb
Wiederwahl (-en) nf re-election n
willkürlich adj arbitrary adj, at random
Wirklichkeit nf actuality n
Wirkung (-en) nf effect n
Wirt (-e) nm landlord n **Hauswirt** nm owner of accomodation for rent
Wirtschaft (-en) nf (system) economy n **sich entwickelnde Wirtschaft** developing economy **fortgeschrittene Wirtschaft** advanced economy **unterentwickelte Wirtschaft** underdeveloped economy
wirtschaftlich adj economic adj **wirtschaftliche Infrastruktur** economic infrastructure
Wirtschaftsanalyse (-n) nf economic analysis n
Wirtschaftsaufschwung (-ünge) nm economic boom n
Wirtschaftsberater (-) nm economic adviser n
Wirtschaftsbericht (-e) nm economic survey n
Wirtschaftsentwicklung nf economic development n
Wirtschaftsgeographie nf economic geography n
Wirtschaftskrieg (-e) nm trade war n
Wirtschaftskrise (-n) nf economic crisis n
Wirtschaftsleistung nf economic performance n
Wirtschaftsplan (-äne) nm economic plan n
Wirtschaftsplanung nf economic planning n

Wirtschaftspolitik nf economic policy n
Wirtschaftsprognose (-n) nf economic forecast n
Wirtschaftsrückgang (-änge) nm economic decline n
Wirtschaftsstrategie nf economic strategy n
Wirtschaftstrend (-s) nm economic trend n
Wirtschaftsunion (-en) nf economic union n
Wirtschaftswachstum nn economic expansion n, economic growth n
Wirtschaftswissenschaftler (-) nm economist n
Wirtschaftsziel (-e) nn economic objective n
Wirtschaftszyklus (-zyklen) nm economic cycle n
Wissen nn knowledge n
Wissensbasis (-basen) nf knowledge base n
Woche (-n) nf week n
Wochenlöhne nmpl weekly wages npl
wöchentlich adj weekly adj
Wohl nn welfare n
wohl adv well adv **wohl informiert** well-informed
wohlerprobt adj well-tried adj
Wohlfahrtsstaat (-en) nm welfare state n
Wohlstandsgesellschaft (-en) nf affluent society n
Wohnsiedlung (-en) nf housing complex n, housing estate n, tenement (US)
Wohnung (-en) nf dwelling n, appartment n **Wohnung auf Timesharing-Basis** timeshare
Wohnungsbauindustrie nf housing industry n
Wohnungsbauprogramm (-e) nn housing scheme n
Wohnungsbauprojekt (-e) nn housing project n
Wohnverhältnisse nnpl living conditions npl
Wort (Wörter, Worte) nn word n
Wortlaut nm wording n
wörtlich adv verbatim adv
Wucher nm usury n
zahlbar adj payable adj **zahlbar an** pay to the order of... **zahlbar sofort ohne Abzug** terms strictly net(t) **zahlbar im voraus** payable in advance
Zahlen nfpl figures npl, numbers npl **in**

den schwarzen Zahlen sein be in the black

zahlen *vb* pay *vb* **eine Gebühr zahlen** pay a fee **im voraus zahlen** pay in advance

Zahlenanalyse (-n) *nf* numerical analysis *n*

Zahltag (-e) *nm* (stock exchange) Account Day *n*

Zahlung (-en) *nf* payment *n* **volle Zahlung** full payment **Zahlung bei Auftragserteilung** cash with order **Zahlung auf Kredit** payment on account **Zahlung bei Warenerhalt** COD (cash on delivery) *abbr*, (collect on delivery) (US)

Zahlungsanweisung (-en) *nf* money order *n*, warrant for payment *n*

Zahlungsaufforderung (-en) *nf* request for payment *n*

Zahlungsbilanz (-en) *nf* balance of payments *n* **günstige Zahlungsbilanz** favourable balance of payments

Zahlungsbilanzdefizit (-e) *nn* balance of payments deficit *n*

Zahlungsbilanzüberschuß (-üsse) *nm* balance of payments surplus *n*

Zahlungsempfänger (-) *nm* payee *n*

zahlungsfähig *adj* solvent *adj*

Zahlungsfähigkeit (-en) *nf* ability to pay *n*, solvency *n*

Zahlungsmethode (-n) *nf* method of payment *n*

zahlungsunfähig *adj* insolvent *adj*

Zahlungsunfähigkeit *nf* insolvency *n*

Zahlungsverpflichtungen *nfpl* obligation/ liability to pay *n* **Zahlungsverpflichtungen nicht nachkommen** default *vb*

Zahlungsverzug (-üge) *nm* default *n*

Zeit (-en) *nf* time *n* **Zeit nehmen** take one's time

Zeitbeschränkung (-en) *nf* time limit *n*

Zeiteinteilung *nf* time management *n*

Zeitkarte (-n) *nf* season ticket *n*

Zeitmaßstab (-stäbe) *nm* timescale *n*

Zeitplan (-pläne) *nm* schedule *n*

zeitraubend *adj* time-consuming *adj*

Zeitraum (-äume) *nm* time frame *n*

Zeitschrift (-en) *nf* (journal) magazine *n*

zeitsparend *adj* time-saving *adj*

Zeitstudie (-n) *nf* work study *n*

Zeitung (-en) *nf* newspaper *n*

Zeitungsanzeige (-n) *nf* newspaper advertisement *n*

Zeitungsbericht (-e) *nm* newspaper report *n*

Zeitvergeudung *nf* waste of time *n*

Zeitzone (-n) *nf* time zone *n*

zentral *adj* central *adj* **zentrale Planwirtschaft** central planned economy

Zentralbank (-en) *nf* central bank *n*

zentralisieren *vb* centralize *vb*

Zentralisierung *nf* centralization *n*

Zentralplanung *nf* central planning *n*

zerstören *vb* wreck *vb*

Zessionsurkunde (-n) *nf* deed of transfer *n*

Zeuge (-n) *nm* witness *n*

Ziel (-e) *nn* objective *n*, target *n* **ein Ziel setzen** set a target

Zielmarkt (-märkte) *nm* target market *n*

Ziffer (-n) *nf* numeric character *n*

Zinsbelastung (eines Sollsaldos) *nf* carrying cost *n*

Zinsen *nmpl* interest *n* **ohne Zinsen** *ex* interest **Zinsen berechnen** charge interest **Zinsen tragen** bear interest **Zinsen zahlen** pay interest

Zinseszins *nm* compound interest *n*

zinsfrei *adj* non-interest-bearing *adj*

Zinskurs (-e) *nm* interest rate *n*, rate of interest *n*

zinslos *adj* interest-free *adj*

Zinsperiode (-n) *nf* interest period *n*

Zinssatz (-sätze) *nm* rate of interest *n* **günstiger Zinssatz** fine rate of interest **veränderlicher Zinssatz** floating rate of interest

zinstragend *adj* interest-bearing *adj*

zirkulieren *vb* **zirkulieren lassen** (document) circulate *vb*

Zivilrecht *nn* civil law *n*

Zoll (Zölle) *nm* customs *npl* (customs) duty *n* **Zölle erhöhen** raise tariffs

Zollabfertigung (-en) *nf* customs check *n*, customs clearance *n*

Zollabfertigungshafen (-häfen) *nm* port of entry *n*

Zollager (-) *nn* bonded warehouse *n*, customs warehouse *n*

Zollamt (-ämter) *nn* customs office *n*

Zollbeamte/r *nmf* customs officer *n*

Zollerklärung (-en) *nf* customs declaration *n*

Zollerlaubnisschein (-e) *nm* clearance certificate *n*

Zollformalitäten *nfpl* customs formalities *npl*

zollfrei *adj* (goods) duty-free **zollfreie Waren** free goods

Zollgebühren *nfpl* customs charges *npl*

Zollinspektor (-en) *nm* customs inspector *n*

Zollkontingent (-e) *nn* tariff quota *n*

Zollkontrolle (-n) *nf* (customs) inspection *n*

Zollmauer (-n) *nf* tariff wall *n*
Zollreform (-en) *nf* tariff reform *n*
Zollschranke (-n) *nf* tariff barrier *n*
Zollunion (-en) *nf* customs union *n*
Zollverhandlungen *npl* tariff
negotiations *npl*
Zollverordnungen *npl* customs
regulations *npl*
Zollverschluß *nm* **unter Zollverschluß** in
bond
Zone (-n) *nf* zone *n* **Einteilung in Zonen**
zoning **in Zonen einteilen** zone *vb*
Zufallschaden (-äden) *nm* accidental
damage *n*
Zugang *nm* access *n*
Zugänglichkeit *nf* accessibility *n*
zugehen *vb* **zugehen auf** head for
Zulage *nf* weighting *n*
Zunahme (-n) *nf* (in inflation) rise *n*
Züricher Gnomen (die) *n* the Gnomes of
Zurich *npl*
zurückgehen *vb* decrease *vb*
zurückhalten *vb* (not release) hold back *vb*
zurückkehren *vb* revert *vb*
zurückkommen *vb* return, come back *vb*
zurückkommen auf refer to
zurücknehmen *vb* (licence) revoke *vb*
zurückrufen *vb* (on phone) call back *vb*
zurücksenden *vb* send back *vb*
zurücktreten *vb* resign *vb* (resign) quit *vb*
zurücktreten von (resign from) leave,
resign from office
zurückweisen *vb* (contract) repudiate *vb*
zurückzahlen *vb* refund *vb*, repay *vb*
zurückziehen *vb* withdraw *vb*
zusammenarbeiten *vb* collaborate *vb*
zusammenarbeiten mit collaborate
with *vb*
Zusammenbruch *nm* (of company, economy) collapse *n*

zusammenhängen *vb* (argument) hang
together *vb*
zusammenrechnen *vb* tally up *vb*
zusätzlich *adj* extra *adj* **zusätzliche Gebühr** additional charge
Zusatzsteuer (-n) *nf* supertax *n*
Zuschauer (-) *nm* viewer *n*
Zuschuß (-üsse) *nm* allowance *n*
Zuständigkeitsbereich *nm* jurisdiction *n*
Zustelldienst *nm* home service *n*
zustimmen *vb* agree *vb*, consent *vb*
Zustimmung *nf* consent *n*
zuteilen *vb* allocate *vb*
zutreffend *adj* applicable *adj* **nicht zutreffend** N/A (not applicable) *abbr*
Zuverlässigkeit *nf* reliability *n*
Zuwachsrate (-n) *nf* rate of accrual *n*
natürliche Zuwachsrate (-n) natural rate
of increase
zuweisen *vb* assign *vb*
Zuweisung *nf* assignment *n*
Zwangswährung (-en) *nf* forced
currency *n*
zweckmäßig *adj* convenient *adj*
zweibahnig *adj* two-way *adj*
Zweigang- *cpd* two-speed *adj*
Zweigniederlassung (-en) *nf* branch
company *n*
Zweigstelle (-n) *nf* branch office *n*
zweijährlich *adj* biennial *adj*
zweimal *adv* twice *adv* **zweimal jährlich**
biannual *adj* **zweimal wöchentlich** twice
a week
zweimonatlich *adj* bimonthly *adj*
zweistufig *adj* two-tier *adj* **zweistufiges
Verwaltungssystem (-e)** two-tier system
Zwischenhändler (-) *nm* middleman *n*
Zwischenlager (-) *nn* entrepôt, intermedi-
ate store *n*

English–German

abandon *vb* aufgeben *vb*
abandoned *adj* **abandoned goods** herrenlose Güter *nnpl*
abate *vb* nachlassen *vb*
abatement *n* Abflauen (-) *nn*
abbreviate *vb* abkürzen *vb*
abbreviated *adj* abgekürzt *adj*
abbreviation *n* Abkürzung (-en) *nf*
abeyance *n* **to fall into abeyance** außer Gebrauch kommen
ability *n* Fähigkeit (-en) *nf* **ability to pay** Zahlungsfähigkeit (-en) *nf*
aboard *adv* **to go aboard** an Bord gehen
abolish *vb* abschaffen *vb*
abolition *n* Abschaffung *nf*
above-mentioned *adj* obenerwähnt *adj*
aboveboard *adj* korrekt *adj*
abroad *adv* **to go abroad** ins Ausland gehen
absence *n* **in the absence of information** in Ermangelung weiterer Information
absent *adj* abwesend *adj*
absentee *adj* abwesend *adj* **absentee landlord** nicht ortsansässiger Hausbesitzer *nm*
absenteeism *n* häufige Abwesenheit *nf*
absolute *adj* absolut *adj*
absorb *vb* absorbieren *vb* **to absorb surplus stock** Überschußwaren aufnehmen
abstract *n* Auszug (-üge) *nm*
abundance *n* Fülle *nf*
abuse **1.** *n* **abuse of power/trust** Machtmißbrauch/Vertrauensmißbrauch *nm/nm* **2.** *vb* mißbrauchen *vb*
accelerate *vb* beschleunigen *vb*
acceleration *n* Beschleunigung *nf*
accept *vb* **accept delivery** die Lieferung annehmen
acceptance *n* **consumer acceptance** Verbraucherakzeptanz *nf* **acceptance house** Akzeptbank (-en) *nf* **market acceptance** Marktakzeptanz *nf*
access **1.** *n* Zugang *nm* **2.** *vb* Zugriff haben auf

accessibility *n* Zugänglichkeit *nf*
accident *n* Unfall (-älle) *nm* **industrial accident** Arbeitsunfall (-älle) *nm*
accidental *adj* **accidental damage** Zufallschaden (-äden) *nm*
accommodation *n* Unterkunft (-ünfte) *nf* **accommodation allowance** Unterkunftszuschuß (-üsse) *nm* **accommodation bill** Gefälligkeitswechsel (-) *nm* **to come to an accommodation** zu einer Einigung kommen
accomplish *vb* schaffen *vb*
accomplishment *n* Leistung (-en) *nf*
accordance *n* **in accordance with** gemäß *prep*
according to *prep* **according to plan** plangemäß **according to the minister** laut Minister
account *n* **bank account** Bankkonto (-konten) *nn* **Account Day** (stock exchange) Zahltag (-e) *nm* **expense account** Spesenkonto (-konten) *nn* **payment on account** Zahlung auf Kredit (-en) *nf* **profit and loss account** Gewinn- und Verlustrechnung (-en) *nf* **savings account** Sparkonto (-konten) *nn* **accounts receivable** ausstehende Forderungen **statement of account** Kontoauszug (-üge) *nm* **to open an account** ein Konto eröffnen **to overdraw on an account** ein Konto überziehen **to settle an account** die Rechnung begleichen **to take sth into account** etwas in Betracht ziehen **trading account** Warenverkaufskonto (-konten) *nn*
account for *vb* erklären *vb*
accountability *n* Verantwortlichkeit (-en) *nf*
accountable *adj* verantwortlich *adj*
accountancy *n* Buchführung *nf*
accountant *n* Buchhalter (-) *nm* **chartered accountant** Bilanzbuchhalter (-) *nm*
accounting *n* **accounting conventions** Buchhaltungsnormen *nfpl* **financial accounting** Finanzbuchhaltung *nf* **manage-**

ment accounting Rechnungswesen für besondere Betriebsprüfungsbedürfnisse *nn* **accounting period** Rechnungsabschnitt (-e) *nm*
accredit *vb* akkreditieren *vb*
accrual *n* Ansammlung *nf* **rate of accrual** Zuwachsrate (-n) *nf*
accrued *adj* **accrued interest** aufgelaufene Zinsen *nmpl*
accumulate *vb* ansammeln *vb*
accumulated *adj* angesammelt *adj*
accuracy *n* Genauigkeit *nf*
accurate *adj* genau *adj*
achieve *vb* erreichen *vb*
achievement *n* Leistung (-en) *nf*
acknowledge *vb* **to acknowledge receipt of sth** den Empfang bestätigen
acknowledgement *n* **acknowledgement of debt** schriftliches Schuldanerkenntnis (-sse) *nn*
acquaintance *n* **business acquaintance** Geschäftsfreund (-e) *nm* **to make the acquaintance of sb** jemanden kennenlernen *vb*
acquire *vb* erwerben *vb*
acquisition *n* Erwerb *nm*
acquisitive *adj* habgierig *adj*
action *n* **industrial action** Arbeitskampf (-kämpfe) *nm* **legal action** Klage (-en) *nf* **out of action** außer Betrieb
actual *adj* tatsächlich *adj*
actuality *n* Wirklichkeit *nf*
actuary *n* Aktuar (-e) *nm*
acumen *n* **business acumen** Geschäftssinn *nm*
additional *adj* **additional charge** zusätzliche Gebühr *nf*
address 1. *n* **home address** Heimatanschrift (-en) *nf* **registered address** eingetragene Anschrift (-en) *nf* **to change address** umziehen *vb* 2. *vb* adressieren *vb*
addressee *n* Empfänger (-) *nm*
adjourn *vb* vertagen *vb* sich vertagen *vb*
adjournment *n* Vertagung (-en) *nf*
adjust *vb* anpassen *vb* **to adjust a claim** einen Versicherungsanspruch regulieren **to adjust the figures** die Zahlen berichtigen
adjustment *n* Anpassung (-en) *nf*, Regulierung (-en) *nf*
administer *vb* verwalten *vb*
administration *n* Verwaltung *nf*
administrative *adj* **administrative costs** Verwaltungskosten *npl*
administrator *n* Verwalter (-) *nm*

advance 1. *adj* **advance notice** Kündigung *nf* **advance payment** Vorauszahlung (-en) *nf* 2. *n* (on salary) Vorschuß (-üsse) *nm* **cash advance** Vorschuß (-üsse) *nm* **payable in advance** zahlbar im voraus 3. *vb* (salary) Vorschuß geben *vb*
advanced *adj* **advanced country** Industriestaat (-en) *nm* **advanced technology** Spitzentechnologie (-n) *nf*
advantage *n* Vorteil (-e) *nm* **comparative advantage** komparativer Vorteil (-e) *nm* **competitive advantage** Wettbewerbsvorteil (-e) *nm*
advantageous *adj* vorteilhaft *adj*
adverse *adj* **adverse balance of trade** ungünstige Handelsbilanz *nf*
advertise *vb* werben (für) *vb*
advertisement *n* Werbung *nf*
advertising *n* **advertising agency** Werbeagentur (-en) *nf* **advertising budget** Werbeetat (-s) *nm* **advertising campaign** Werbekampagne (-n) *nf* **advertising medium** Werbemittel (-) *nn* **advertising revenue** Werbeeinkommen (-) *nn*
advice *n* Rat (Ratschläge) *nm*
advise *vb* beraten *vb* **to advise sb about sth** jemanden über etwas beraten
adviser/advisor *n* Berater (-) *nm*
advisory *adj* beratend *adj*, Beratungs- *cpd*
advocate *vb* befürworten *vb*
aerospace *adj* **aerospace industry** Luftfahrtindustrie (-n) *nf*
affidavit *n* eidesstattliche Versicherung (-en) *nf*
affiliated *adj* **affiliated company** Schwestergesellschaft (-en) *nf*
affluent *adj* **affluent society** Wohlstandsgesellschaft (-en) *nf*
afford *vb* **I can't afford (to buy a new printer)** ich kann mir (einen neuen Drucker) nicht leisten **we cannot afford (to take) the risk** wir können das Risiko nicht eingehen
after-sales service *n* Kundendienst *nm*
agency *n* **advertising agency** Werbeagentur (-en) *nf* **employment agency** Stellenvermittlung (-en) *nf* **travel agency** Reisebüro (-s) *nn*
agenda *n* Tagesordnung (-en) *nf*
agent *n* Vertreter (-) *nm*
AGM (Annual General Meeting) *abbr* Jahreshauptversammlung (-en) *nf*
agrarian *adj* Agrar- *cpd*
agree *vb* zustimmen *vb*
agreed *adj* einverstanden *adj*

agreement *n* **by mutual agreement** in gegenseitigem Einverständnis **verbal agreement** mündliche Absprache (-n) *nf* **wage agreement** Lohnvertrag (-äge) *nm*
agribusiness *n* Agrargeschäft (-e) *nn*
agriculture *n* Landwirtschaft *nf*
agronomist *n* Agronom (-e) *nm*
aid *n* **financial aid** Finanzhilfe *nf*
air *n* **by air** auf dem Luftweg **air freight** Luftfracht *nf* **air traffic controller** Fluglotse (-n) *nm*
air-conditioned *adj* klimatisiert *adj*
airline *n* Fluggesellschaft (-en) *nf*
airmail *n* Luftpost *nf*
airport *n* Flughafen (-häfen) *nm*
allocate *vb* zuteilen *vb*
allowance *n* Zuschuß (-üsse) *nm*, Zulage (-n) *nf* **family allowance** Kindergeld *nn*
amalgamate *vb* fusionieren *vb*
amalgamation *n* Fusion (-en) *nf*
amend *vb* ändern *vb*
amendment *n* Änderung (-en) *nf*
amends *npl* **to make amends** wiedergutmachen *vb*
amenities *npl* Einrichtungen *nfpl*
amortization *n* Amortisation *nf*
amortize *vb* amortisieren *vb*
amount *n* Betrag (-äge) *nm*
amount to *vb* betragen *vb*
analysis *n* **cost-benefit analysis** Kosten-Nutzen-Analyse (-n) *nf* **systems analysis** Systemanalyse *nf*
analyze *vb* analysieren *vb*
annual *adj* **annual general meeting (AGM)** Jahreshauptversammlung (-en) *nf* **annual report** Jahresbericht (-e) *nm*
annuity *n* Rente (-n) *nf*
annulment *n* Annullierung (-en) *nf*
Ansaphone (R) *n* Anrufbeantworter (-) *nm*
answer 1. *n* Antwort (-en) *nf* 2. *vb* beantworten *vb* antworten *vb*
answering *adj* **answering machine** Anrufbeantworter (-) *nm*
anti-inflationary *adj* **anti-inflationary measures** antiinflationäre Maßnahmen *nfpl*
antitrust *adj* **antitrust laws** Antitrustgesetze *nnpl*, Kartellgesetze *nnpl*
appeal 1. *n* Appell (-e) *nm*, Bitte (-n) *nf* 2. *vb* bitten *vb*
application *n* **application form** Bewerbungsformular (-e) *nn* **letter of application** Bewerbungsschreiben (-) *nn*
apply for *vb* sich bewerben um *vb*
appoint *vb* **to appoint sb to a position** einstellen *vb*

appointment *n* (meeting) Termin (-e) *nm* (to a position) Einstellung (-en) *nf* **to make an appointment** einen Termin vereinbaren
appraisal *n* Abschätzung (-en) *nf*
appreciate *vb* (rise in value) im Wert steigen *vb*
appreciation *n* (in value) Wertsteigerung *nf*
apprentice *n* Lehrling (-e) *nm*
apprenticeship *n* Lehre *nf*
appropriation *n* Beschlagnahme *nf*
approval *n* Billigung *nf* **on approval** auf Probe
approve *vb* billigen *vb*
approximate *adj* ungefähr *adj*
approximately *adv* ungefähr *adv*
arbitrage *n* Arbitrage (-n) *nf*, Schiedsspruch (-üche) *nm*
arbitrary *adj* willkürlich *adj*
arbitrate *vb* vermitteln *vb*
arbitration *n* Schlichtung *nf*
arbitrator *n* Schlichter (-) *nm*
area *adj* **area manager** Regionalleiter (-) *nm*
arithmetic *n* Mathematik *nf*
arithmetical *adj* **arithmetical mean** arithmetisches Mittel (-) *nn*
arms *npl* **arms trade** Waffenhandel *nm*
arrangement *n* (agreement) Verabredung (-en) *nf*
arrears *npl* Rückstände *nmpl* **in arrears** im Rückstand **to fall/get into arrears** in Rückstand kommen
articulated *adj* **articulated lorry** Sattelschlepper (-) *nm*
asap (as soon as possible) *abbr* so bald wie möglich
asking *adj* **asking price** Angebotspreis (-e) *nm*
assembly *n* **assembly line** Montageband (-bänder) *nn*
assess *vb* einschätzen *vb*
assessment *n* Einschätzung (-en) *nf*
asset *n* Vermögen (-) *nn* **capital assets** Kapitalvermögen *nn* **asset stripping** Anlagenausschlachtung *nf*
assign *vb* zuweisen *vb*
assignee *n* Forderungsübernehmer (-) *nm*
assignment *n* Zuweisung *nf*
assistant *adj* **assistant manager** stellvertrender Leiter *nm*
associate 1. *adj* **associate director** außerordentliches Mitglied des Aufsichtsrats *nn*, Gesellschafter (-) *nm* 2. *n* Partner *nm*

attestation n Bestätigung (-en) nf, Bescheinigung (-en) nf
attorney n **power of attorney** Vollmacht nf
auction 1. n Versteigerung (-en) nf **2.** vb versteigern vb
auctioneer n Auktionator (-en) nm
audit n Buchprüfung (-en) nf
auditor n Buchprüfer (-) nm
authority n (official) Behörde (-n) nf
authorize vb ermächtigen vb
authorized adj **authorized dealer** Vertragshändler (-) nm
automatic adj automatisch adj **automatic cash dispenser** Geldautomat (-en) nm
automation n Automatisierung nf
automobile n **automobile industry** Autoindustrie (-n) nf
autonomous adj autonom adj
auxiliary adj Hilfs- cpd
average adj Durschnitt (-e) nm **average unit** Durchschnittskosten pro Einheit npl
avoid vb vermeiden vb
avoidance n **tax avoidance** Steuerbetrug nm
axe, ax (US) vb **to axe expenditure** Ausgaben reduzieren
back vb **to back a venture** eine Initiative finanziell unterstützen
back pay n Nachzahlung nf
backdate vb rückdatieren vb **to backdate a cheque** einen Scheck rückdatieren
backer n Geldgeber nm
backhander* n Schmiergeld nn
backing n Unterstützung nf
backlog n Rückstände nmpl
bad adj **bad cheque** ungültiger Scheck (-s) nm **bad debt** uneinbringliche Schuld (-en) nf
bail n Kaution nf
bailiff n Gerichtsvollzieher (-) nm
balance 1. n (financial) Bilanz nf **bank balance** Kontostand (-ände) nm **final balance** Schlußbilanz (-en) nf **balance in hand** Guthaben (-) nn **balance of payments** Zahlungsbilanz (-en) nf **balance of payments deficit** Zahlungsbilanzdefizit (-e) nn **balance of payments surplus** Zahlungsbilanzüberschuß (-üsse) nm **balance of trade** Handelsbilanz (-en) nf **balance sheet** Bilanz (-en) nf **trade balance** Handelsbilanz (-en) nf **2.** vb **to balance the books** die Bilanz ziehen vb **to balance the budget** den Etat ausgleichen
bank 1. n Bank (-en) nf **bank account** Bankkonto (-konten) nn **bank balance** Bankguthaben (-) nn **bank card** Kreditkarte (-en) nf **bank charges** nf **bank clerk** Bankangestellte/r nmf **bank draft** Bankwechsel (-) nm **bank holiday** Bankfeiertag (-e) nm **bank loan** Bankdarlehen (-) nn **bank manager** Bankdirektor (-en) nm **bank overdraft** Überziehungskredit (-e) nm **bank rate** Diskontsatz (-sätze) nm **bank statement** Kontoauszug (-üge) nm **2.** vb **to bank a cheque** einen Scheck einzahlen
banker n Bankier (-s) nm **banker's order** Dauerauftrag (-äge) nm
banking n **banking circles** Bankkreise nmpl **banking hours** Schalterstunden nfpl
banknote n Banknote (-n) nf
bankrupt adj bankrott adj **to be bankrupt** bankrott sein
bankruptcy n Konkurs nm
bar code n Strichcode (-s) nm
bargain 1. adj **bargain offer** adj Sonderangebot (-e) nn **bargain price** adj niedriger Preis (-e) nm, Spottpreis **2.** n Geschäft (-e) nn **bargain** günstiges Kaufobjekt (-e) nn **3.** vb feilschen vb
barrier n Barriere (-n) nf, Schranke nf **trade barrier** Handelsschranke (-n) nf
barrister, lawyer (US) n Rechtsanwalt (-älte) nm
barter 1. adj **barter agreement** Tauschhandelsabkommen (-) nn **barter transaction** Tauschhandel nm **2.** n Tauschhandel nm **3.** vb tauschen vb
base adj **base lending rate** Eckzins der Clearing-Banken für Ausleihungen nm
basic adj **basic commodity** Grundstoff (-e) nm **basic income** Basiseinkommen nn **basic rate** Eckzins für Ausleihungen nm **basic training** Grundausbildung nf
basis n **basis of assessment** Bemessungsgrundlage (-n) nf
basket n **basket of currencies** Währungskorb nm
batch n (of goods) Sendung (-en) nf **batch processing** (DP) Serienverarbeitung nf
bear 1. n (stock exchange) Baissier (-s) nm **bear market** n Baissemarkt (-märkte) nm **2.** vb **to bear interest** Zinsen tragen vb
bearer n Inhaber (-) nm **bearer bond** Inhaberschuldverschreibung (-en) nf **bearer cheque** Inhaberscheck (-s) nm **bearer share** Inhaberaktie (-n) nf
bench n **bench mark** Maßstab (-stäbe) nm **bench mark price** Richtpreis (-e) nm

benefactor n Gönner (-e) nm
benefit 1. n (social security) Nutzen (-) nm
2. vb profitieren vb nützen vb
bequeath vb vermachen vb
bequest n Vermachen (-) nn
best adj best-before date
Verbrauchsdatum nn best seller Verkaufsschlager (-) nm, Bestseller (-) nm
biannual adj zweimal jährlich
bid 1. n Angebot (-e) nn 2. vb (auction) bieten vb
biennial adj zweijährlich adj
bilateral adj bilateral trade der bilaterale Handel
bill 1. n (invoice) Rechnung (-en) nf bill of exchange Wechsel (-) nm bill of lading Konnossement (-s) nn, Ladeschein (-e) nm bill of sale Verkaufsurkunde (-n) nf bills discounted Wechselobligo nn to pay a bill die Rechnung begleichen 2. vb (invoice) in Rechnung stellen vb
bimonthly adj zweimonatlich adj
binding adj verbindlich adj legally binding rechtsverbindlich adj
biweekly adj vierzehntäglich adj
black adj black economy Schwarzhandel nm, Schwarzmarkt nm
black market Schwarzmarkt (-märkte) nm to be in the black in den schwarzen Zahlen sein, Geld auf dem Konto haben
blank adj blank cheque Blankoscheck (-s) nm
block 1. n Block (-öcke) nm 2. vb sperren vb
blockade 1. n Blockade (-n) nf 2. vb blockieren vb
blocked adj blocked account Sperrkonto (-konten) nn
blue adj blue-chip company erstklassiges Unternehmen (-) nn blue-collar worker Arbeiter (-) nm blue-chip securities erstklassige Wertpapiere nn
board n Vorstand (-ände) nm Board of Trade (GB) Handelsministerium nn board meeting (GB) Vorstandssitzung (-en) nf
board of directors (GB) Vorstand (-ände) nm board room (GB) Sitzungssaal (-äle) nn
bona fide adj gutgläubig adj, guten Glaubens adj
bond n Schuldverschreibung (-en) nf, Obligation (-en) nf bond certificate Bond-Zertifikat (-e) nn government bond Staatsanleihe (-n) nf in bond unter Zollverschluß

bonded adj bonded warehouse Zollager (-) nn
bondholder n Obligationär (-e) nm, Anleihegläubiger (-) nm
bonus n Prämie (-n) nf
book 1. n cheque book Scheckheft (-e) nn book profit Buchgewinn nm the books die Bücher nnpl book value Buchwert (-e) nm 2. vb to book a hotel room ein Hotelzimmer reservieren vb to book in advance im voraus buchen
book-keeper n Buchhalter (-) nm
book-keeping n Buchhaltung nf
booking n (reservation) Reservierung (-en) nf
bookseller n Buchhändler nm
bookshop, bookstore (US) n Buchhandlung (-en) nf
boom 1. n economic boom Wirtschaftsaufschwung (-ünge) nm boom in demand Nachfrageboom (-s) nm 2. vb einen Aufschwung nehmen vb
booming adj florierend
boost 1. n Ankurbelung nf 2. vb to boost demand die Nachfrage ankurbeln vb to boost morale die Moral heben vb to boost production die Produktion steigern vb to boost sales den Absatz steigern vb
boot vb to boot a computer vb einen Computer laden vb
booth n (voting) Stand (-ände) nm
borrow vb leihen vb
borrowing n Kreditaufnahme nf
boss n Chef (-s) nm
bottleneck n Engpaß (-pässe) nm bottleneck inflation Engpaßinflation nf
bottom 1. adj niedrig adj bottom price niedrigster Preis (-e) nm 2. n at the bottom unten prep 3. vb to bottom out den tiefsten Stand erreichen
bought adj bought ledger Wareneinkaufsbuch (-bücher) nn
bounce* vb (cheque) platzen vb
bound n out of bounds verboten adj
box 1. n box number Chiffre (-n) nf, Postfach (-fächer) nn box office Kasse (-n) nf PO box Postfach (-fächer) nn 2. vb to box sth up in eine(r) Kiste verpacken vb
boycott 1. n Boykott (-s) nm 2. vb boykottieren vb
bracket n Träger (-) nm, Klammer (-n) nf tax bracket Steuerklasse (-n) nf
branch n Filiale (-n) nf branch company Zweigniederlassung (-en) nf branch ma-

nager Filialleiter (-) *nm* **branch office** Zweigstelle (-n) *nf*
brand *n* Marke (-n) *nf* **brand image** Markenbild (-er) *nn* **brand leader** Markenführer (-) *nm*
breach *n* Vertragsverletzung (-en) *nf* **breach of contract** Vertragsverletzung (-en) *nf*
break 1. *n* **to take a break** Pause machen, Urlaub nehmen **2.** *vb* **to break an agreement** einen Vertrag brechen *vb*
break even *vb* kostendeckend arbeiten *vb*
break up *vb* auflösen *vb*
break-even *adj* **break-even point** Gewinnschwelle (-n) *nf*
breakdown *n* (of figures) Aufgliederung der Zahlen *nf* **breakdown service** Pannendienst (-e) *nm*
breakthrough *n* Durchbruch (-brüche) *nm* **to make a breakthrough** durchbrechen *vb*
breakup *n* Auflösung (-en) *nf*, Liquidation (-en) *nf*
bribe 1. *n* Bestechungsgeld (-er) *nn* **2.** *vb* bestechen
bribery *n* Bestechung *nf*
bridging *adj* **bridging loan, bridge loan** (US) Überbrückungskredit (-e) *nm*
brief 1. *n* Auftrag (-äge) *nm* **2.** *vb* instruieren *vb*, beauftragen *vb*
briefing *n* Einsatzbesprechung (-en) *nf*
bring down *vb* (prices) herabsetzen *vb*, reduzieren *vb*
bring forward *vb* vorverlegen *vb*
bring out *vb* (product) herausbringen *vb*, auf den Markt bringen *vb*
brinkmanship *n* Krisenpolitik *nf*
Britain *n* Großbritannien *nn*
British *adj* britisch *adj* **British Council** British Council *nm* **British Isles** die Britischen Inseln *nf*
broad *adj* **broad market** aufnahmefähiger Markt (-märkte) *nm*
broadcast 1. *n* Sendung (-en) *nf* **2.** *vb* senden *vb*
broadsheet *n* Handzettel (-) *nm*
brochure *n* Prospekt (-e) *nm*
broker *n* Makler (-) *nm*, Broker (-) *nm*
brokerage *n* Maklergeschäft *nn* **brokerage firm** Maklerfirma (-firmen) *nf*
buck* (US) *n* Dollar *nm* **to pass the buck*** die Verantwortung abschieben
budget *n* Budget (-s) *nn* **to draw up a budget** den Haushaltsplan erstellen
budget for *vb* im Budget einplanen
budgetary *adj* **budgetary deficit** Defizit (-e) *nn* **budgetary policy** Finanzpolitik *nf*

bug 1. *n* (listening device) Wanze (-n) *nf*, Programmfehler *nm* **2.** *vb* stören *vb* **to bug a call** ein Gespräch abhören
build *vb* **to build a reputation** sich einen Ruf schaffen
builder *n* Bauunternehmer (-) *nm*
building *n* **building contractor** Bauunternehmer (-) *nm* **building firm** Baufirma (-firmen) *nf* **building industry/trade** Bauindustrie *nf* **building permit** Baugenehmigung (-en) *nf* **building site** Baustelle (-n) *nf* **building society** Bausparkasse (-n) *nf*
built-in *adj* eingebaut *adj*
built-up *adj* **built-up area** bebautes Gebiet (-e) *nn*
bulk *n* Massen- *cpd* **the bulk of** der größte Teil *nm* **to buy in bulk** *vb* in Mengen einkaufen *vb*
bull 1. *n* (stock exchange) Haussier (-s) *nm* **bull market** (stock exchange) Haussemarkt (-märkte) *nm* **2.** *vb* (stock exchange) auf Hausse spekulieren *vb*
bulletin *n* Nachricht (-en) *nf*, Nachrichtensendung (-en) *nf* **bulletin board** schwarzes Brett (-er) *nn*
bullion *n* Edelmetallbarren *nm*
bump up *vb* (prices) Preise erhöhen
bundle *n* Paket (-e) *nn*, Bündel (-) *nn*
bundle up *vb* bündeln *vb*
buoyant *adj* **buoyant market** eine feste Börse (-n) *nf*
bureau *n* **bureau de change** Wechselstube (-n) *nf* **Federal Bureau (US)** Bundesamt *nn*
bureaucracy *n* Bürokratie *nf*
bureaucrat *n* Bürokrat (-en) *nm*
bureaucratic *adj* bürokratisch *adj*
bursar *n* Finanzverwalter (-) *nm*
bus *n* **bus station** Busbahnhof (-höfe) *nm*
business *n* Geschäft (-e) *nn* **to go out of business** Konkurs melden **business address** Geschäftsadresse (-n) *nf* **business associate** Geschäftsfreund (-e) *nm* **big business** Großindustrie *nf* **business consultant** Unternehmensberater (-) *nm* **business expenses** Spesen *npl* **family business** Familiengeschäft (-e) *nn* **business hours** Geschäftsstunden *nfpl* **business premises** Geschäftsräume *nmpl* **business studies** Betriebswirtschaftslehre *nf* **business suit** Geschäftsanzug (-züge) *nm* **to set up in business** ein Geschäft gründen **business transaction** Geschäft (-e) *nn* **business trip** Geschäftsreise (-n) *nf*

businesslike *adj* geschäftstüchtig *adj*
busy *adj* beschäftigt *adj* busy signal (US)
Besetztton (-töne) *nm*
buy 1. *n* a good buy ein gutes Geschäft
2. *vb* to buy sth at a high price zu einem
hohen Preis kaufen to buy sth on credit
auf Kredit kaufen to buy sth second hand
aus zweiter Hand kaufen *vb* to buy sth
wholesale im Großhandel kaufen *vb*
buy out *vb* aufkaufen *vb*
buy-out *n* Aufkauf (-käufe) *nm*, Übernahme (-n) *nf*
buyer *n* Käufer (-) *nm* buyer's market
Käufermarkt (-märkte) *nm*
buying *n* buying and selling Kauf und
Verkauf *nm* buying power Kaufkraft *nf*
buying price Kaufpreis (-e) *nm* buying
rate Ankaufskurs *nm*
by-product *n* Nebenprodukt (-e) *nn*
bypass *vb* umgehen *vb*
byte *n* Byte *nn*
c.i.f. (cost, insurance and freight) *abbr* cif
(Kosten, Versicherung, Fracht) *abbr*
CAD (computer-aided or assisted
design) *abbr* computergestütztes Design
calculate *vb* berechnen *vb*
calculation *n* Berechnung (-en) *nf*
calculator *n* Rechner (-) *nm*
call 1. *n* call money Tagesgeld *nn* person-
to-person call Gespräch mit Voranmeldung (-e) *nn* reverse-charge call, collect
call (US) R-Gespräch (-e) *nn* 2. *vb* to call
a meeting eine Sitzung einberufen to call
it a deal eine Abmachung treffen
call back *vb* (on phone) zurückrufen *vb*
call for *vb* verlangen *vb*, rufen *vb*
call in *vb* (demand the repayment of a
loan) ein Darlehen kündigen
campaign *n* Kampagne (-n) *nf* advertising
campaign Werbekampagne (-n) *nf* publicity campaign Werbekampagne (-n) *nf*
sales campaign Verkaufskampagne (-n) *nf*
to run a campaign eine Werbekampagne
führen
cancel *vb* annullieren *vb* cancel a contract
einen Vertrag aufheben cancel an appointment absagen *vb*
cancellation *n* Stornierung (-en) *nf*, Rückgängigmachung (-en) *nf* cancellation
charge Stornogebühr (-en) *nf*
candidate *n* (for job) Kandidat (-en) *nm*,
Bewerber (-) *nm*
cap *vb* to cap the interest rate die Zinsen
begrenzen
CAP (Common Agricultural Policy) *abbr*
Gemeinsame Agrarpolitik *nf*

capacity *n* earning capacity
Ertragsfähigkeit *nf* industrial capacity
Industriekapazität *nf* in my capacity as
chairman in meiner Eigenschaft als
Vorsitzender manufacturing capacity
Produktionskapazität *nf* storage capacity
Lagerkapazität *nf* to expand capacity die
Kapazität erweitern to work to full capa-
city voll ausgelastet sein
capital *n* Kapital *nn* capital assets
(Kapital)vermögen *nn* capital budget In-
vestitionsplan (-pläne) *nm* capital cost
Kapitalkosten *npl* capital expenditure
Investitionsausgaben *nfpl* capital exports
Kapitalausfuhr *nf* fixed capital
Anlagevermögen *nn* capital funds
Eigenmittel *nnpl* capital gains
Kapitalgewinne *nmpl,*
Veräußerungsgewinne *nmpl* capital
gains tax Kapitalgewinnsteuer (-n) *nf*
capital goods Kapitalgüter *nnpl* initial
capital Anfangskapital *nn* invested capital Investitionskapital *nn* capital loss
Kapitalverlust (-e) *nm* capital market
Kapitalmarkt (-märkte) *nm* to raise capital Kapital aufbringen capital turnover
Kapitalumschlag *nm* venture capital
Spekulationskapital *nn* working capital
Betriebskapital *nn*
capitalism *n* Kapitalismus *nm*
capitalist *n* Kapitalist (-en) *nm*
capitalize *vb* kapitalisieren *vb*
card *n* bank card Kreditkarte (-n) *nf*
business card Geschäftskarte (-n) *nf*
chargecard Kundenkreditkarte (-n) *nf*
cheque card Scheckkarte (-n) *nf* credit
card Kreditkarte (-n) *nf* identity card
Ausweis (-e) *nm* smart card Smart-
Card *nf*
career *n* Karriere (-n) *nf* careers advice
Berufsberatung *nf*
cargo *n* Fracht (-en) *nf* bulk cargo
Massengutladung *nf* cargo ship Frachtschiff (-e) *nn*
carriage *n* carriage charge Frachtgebühr
(-en) *nf* carriage costs Frachtkosten *npl*
carriage forward per Frachtnachnahme
carriage included frachtfrei carriage paid
frachtfrei
carrier *n* Spediteur (-e) *nm* bulk carrier
Massengutfrachter *nm* express carrier
Eiltransporter *nm*
carry *vb* (stock) führen *vb*
carry forward *vb* übertragen *vb*
carry out *vb* ausführen *vb*

carry over *vb* (to next month)
prolongieren *vb*
carrying *adj* carrying cost Zinsbelastung
(eines Sollsaldos) *nf*
cartel *n* Kartell (-e) *nn*
cash 1. *n* Bargeld *nn* cash and carry
Selbstabholung gegen Kasse *nf* cash
before delivery Barzahlung vor
Lieferung *nf* cash crop zum Verkauf
bestimmte Ernte *nf* cash desk Kasse (-n)
nf cash discount Barrabatt *nm* cash flow
Cashflow *nm*, Kapitalfluß *nm* for cash
gegen Barzahlung cash machine/di-
spenser Geldautomat (-en) *nm* cash offer
Barangebot (-e) *nn* cash on delivery
(COD) Barzahlung bei Lieferung *nf* cash
on receipt of goods Barzahlung bei Erhalt
der Ware *nf* cash payment Barzahlung
(-en) *nf* cash sale Kassageschäft (-e) *nn*
to pay in cash bar zahlen cash transaction Kassageschäft (-e) *nn* cash with
order Zahlung bei Auftragserteilung *nf*
2. *vb* einlösen *vb*, kassieren to cash a
cheque einen Scheck einlösen
cash up *vb* Kasse machen *vb*, kassieren *vb*
cashier *n* Kassierer/in *nm/nf*
cater for *vb* eingestellt sein auf *vb*
caution *n* caution money Kaution *nf*
ceiling *n* (on prices) Preisobergrenze *nf* to
put a ceiling on sth eine Höchstgrenze
festsetzen
central *adj* central bank Zentralbank (-en)
nf central planned economy zentrale
Planwirtschaft (-en) *nf* central planning
Zentralplanung *nf* central processing
unit (CPU) (DP) Zentraleinheit (-en) *nf*,
CPU (-s) *nf*
centralization *n* Zentralisierung *nf*
centralize *vb* zentralisieren *vb*
centre *n* business centre Geschäftszentrum (-en) *nn* Jobcentre Arbeitsamt
(-ämter) *nn*
certificate 1. *n* Bescheinigung (-en) *nf*,
Zeugnis (-se) *nn* clearance certificate
Zollerlaubnisschein (-e) *nm* marriage
certificate Trauschein (-e) *nm* certificate
of employment Arbeitszeugnis (-se) *nn*
certificate of origin Ursprungszeugnis
(-se) *nn* certificate of ownership Eigentumsurkunde (-n) *nf* share certificate,
stock certificate (US) Aktienzertifikat (-e)
nn 2. *vb* bescheinigen *vb*
certified *adj* certified cheque gedeckter
Scheck (-s) *nm*
certify *vb* bescheinigen *vb*
chain *n* chain of shops Ladenkette (-n) *nf*

retail chain Einzelhandelskette (-n) *nf*
chain store Filialgeschäft (-e) *nn*
chair *vb* to chair a meeting (bei einer
Sitzung) Vorsitz führen
chamber *n* Chamber of Commerce Handelskammer (-n) *nf*
chancellor *n* Chancellor of the Exchequer
(GB) Finanzminister (-) *nm*
change *n* (from purchase) Wechselgeld *nn*
bureau de change Wechselstube (-n) *nf*
loose/small change (coins) Kleingeld *nn*
charge 1. *n* charge account Kreditkonto
(-konten) *nn* bank charges
Bankspesen *npl* delivery charges
Liefergebühren *nfpl* handling charges
Ladekosten (-) *npl* legal charge
Rechtskosten *npl* to be in charge verantwortlich sein 2. *vb* charge a price
berechnen to charge commission Provision berechnen to charge for sth
berechnen to charge sth to an account
ein Konto mit etwas belasten to take
charge of sth etwas übernehmen to
charge sb with sth jemanden anklagen
(wegen)
chargeable *adj* anrechenbar *adj*
charitable *adj* charitable trust karitative
Organisation (-en) *nf*
charity *n* karitative Organisation (-en) *nf*
chart *n* Tabelle (-n) *nf* bar chart Balkendiagramm (-e) *nn* flow chart Flow-Chart
(-s) *nm* pie chart Kreisdiagramm (-e) *nn*
charter *n* Charter (-s) *nm* charter flight
Charterflug (-üge) *nm*
chartered *adj* chartered accountant Bilanzbuchhalter (-) *nm* chartered bank
konzessionale Bank (-en) *nf* chartered
surveyor Landvermesser (-) *nm*
chattels *npl* bewegliche Sachen *nfpl*
check 1. *n* customs check Zollabfertigung (-en) *nf* to make a check on sth
prüfen *vb* 2. *vb* prüfen *vb*
check in *vb* (at airport) einchecken *vb*
(register in an hotel) sich anmelden *vb*
check out *vb* (pay the hotel bill)
abreisen *vb*
checkbook (US) *n* Scheckbuch (-ücher) *nn*
chemical *adj* chemical industry Chemieindustrie (-n) *nf* chemical products
Chemieprodukte *nnpl*
cheque, check (US) *n* Scheck (-s) *nm* to
return a cheque to drawer einen Scheck
an den Austeller zurückgeben blank
cheque Blankoscheck (-s) *nm* cheque
book Scheckbuch (-bücher) *nn* crossed
cheque gekreuzter Scheck (-s) *nm* dud

cheque geplatzter Scheck (-s) *nm* a
cheque for the amount of £100 Scheck in
Höhe von £100 (-s) *nm* to bounce a
cheque einen Scheck platzen lassen to
cash a cheque einen Scheck einlösen to
make out a cheque einen Scheck
ausstellen to pay by cheque per Scheck
zahlen to sign a cheque einen Scheck
unterschreiben to stop a cheque einen
Scheck sperren traveller's cheque, traveler's cheque (US) Reisescheck (-s) *nm*
chief *adj* chief accountant
Hauptbuchhalter *nm* chief cashier
Hauptkassierer (-) *nm* chief financial
officer Finanzleiter (-) *nm*
circular *n* (letter) Rund- *cpd*
circulate *vb* (document) zirkulieren
lassen *vb*
circulation *n* in circulation im Umlauf
circumstance Umstand (-ände) *nm* circumstances beyond our control nicht in
unserer Hand liegende Umstände due to
unforeseen circumstances aus nicht vorhersehbaren Gründen under no circumstances unter keinen Umständen
civil *adj* civil engineering Tiefbau *nm* civil
servant Beamte/r *nmf* civil service
Staatsdienst *nm*
claim 1. *n* claim form Antragsformular
(-e) *nn* claims department Reklamationsabteilung (-en) *nf* claims procedure
Reklamationsverfahren (-) *nn* to put in a
claim Ansprüche geltend machen to
settle a claim begleichen *vb* wage claim
Lohnforderung (-e) *nf* 2. *vb* (demand)
beanspruchen *vb* to claim for damages
Schadenersatzansprüche geltend machen
claimant *n* Antragsteller (-) *nm*
class *n* business class (plane) Business-
Class first class (plane) erste Klasse *nf*
classified *adj* classified advertisement
Anzeige (-n) *nf* classified information
streng vertrauliche Information *nf*
clause *n* (in contract) Klausel (-n) *nf*
escape clause Ausweichklausel (-n) *nf*
option clause Optionsklausel (-n) *nf*
clear 1. *adj* clear loss Nettoverlust *nm* to
make oneself clear sich klar ausdrücken
2. *vb* (cheque) abrechnen *vb* to clear sth
through customs abfertigen *vb*
clearance *n* clearance offer Sonderangebot (-e) *nn* clearance sale Ausverkauf
(-äufe) *nm*
clearing *adj* clearing bank Clearingbank
(-en) *nf*, Geschäftsbank (-en) *nf* clearing
house Clearing House (-s) *nn*, Clearing-

stelle (-n) *nf* clearing payment Abrechnungszahlung (-en) *nf*
clerical *adj* clerical error Schreibfehler (-)
nm clerical work Büroarbeit *nf*
clerk *n* Büroangestellte/r *nmf*
client *n* Kunde (-n) *nm*
clientele *n* Kundschaft *nf*
clinch *vb* abschließen *vb* clinch a deal ein
Geschäft abschließen
clock in *vb* den Arbeitsbeginn stempeln
clock out *vb* das Arbeitsende stempeln
close *vb* to close a business ein Geschäft
aufgeben stilligen to close a deal ein
Geschäft abschließen, to close a meeting
eine Sitzung aufgeben to close an account ein Konto auflösen
closed *adj* geschlossen *adj* closed ses-
sion/meeting geschlossene Sitzung (-en)
nf closed shop gewerkschaftsgebundene
Firma (-en) *nf*
closing *adj* closing bid Höchstgebot (-e)
nn closing price Schlußkurs (-e) *nm*
closing time Geschäftsschluß *nm*
closure *n* Stillegung (-en) *nf* closure of a
company Betriebsstillegung (-en) *nf*
COD (cash on delivery), (collect on delivery) (US) *abbr* Zahlung bei Warenerhalt
code *n* bar code Strichcode (-s) *nf* professional code of practice Ehrenkodex (-e)
nm, Verhaltenskodex (-e) *nm* post code,
zip code (US) Postleitzahl (-en) *nf* telephone code Ortsnetzkennzahl (-en) *nf* tax
code Abgabenordnung (-en) *nf*
collaborate *vb* zusammenarbeiten mit *vb*
collaborative *adj* collaborative venture
Gemeinschaftsprogramm (-e) *nn*, Gemeinschaftsunternehmen (-) *nn*
collapse *n* (of economy, company) Zusammenbruch (-üche) *nm* (on stock market) Kursverfall *nm*
collateral 1. *adj* collateral security
akzessorische Sicherheit *nf* 2. *n*
Sicherungsgegenstand *nm*, akzessorische Sicherheit *nf*
colleague *n* Kollege (-n) *nm*
collect *vb* einziehen *vb* to collect a debt
eine Schuld einziehen *vb*
collecting *adj* collecting agency Inkassoagentur (-en) *nf*, Inkassobüro (-s) *nn*
collection *n* Inkasso *nn*, Einziehung *nf*
debt collection Schuldeneinziehung *nf*
collective 1. *adj* collective agreement
Tarifabkommen (-) *nn* collective bargaining Tarifverhandlung (-en) *nf* 2. *n* Kollektiv (-e) *nn* workers' collective
Arbeitsgemeinschaft (-en) *nf*

colloquium *n* Kolloquium (-ien) *nn*
comment *n* Bemerkung (-en) *nf*
commerce *n* Handel *nm*
commercial *adj* kaufmännisch *adj*,
kommerziell *adj* **commercial bank** Geschäftsbank (-en) *nf* **commercial traveller, commercial traveler (US)**
Geschäftsreisende/r *nmf* **commercial vehicle** Nutzfahrzeug (-e) *nn*
commission *n* Provision *nf* **commission agent** Provisionsvertreter (-) *nm* **commission broker** Aktienmakler (auf Provisionsbasis) (-) *nm* **commission fee**
Provisionsgebühr (-en) *nf* **to charge commission** Provision berechnen
commit *vb* (sich) verpflichten *vb*
commitment *n* Verpflichtung (-en) *nf*
committee *n* Ausschuß (-üsse) *nm* **advisory committee** Beirat (-äte) *nm* **committee meeting** Ausschußsitzung (-en) *nf*
common *adj* **Common Agricultural Policy (CAP)** Gemeinsame Agrarpolitik *nf*
Common Market Gemeinsamer Markt *nm*
common law Gewohnheitsrecht *nn*
communication *n* Kommunikation *nf*
communication network Kommunikationsnetz (-e) *nn*
company *n* Gesellschaft (-en) *nf*, Unternehmen (-) *nn*, Betrieb (-e) *nm* **holding company** Holding-Gesellschaft (-en) *nf*
incorporated company (US) Aktiengesellschaft (-en) *nf* **joint-stock company**
Aktiengesellschaft (-en) *nf* **company law**
Gesellschaftsrecht *nn* **limited company**
Gesellschaft mit beschränkter Haftung
(-en) *nf* **parent company** Muttergesellschaft (-en) *nf* **company policy**
Unternehmenspolitik *nf* **private limited company** Gesellschaft mit beschränkter
Haftung (in privater Hand) (-en) *nf* **public limited company** Gesellschaft mit beschränkter Haftung (-en) *nf* **registered company** eingetragene Firma (-en) *nf*
company secretary höchster Verwaltungsbeamter (-en) *nm* **sister company**
Schwestergesellschaft (-en) *nf* **subsidiary company** Tochtergesellschaft (-en) *nf*
comparative *adj* vergleichend *adj*
compatible *adj* kompatibel *adj*
compensate for *vb* entschädigen *vb*
compensation *n* Entschädigung *nf* **to claim compensation** Entschädigung
verlangen **to pay compensation** Entschädigung zahlen
compete *vb* konkurrieren (mit) *vb* **to compete with a rival** konkurrieren (mit)

competing *adj* **competing company** konkurrierende Gesellschaft (-en) *nf*, Konkurrent (-en) *nm*
competition *n* Konkurrenz *nf*,
Wettbewerb *nm* **cut-throat competition**
ruinöse Konkurrenz *nf* **market competition** Konkurrenz auf dem Markt *nf* **unfair competition** unlauterer Wettbewerb *nm*
competitive *adj* wettbewerbsfähig *adj*
competitiveness *n*
Wettbewerbsfähigkeit *nf*,
Konkurrenzfähigkeit *nf*
competitor *n* Konkurrent (-en) *nm*
complain *vb* **to complain about sth**
beanstanden *vb*, sich beschweren über *vb*
complaint *n* Mangelrüge (-n) *nf* **to make a complaint** Beschwerde einlegen **complaints department** Beschwerdeabteilung (-en) *nf*
complete *vb* vollenden *vb*
complex 1. *adj* komplex *adj*,
kompliziert *adj* 2. *n* Komplex (-e) *nm*
housing complex Wohnsiedlung (-en) *nf*
complimentary *adj* frei *adj*, kostenlos *adj*
comply *vb* **to comply with legislation** die
Bedingungen erfüllen, den Anordnungen
nachkommen **to comply with the rules**
sich an die Regeln halten
compound *adj* **compound interest**
Zinseszins *nm*
comprehensive *adj* umfassend *adj* **comprehensive insurance policy**
Vollkaskoversicherung *nf*
compromise *n* Kompromiß (-sse) *nm* **to reach a compromise** einen Kompromiß
schließen
computer *n* Computer (-) *nm* **computer-aided design (CAD)** computergestütztes
Design *nn*, CAD *nn* **computer-aided learning (CAL)** computergestütztes
Lernen *nn*, CAL *nn* **computer-aided manufacture (CAM)** computergestützte
Fertigung *nf*, CAM *nf* **computer centre, center (US)** Computerzentrum (-en) *nn*
computer file Datei (-en) *nf* **computer language** Computersprache (-n) *nf* **laptop computer** Laptop-Computer (-) *nm*
(be) computer literate sich mit Computern auskennen **mainframe computer**
Großrechner (-) *nm* **computer operator**
Computer-Operator (-en) *nm* **personal computer (PC)** Personalcomputer (-) *nm*,
PC (-s) *nm* **portable computer** tragbarer
Computer (-) *nm* **computer program**
Computerprogramm (-) *nn* **computer**

programmer Programmierer (-) *nm*
computer terminal Terminal (-s) *nn*
concern 1. *n* Unternehmen (-) *nn* **going
concern** arbeitendes Unternehmen *nn*
2. *vb* (be of importance to) betreffen *vb*
concur *vb* übereinstimmen *vb*
condition *npl* **living conditions**
Wohnverhältnisse *nnpl* **conditions of
purchase** Kaufbedingungen *nfpl* **conditions of sale** Verkaufsbedingungen *nfpl*
working conditions
Arbeitsverhältnisse *nnpl*,
Arbeitsbedingungen *nfpl*
conference *n* Konferenz (-en) *nf* **conference proceedings** Tagungsbericht (-e) *nm*
to arrange a conference eine Konferenz
veranstalten, organisieren **conference
venue** Tagungsort (-e) *nm*
confidence *n* **in strictest confidence**
streng vertraulich
confidential *adj* vertraulich *adj*
confirm *vb* **to confirm receipt of sth** den
Empfang bestätigen
confirmation *n* Bestätigung *nf*
conglomerate *n* Konglomerat (-e) *nn*,
Mischkonzern (-e) *nm*
congress *n* Kongreß (-sse) *nm*
connect *vb* **could you connect me to...**
(telephone) könnten Sie mich bitte mit X
verbinden?
connection *n* **business connections**
Geschäftsbeziehungen *nfpl*
consent 1. *n* Zustimmung *nf* **2.** *vb*
zustimmen *vb*
consequence *n* Folge (-n) *nf*
consideration *n* (for contract) Überlegung
(-en) *nf*
consignee *n* Empfänger (-) *nm*, Konsignatar (-e) *nm*
consigner/or *n* Absender (-) *nm*
consignment *n* Sendung (-en) *nf*
consolidate *vb* konsolidieren *vb*
consolidated *adj* konsolidiert *adj* **consolidated figures** konsolidierte Zahlen *nfpl*,
konsolidierte Bilanz *nf*
consortium *n* Konsortium (-ien) *nn*
construction *n* **construction industry**
Bauindustrie (-n) *nf*
consul *n* Konsul (-n) *nm*
consulate *n* Konsulat (-e) *nn*
consult *vb* beraten *vb*, konsultieren *vb* **to
consult with sb** sich mit jemandem
beraten
consultancy, consulting (US) *adj* **consultancy firm** *n* Beratung *nf* **consultancy**

fees Beratungsgebühren *nfpl* **consultancy work** Beratungstätigkeit *nf*
consultant *n* Berater (-) *nm*
consumer *n* Verbraucher (-) *nm*, Konsument (-en) *nm* **consumer credit**
Konsumkredit *nm* **consumer demand**
Konsumnachfrage *nf* **consumer habits**
Verbrauchsgewohnheiten *nfpl* **consumer
research** Konsumforschung *nf* **consumer
satisfaction** Verbraucherzufriedenheit *nf*
consumer survey Konsumumfrage (-n) *nf*
consumer trends Konsumtrends *nmpl*,
Konsumtendenzen *nfpl*
consumerism *n* Konsumdenken *nn*
contact 1. *n* **to get in contact with sb** sich
mit jemandem in Verbindung setzen
business contacts Geschäftsfreunde *nmpl*
2. *vb* kontaktieren *vb*
container *n* Container (-e) *nm*, Behälter (-e)
nm **container depot** Containerdepot (-s)
nn **container ship** Containerschiff (-e) *nn*
container terminal Containerlager (-) *nn*
contract *n* Vertrag (-äge) *nm* **breach of
contract** Vertragsverletzung (-en) *nf* **draft
contract** Vertragsentwurf (-ürfe) *nm* **contract labour** Akkordarbeit *nf* **law of
contract** Vertragsrecht *nn* **the terms of
the contract** die
Vertragsbedingungen *nfpl* **the signatories to the contract** die
Unterzeichner *nmpl* **to cancel a contract**
einen Vertrag stornieren **to draw up a
contract** einen Vertrag entwerfen **to sign
a contract** einen Vertrag unterzeichnen **to
tender for a contract** einen Vertrag
ausschreiben **under the terms of the
contract** nach den Vertragsbedingungen
contract work Vertragsarbeit *nf*
contracting *adj* **the contracting parties**
die Vertragsparteien *nfpl*
contractor *n* Auftragnehmer (-) *nm* **building contractor** Bauunternehmer (-) *nm*
haulage contractor Kraftverkehrspedition
(-en) *nf*
contractual *adj* **contractual obligations**
Vertragspflichten *nfpl*
contravene *vb* verletzen *vb*
contravention *n* Verletzung (-en) *nf*
contribute *vb* beitragen *vb*
contribution *n* **social security contributions** Sozialversicherungsbeiträge *nmpl*
control *n* **financial control**
Finanzkontrolle *nf* **production control**
Produktionskontrolle (-n) *nf* **quality control** Qualitätskontrolle (-n) *nf* **stock control** Lagerwirtschaft *nf*

convene *vb* **to convene a meeting** eine Sitzung einberufen
convenience *n* **at your earliest convenience** möglichst bald
convenient *adj* zweckmäßig *adj*
convertible *adj* **convertible currency** konvertierbare Währung (-en) *nf*
copier *n* (photocopier) Kopierer (-) *nm*
copy 1. *n* Kopie (-n) *nf* 2. *vb* (photocopy) kopieren *vb*
copyright *n* Copyright *nn* **copyright law** Urheberrecht (-e) *nn*
corporate *adj* korporativ *adj* **corporate image** Unternehmens-Image (-s) *nn* **corporate investment** Unternehmensinvestitionen *nfpl*
corporation *n* Körperschaft (-en) *nf* **corporation tax** Körperschaftssteuer (-n) *nf*
correspondence *n* Korrespondenz *nf*, Briefwechsel *nm*
corruption *n* Korruption *nf*
cosignatory *n* Mitunterzeichner (-) *nm*
cost 1. *n* Kosten *npl* **cost breakdown** Kostenaufstellung *nf* **cost centre** Kostenstelle (-n) *nf* **cost-cutting** Kostensenkung *nf* **cost of living** Lebenshaltungskosten *npl* **operating cost** betriebliche Aufwendungen *nfpl* **cost price** Herstellungspreis (-e) *nm* **running cost** Betriebskosten *npl* 2. *vb* **to cost a job** die Kosten einer Arbeit ermitteln
counterfeit 1. *n* Fälschung *nf* 2. *vb* fälschen *vb*
counterfoil *n* Kontrollabschnitt (-e) *nm*
countersign *vb* gegenzeichnen *vb*
country *n* Land (-änder) *nn* **developing country** Entwicklungsland (-änder) *nn* **third-world country** Land der Dritten Welt (-änder) *nn*, Entwicklungsland (-änder) *nn*
coupon *n* Kupon (-s) *nm*
courier 1. *n* Kurier (-e) *nm*, Reiseleiter (-) *nm* **by courier service** per Kurierdienst 2. *vb* per Eilboten senden
court *n* Gerichtshof (-öfe) *nm* **Court of Appeal, Court of Appeals** (US) Rechtsmittelinstanz *nf* **criminal court** Strafgericht *nn* **in court** vor dem Gericht
covenant *n* Verpflichtung (-en) *nf*
covenantee *n* Vertragsberechtigte/r *nmf*
covenantor *n* Kontrahent/in (-en/-innen) *nm/nf*
cover *n* **insurance cover** Versicherung *nf* **cover note** Deckungszusage *nf*
credit 1. *n* Kredit *nm* **credit agency**

Kreditauskunftei (-en) *nf* **to buy sth on credit** auf Kredit kaufen **credit card** Kreditkarte (-n) *nf* **credit company** Finanzierungsinstitut (-e) *nn* **credit control** Kreditkontrolle *nf* **credit enquiry** Kreditwürdigkeitsprüfung *nf* **in credit** in den schwarzen Zahlen **letter of credit** Akkreditiv (-e) *nn* **long credit** langfristiger Kredit *nm* **credit note** Gutschriftsanzeige (-n) *nf* **credit rating** Bonität *nf* **credit terms** Kreditkonditionen *nfpl* 2. *vb* **to credit sth to an account** einem Konto gutschreiben
creditor *n* Gläubiger (-) *nm*
creditworthiness *n* Kreditwürdigkeit *nf*
creditworthy *adj* kreditwürdig *adj*
crossed *adj* **crossed cheque** gekreuzter Scheck (-s) *nm*
currency *n* Währung (-en) *nf* **convertible currency** konvertierbare Währung (-en) *nf* **foreign currency** Fremdwährung (-en) *nf* **hard currency** harte Währung (-en) *nf* **legal currency** gesetzliche Währung (-en) *nf* **paper currency** Papierwährung (-en) *nf* **soft currency** weiche Währung (-en) *nf* **currency transfer** Währungsüberweisung (-en) *nf*
current *adj* **current account** Girokonto (-konten) *nn*
curriculum vitae (CV), résumé (US) *n* Lebenslauf (-äufe) *nm*
customer *n* Kunde (-n) *nm* **customer loyalty** Kundentreue *nf* **regular customer** Stammkunde (-n) *nm* **customer relations** Kundenbeziehungen *nfpl*
customs *npl* Zoll *nm* **customs charges** Zollgebühren *nfpl* **customs clearance** Zollabfertigung *nf* **customs declaration** Zollerklärung (-en) *nf* **customs office** Zollamt (-ämter) *nn* **customs officer** Zollbeamte/r *nmf* **customs regulations** Zollverordnungen *nfpl* **to clear sth through customs** abfertigen *vb* **customs union** Zollunion (-en) *nf* **customs warehouse** Zollager (-) *nn*
cut 1. *n* **tax cut** Steuersenkung (-en) *nf* 2. *vb* (reduce) kürzen *vb*
damage 1. *n* Schaden (-äden) *nm* **to cause extensive damage** beträchtlichen Schaden verursachen **to claim damages** (legal) Schadenersatz beanspruchen **damage to goods in transit** Transitschäden *nmpl* **damage to property** Eigentumsschaden *nm* 2. *vb* beschädigen *vb*
data *npl* Daten *nnpl* **data bank** Datenbank

(-en) *nf* **database** Datenbank (-en) *nf* **data capture** Datenerfassung *nf* **data processing** Datenverarbeitung *nf*
date *n* Datum (-en) *nn* **delivery date** Liefertermin (-e) *nm* **out of date** veraltet *adj*, überholt *adj* **up to date** aktuell *adj*
deal *n* Geschäft (-e) *nn* **it's a deal!** abgemacht!
dealer *n* Händler (-) *nm* **foreign exchange dealer** Devisenhändler (-) *nm*
dealing, trading (US) *n* Handel *nm* **foreign exchange dealings** Devisenhandel *nm* **insider dealing** Insiderhandel *nm*
debenture *n* gesicherte Schuldverschreibung (-en) *nf* **debenture bond** gesicherte Anleihe (-n) *nf* **debenture capital, debenture stock** (US) Anleihekapital *nn* **debenture loan** Obligationsanleihe (-n) *nf*
debit 1. *n* Debit *nn* **debit balance** Belastungssaldo (-en) *nm* 2. *vb* (account) belasten *vb*
debiting *n* **direct debiting** Einzugsermächtigung *nf*
debt *n* Schuld (-en) *nf* **corporate debt** Firmenschulden *nfpl* **to get into debt** in Schuld geraten **to pay off a debt** eine Schuld tilgen **to reschedule a debt** umschulden *vb* **debt service** Schuldendienst (-e) *nm*
debtor *n* Schuldner (-) *nm*
decline *n* (economic) Rückgang (-änge) *nm*
decrease 1. *n* Rückgang (-änge) *nm* 2. *vb* zurückgehen *vb*
deduct *vb* abziehen *vb*
deductible *adj* abziehbar *adj*
deduction *n* Abzug (-üge) *nm*
deed *n* (law) Übertragungsurkunde (-n) *nf* **deed of sale** Verkaufsurkunde (-n) *nf* **deed of transfer** Zessionsurkunde (-n) *nf*
default 1. *n* Zahlungsverzug (-üge) *nm* 2. *vb* Zahlungsverpflichtungen nicht nachkommen
defect *n* Fehler (-) *nm*
defective *adj* fehlerhaft *adj*
defer *vb* (postpone) aufschieben *vb*
deferment *n* Aufschub (-übe) *nm*
deferred *adj* (tax) aufgeschoben *adj*
deficiency *n* Fehlbetrag (-äge) *nm*, Mangel (Mängel) *nm*
deficient *adj* mangelhaft *adj*
deficit *n* Defizit (-e) *nn* **deficit financing** Defizitwirtschaft *nf*
deflation *n* Deflation *nf*
deflationary *adj* deflationär *adj*
defraud *vb* betrügen *vb*

del credere *adj* **del credere agent** Garantievertreter (-) *nm*
delay 1. *n* Verzögerung (-en) *nf* **without delay** unverzüglich *adj* 2. *vb* verzögern *vb*
delegate 1. *n* Delegierte/ r *nmf* 2. *vb* delegieren *vb*
delegation *n* Delegation *nf*
deliver *vb* (goods) liefern *vb*
delivery *n* Lieferung (-en) *nf* **cash on delivery** Barzahlung bei Lieferung **delivery date** Liefertermin (-e) *nm* **free delivery** Lieferung gratis **general delivery** (US) postlagernd *adj* **recorded delivery** Bestätigung der Auslieferung einer Sendung *nf* **delivery time** Lieferzeit (-en) *nf*
demand 1. *n* Nachfrage *nf* **supply and demand** Angebot und Nachfrage *nn* 2. *vb* fordern *vb*
demography *n* Demographie *nf*
demote *vb* (employee) degradieren *vb*
denationalize *vb* entnationalisieren *vb*
department *n* Abteilung (-en) *nf* **government department** Regierungsabteilung (-en) *nf* **personnel department** Personalabteilung (-en) *nf* **department store** Kaufhaus (-äuser) *nn*
depletion *n* Erschöpfung *nf*
deposit *n* Einzahlung (-en) *nf* einzahlen *vb* **deposit account** Einlagenkonto (-konten) *nn*
depository *n* einlagennehmendes Institut (-e) *nn*
depreciate *vb* an Wert verlieren *vb*
depreciation *n* Wertverlust *nm*
depression *n* (economic) Flaute (-n) *nf*
deputy 1. *adj* stellvertretend *adj* **deputy director** stellvertretender Direktor *nm* 2. *n* Stellvertreter (-) *nm*
design 1. *n* Design (-s) *nn* **a machine of good/bad design** eine gut/schlechte konstruierte Maschine *nf* 2. *vb* konstruieren *vb*
designer *n* (commercial) Designer (-) *nm*
devaluation *n* Abwertung (-en) *nf*
developer *n* Erschließungsunternehmen (-) *nn*
digital *adj* digital *adj*
diminishing *adj* **diminishing returns** Ertragsrückgang *nm*
director *n* Direktor (-en) *nm* **board of directors** Vorstand (-ände) *nm*, Direktorium (-ien) *nn* **managing director** Vorstandsvorsitzende/r *nmf*
disburse *vb* auszahlen *vb*
discount *n* Rabatt (-e) *nm* **at a discount**

mit Rabatt **discount rate** Diskontsatz
(-ätze) *nm*
discounted *adj* **discounted cash flow**
(DCF) diskontierter Einnahmeüberschuß
(-üsse) *nm*
disk *n* Diskette (-n) *nf* **disk drive** (Disk-
etten)laufwerk (-e) *nn* **floppy disk** Diskette (-n) *nf* **hard disk** Festplatte (-n) *nf*
magnetic disk Diskette (-n) *nf*
dismiss *vb* (employee) entlassen *vb*
dispatch 1. *n* **date of dispatch** Versanddatum (-en) *nn* **2.** *vb* (goods)
absenden *vb*
dispatcher *n* Absender (-) *nm*
display 1. *n* (of goods) Ausstellung (-en)
nf **2.** *vb* ausstellen
disposable *adj* (not for re-use) Wegwerf-
cpd **disposable income**
Nettoeinkommen *nn*
dispute *n* Streit (-e) *nm* **industrial dispute**
Arbeitsstreitigkeit (-en) *nf*
distribution *n* Vertrieb *nm*, Verteilung *nf*
distributor *n* Händler (-) *nm*
diversification *n* Diversifikation *nf*
diversify *vb* diversifizieren *vb*
dividend *n* Dividende (-n) *nf*
division *n* (of company) Geschäftsbereich
(-e) *nm* **division of labour**
Arbeitsaufteilung *nf*
dock 1. *n* (for berthing) Hafen (Häfen) *nm*
2. *vb* (ship) anlegen *vb*, docken *vb*
dockyard *n* Werft (-en) *nf*
document *n* Dokument (-e) *nn* **document
retrieval** Dokumentenauffindung *nf*
domestic *adj* inländisch *adj* **domestic
policy** Inlandspolitik *nf*
door *n* **door-to-door selling**
Haustürverkauf *nm*
double *adj* **double-entry** (bookkeeping)
doppelte Buchhaltung *nf*
Dow-Jones average (US) *n* Dow-Jones
Durchschnitt *nm*
down *adj* **down payment** Anzahlung (-en)
nf
downturn *n* (economic) Abschwung
(-ünge) *nm*
downward 1. *adj* absteigend *adj* **2.** *adv*
nach unten *adv*
draft *n* (financial) Tratte (-n) *nf,* Wechsel (-)
nm
draw *vb* (cheque) ausstellen *vb*
dry *adj* **dry goods** Kurzwaren *nfpl*
dumping *n* Dumping *nn*
durable *adj* haltbar *adj* **durable goods**
Gebrauchsgüter *nnpl*

duty *n* (customs) Zoll *nm* **duty-free**
(goods) zollfrei *adj*
dynamic *adj* dynamisch *adj*
dynamics *npl* Dynamik *nf*
early *adj* **early retirement**
Vorruhestand *nm*
earn *vb* verdienen *vb*
earned *adj* **earned income**
Arbeitseinkommen *nn* **earned surplus**
freie Rücklage (-n) *nf*
earnest *adj* **earnest money** Angeld (-er)
nn
earning *adj* **earning capacity**
Ertragsfähigkeit *nf* **earning power**
Ertragsfähigkeit *nf*
earnings *npl* Ertrag *nm* **earnings drift**
Ertragstendenz *nf* **loss of earnings**
Einkommensverlust *nm* **earnings-related pension** gehaltsabhängige Rente
(-n) *nf* **earnings yield** Gewinn je
Stammaktie *nm*
easy *adj* **easy-money policy** leichtverdientes Geld *nn*
EC (European Community) *abbr* EG
(Europäische Gemeinschaft) *nf*
econometrics *npl* Ökonometrie *nf*
economic *adj* **economic adviser** Wirtschaftsberater (-) *nm* **economic analysis**
Wirtschaftsanalyse (-n) *nf* **economic crisis** Wirtschaftskrise (-n) *nf* **economic
cycle** Wirtschaftszyklus (-en) *nm* **economic decline** Wirtschaftsrückgang
(-änge) *nm* **economic development**
Wirtschaftsentwicklung *nf* **Economic and
Monetary Union** Wirtschafts- und
Währungsgemeinschaft *nf* **economic
expansion** Wirtschaftswachstum *nn*
economic forecast Wirtschaftsprognose
(-n) *nf* **economic geography**
Wirtschaftsgeographie *nf* **economic
growth** Wirtschaftswachstum *nn* **economic infrastructure** wirtschaftliche
Infrastruktur *nf* **economic integration**
wirtschaftliche Integration *nf* **economic
objective** Wirtschaftsziel (-e) *nn*
economic performance
Wirtschaftsleistung *nf* **economic planning** Wirtschaftsplanung *nf* **economic
policy** Wirtschaftspolitik *nf* **economic
sanction** wirtschaftliche Sanktion (-en) *nf*
economic slowdown konjunkturelle
Abkühlung *nf* **economic strategy**
Wirtschaftsstrategie *nf* **economic superpower** wirtschaftliche Supermacht
(-mächte) *nf* **economic survey** Wirtschaftsbericht (-e) *nm* **economic trend**

Wirtschaftstrend (-s) *nm* **economic union**
Wirtschaftsunion (-en) *nf*
economical *adj* wirtschaftlich *adj*
economics *npl* Volkswirtschaft *nf*
economist *n* Wirtschaftswissenschaftler (-)
nm
economy *n* Wirtschaft (-en) *nf* **advanced**
economy fortgeschrittene Wirtschaft *nf*
developing economy sich entwickelnde
Wirtschaft *nf* **free market economy** freie
Marktwirtschaft (-en) *nf* **global economy**
Weltwirtschaft (-) *nf* **economies of scale**
Kostendegression *nf* **national economy**
Staatswirtschaft *nf* **planned economy**
Planwirtschaft (-en) *nf* **underdeveloped**
economy unterentwickelte Wirtschaft
(-en) *nf*
ECSC (European Coal and Steel
Community) *abbr* Montanunion *nf*
ECU (European Currency Unit) *abbr* ECU
(Europäische Währungseinheit) (-s) *nm*
edge *n* **competitive edge** Wettbewerbs-
vorteil (-e) *nm*
effect *n* Wirkung (-en) *nf* **financial effects**
die finanziellen Auswirkungen *nfpl*
efficiency *n* Leistungsfähigkeit *nf*
efficient *adj* leistungsfähig *adj*
EFT (electronic funds transfer) *abbr* EFT
(Europäischer Elektronischer
Geldverkehr) *nm*
EFTA (European Free Trade
Association) *abbr* EFTA (Europäische
Freie Handelsgemeinschaft) *nf*
elasticity *n* Elastizität *nf* **income elasticity**
Einkommenselastizität *nf* **elasticity of**
demand Nachfragenelastizität *nf*
elasticity of production Produktionselastizität *nf*
election *n* Wahl (-en) *nf* **general election**
Bundestagswahl (-en) *nf* **local election**
Landtagswahl (-en) *nf*, Gemeinderatswahl
(-en) *nf*
electronic *adj* elektronisch *adj* **electronic**
banking elektronische Abwicklung von
Bankgeschäften *nf* **electronic data pro-**
cessing elektronische
Datenverarbeitung *nf* **electronic mail**
elektronische Post *nf*
elimination *n* **elimination of tariffs**
Tarifabbau *nm*
email *n* elektronische Post *nf*
embargo *n* Embargo (-s) *nn* **to impose an**
embargo etwas mit einem Embargo
belegen **to lift an embargo** ein Embargo
aufheben **trade embargo** Handelsembargo (-s) *nn*

embassy *n* Botschaft (-en) *nf*
embezzle *vb* unterschlagen *vb*
embezzlement *n* Unterschlagung *nf*
embezzler *n* (jemand, der eine Unterschlagung begeht)
emergency *n* Notfall (-fälle) *nm* **emer-**
gency fund Hilfsfonds *nm*
emigration *n* Auswanderung *nf*
employ *vb* beschäftigen *vb*
employee *n* Arbeitnehmer (-) *nm* **em-**
ployee recruitment Anwerbung *nf* **em-**
ployee training Personalausbildung *nf*
employer *n* Arbeitgeber (-) *nm* **employers'**
liability insurance Arbeitgeberhaftpflicht-
versicherung *nf* **employers' federation**
Arbeitgeberverband (-ände) *nm*
employment *n* Arbeit *nf* **employment**
agency Arbeitsvermittlung *nf* **employ-**
ment contract Arbeitsvertrag (-äge) *nm*
full employment Vollbeschäftigung *nf*
employment law Arbeitsrecht (-e) *nn*
encashment *n* Einlösung *nf*
enclose *vb* beilegen *vb*
enclosure *n* Anlage (-n) *nf*
end *n* **end consumer** Endverbraucher (-)
nm **end user** Endabnehmer (-) *nm*
endorse *vb* (cheque) unterzeichnen *vb*
endorsement *n* Indossament *nn*
endowment *n* Stiftung (-en) *nf* **endow-**
ment insurance Lebensversicherung *nf*
endowment policy Lebensversicherungspolice (-n) *nf*
enforce *vb* (policy) durchsetzen *vb*
enforcement *n* Durchführung *nf*
engagement *n* (meeting) Termin (-e) *nm*
engineering *n* Maschinenbau *nm* **civil**
engineering Tiefbau *nm* **electrical eng-**
ineering Elektrotechnik *nf* **mechanical**
engineering Maschinenbau *nm* **precision**
engineering Feinmechanik *nf*
enhance *vb* (value) erhöhen *vb*
enlarge *vb* vergrößern *vb*
enquire *vb* fragen *vb*
enquiry *n* Anfrage (-n) *nf*
enterprise *n* (project) Unternehmen (-) *nn*
private enterprise Privatunternehmen (-)
nn
entertain *vb* **to entertain a client**
bewirten *vb*
entrepôt *n* Zwischenlager (-) *nn*
entrepreneur *n* Unternehmer (-) *nm*
entrepreneurial *adj* unternehmerisch *adj*
entry *n* **entry for free goods** Deklaration
für zollfreie Waren **entry into force**
Inkrafttreten *nn* **port of entry** Zollabferti-

gungshafen (-häfen) *nm* **entry visa** Einreisevisum (-a) *nn*
equalization *n* **equalization of burdens** Lastenausgleich *nm*
equalize *vb* ausgleichen *vb*
equilibrium *n* Gleichgewicht *nn*
equip *vb* ausstatten *vb*
equipment *n* Ausstattung *nf* **equipment leasing** Investitionsgüterleasing *nn*
equity *n* Eigenkapital *nn* **equity capital** Eigenkapital *nn* **equity financing** Eigenfinanzierung *nf* **equity interests** Kapitalbeteiligung *nf* **equity share** Stammaktie (-n) *nf* **equity trading** Aktienhandel *nm* **equity transaction** Kapitalhandel *nm*
ergonomics *npl* Ergonomik *nf*
escalate *vb* eskalieren *vb*
escalation *n* (prices) Erhöhung (-en) *nf*
escalator *n* Rolltreppe (-n) *nf*
escudo *n* Escudo *nm*
establish *vb* gründen *vb*
establishment *n* Gründung *nf*
estate *n* **estate agency, real estate agency** (US) Immobiliengesellschaft (-en) *nf* **estate agent, real estate agent** (US) Immobilienmakler (-) *nm*
estimate 1. *n* Schätzung (-en) *nf* **estimate of costs** Schätzkosten *npl* 2. *vb* schätzen *vb*
eurobond *n* Eurobond (-s) *nm*
eurocapital *n* Eurokapital *nn*
eurocheque *n* Euroscheck (-s) *nm*
eurocracy *n* Eurokratie *nf*
eurocrat *n* Eurokrat (-en) *nm*
eurocredit *n* Eurokredit (-e) *nm*
eurocurrency *n* Eurowährung (-en) *nf* **eurocurrency market** Eurogeldmarkt (-märkte) *nm*
eurodollar *n* Eurodollar (-s) *nm*
eurofunds *npl* Eurokapital *nn*
euromarket *n* Euromarkt (-märkte) *nm*
euromerger *n* Eurofusion (-en) *nf*
euromoney *n* Eurogeld (-er) *nn*
European *adj* europäisch *adj* **Council of Europe** Europarat (-äte) *nm* **European Advisory Committee** Europäischer Beratungsausschuß (-üsse) *nm* **European Commission** EG-Kommission *nf* **European Community (EC)** Europäische Gemeinschaft (EG) *nf* **European Court of Justice (ECJ)** Europäischer Gerichtshof *nm* **European Development Fund (EDF)** Europäischer Entwicklungsfonds *nm* **European Investment Bank (EIB)** Europäische

Investitionsbank *nf* **European Monetary Agreement (EMA)** Europäisches Währungsabkommen *nn* **European Monetary Cooperation Fund (EMCF)** Europäischer Fonds (in währungspolitischer Zusammenarbeit) *nm* **European Monetary System (EMS)** Europäisches Währungssystem *nn* **European Monetary Union (EMU)** Europäische Währungsunion *nf* **European Parliament** Europaparlament *nn* **European Recovery Plan** Europäischer Wiederaufbauplan *nm* **European Regional Development Fund (ERDF)** Europäischer Regionalentwicklungsfonds *nm* **European Social Fund (ESF)** Europäischer Sozialfonds *nm* **European Unit of Account (EUA)** Europäische Rechnungseinheit (-en) *nf*
eurosceptic *n* Euroskeptiker *nm*
evade *vb* ausweichen (+ dat) *vb*
evasion *n* **tax evasion** Steuerhinterziehung *nf*
eviction *n* Exmittierung *nf*
ex *prep* **ex factory/works** ab Werk **ex gratia payment** Sonderzahlung (-en) *nf* **ex interest** ohne Zinsen **ex quay** ab Hafen **ex repayment** ohne Rückzahlung **ex ship** ab Schiff **ex stock** ab Lager **ex store/warehouse** ab Lager **ex wharf** ab Hafen
examination *n* Prüfung (-en) *nf*
examine *vb* prüfen *vb*
exceed *vb* überschreiten *vb*
excess *adj* **excess capacity** Überkapazität *nf* **excess demand inflation** Übernachfrageinflation *nf* **excess profit(s) tax** Mehrgewinnsteuer *nf* **excess reserves** Sonderrücklage *nf*
exchange *n* **exchange broker** Devisenmakler (-) *nm* **exchange cheque** Austauschscheck (-s) *nm* **exchange clearing agreement** Devisenverrechnungsabkommen *nn* **exchange control** Devisenkontrolle *nf* **foreign exchange** Devisen *nfpl* **exchange market** Devisenmarkt (-märkte) *nm* **exchange rate** Wechselkurs (-e) *nm* **exchange rate mechanism (ERM)** Wechselkursmechanismus *nm* **exchange restrictions** Devisenbeschränkungen *nfpl* **exchange risk** Kursrisiko (-iken) *nn* **Stock Exchange** Wertpapierbörse (-n) *nf*
excise *n* **excise duty** Verbrauchssteuer (-n) *nf* **the Board of Customs and Excise** Ministerialabteilung für Zölle und Verbrauchssteuern *nf*

exclude vb ausschließen vb
exclusion n **exclusion clause** Ausschlußklausel (-n) nf **exclusion zone** Sperrzone
(-n) nf
executive 1. adj **executive committee**
Leitungsausschuß (-üsse) nm **executive
compensation** Vergütung für leitende
Angestellte nf **executive duties**
Führungsaufgaben nfpl **executive hierarchy** Leitungspyramide nf **executive
personnel** Führungskräfte nfpl 2. n lei-
tend/e Angestellte/r nfm
exempt adj befreit von adj **tax-exempt**
steuerfrei adj
exemption n Befreiung nf
exhaust vb (reserves) erschöpfen vb
exhibit vb ausstellen vb
exhibition n Ausstellung (-en) nf
exorbitant adj maßlos adj
expand vb erweitern vb
expansion n Erweiterung nf **expansion of
capital** Kapitalsteigerung nf **expansion of
trade** Handelserweiterung nf
expectation n Erwartung (-en) nf **consumer expectations**
Verbrauchererwartungen nfpl
expedite vb beschleunigen vb
expenditure n Ausgaben nfpl **expenditure
rate** Unkostensatz (-sätze) nm **state expenditure** Staatsausgaben nfpl **expenditure taxes** Ausgabesteuern nfpl
expense n Kosten npl **expense account**
Spesenkonto (-s) nn **expense control**
Kostenkontrolle (-n) nf **entertainment
expenses** Unterhaltungskosten npl **travelling expenses, travel expenses** (US)
Reisekosten npl
experience 1. n Erfahrung (-en) nf
experience curve Lernkurve nf 2. vb
erfahren vb
experienced adj erfahren adj
expert 1. adj Fach- cpd 2. n Experte (-n)
nm
expertise n Fachwissen nn
expiration n Verfall nm
expire vb auslaufen vb
expiry, expiration (US) n Ablauf nm **expiry
date, expiration** (US) Verfallstag (-e) nm
export 1. adj **export bill of lading**
Konnossement (-s) nn **export credit** Exportkredit (-e) nm **export credit insurance**
Exportkreditversicherung nf **export department** Exportabteilung (-en) nf **export-led growth** durch Export bedingtes
Wachstum nn **export licence**
Exportlizenz nf **export marketing**

Exportmarketing nn **export operations**
Exporttätigkeiten nfpl **export strategy**
Exportstrategie (-n) nf **export subsidies**
Exportzuschüsse nmpl **export surplus**
Exportüberschuß nm **export tax** Ausfuhrsteuer (-n) nf **export trade**
Exporthandel nm 2. n Export nm **export
of capital** Kapitalausfuhr nf 3. vb
exportieren vb
exporter n Exporteur (-e) nm
express adj **express agency**
Schnelldienst nm **express delivery** Eilzustellung (-en) nf **express service**
Eildienst nm
expropriate vb enteignen vb
expropriation n Enteignung nf
extend vb **to extend a contract** einen
Vertrag verlängern **to extend credit** Kredit gewähren **to extend the range** die
Reihe erweitern
extension n (of contract) Verlängerung
(-en) nf
extent n **extent of cover** (insurance)
Versicherungsausmaß nn
external adj Auslands- cpd **external audit**
Buchprüfung nf
extortion n Erpressung nf
extra adj zusätzlich adj **extra cost**
Mehrkosten npl **extra profit**
Mehrgewinn nm
extraordinary adj **extraordinary meeting**
außerordentliche Versammlung (-en) nf
extraordinary value außerordentlicher
Wert (-e) nm
facility n (plant) Anlage (-n) nf **facility
planning** Werksplanung nf
facsimile (fax) n Faxgerät (-e) nn
factor 1. adj **factor income** Factoring-
Einkommen nn **factor market** Factoring-
Markt (-märkte) nm **factor price** Erzeugerpreis (-e) nm 2. n (buyer of debts)
Faktor (-en) nm **limiting factor**
Einschränkung nf **factor of production**
Produktionsfaktor (-en) nm 3. vb (debts)
fakturieren vb
factoring n (of debts) Factoring nn
factory n **factory board** Vorstand (-ände)
nm, Aufsichtsrat (-räte) nm **factory costs**
Fertigungskosten npl **factory inspector**
Gewerbeaufsichtsbeamte/r nmf **factory
ledger** Hauptbuch (-bücher) nn **factory
overheads** Fertigungsgemeinkosten npl
factory price Preis ab Werk (-e) nm
fail vb (negotiations) versagen vb (attempts) versagen vb
failure n Versagen nn

fair *adj* fair *adj* **fair competition** lauterer Wettbewerb *nm* **fair market value** angemessener Marktpreis (-e) *nm* **fair rate of return** angemessene Verzinsung *nf* **fairtrade agreement** Preisbindungsabkommen (-) *nn* **fair-trade policy** Außenhandelspolitik auf der Basis gegenteiliger Vorteile *nf* **fair-trade practice** lautere Wettbewerbsmethode (-n) *nf* **fair trading** vertikale Preisbindung *nf* **fair wage** angemessener Lohn *nm*
fall due *vb* fällig werden *vb*
falling *adj* **falling prices** fallende Preise *nmpl* **falling rate of profit** fallende Gewinnspanne *nf*
false *adj* **false representation** Vorspiegelung falscher Tatsachen *nf*
falsification *n* Verfälschung *nf* **falsification of accounts** Kontenfälschung *nf*
family *n* Familie (-n) *nf* **family allowance** Kindergeld *nn* **family branding** Familienmarke *nf* **family corporation** Familien-Aktiengesellschaft (-en) *nf* **family income** Familieneinkommen *nn* **family industry** Familienindustrie *nf*
farm out *vb* an Subunternehmer vergeben *vb*
farming *n* Landwirtschaft *nf* **farming of taxes** Verpachtung von Steuern *nf* **farming subsidies** Agrarsubventionen *nfpl*
FAS (free alongside ship) *abbr* frei Längsseite Schiff
fast *adj* **fast-selling goods** Schnelldreher *npl* **fast track** Schnellspur *nf*
fault *n* Fehler (-) *nm* **minor fault** Kleinfehler (-) *nm* **serious fault** schwerer Defekt (-e) *nm* **to find fault with** kritisieren *vb*
faulty *adj* **faulty goods** fehlerhafte Ware (-n) *nf* **faulty workmanship** Herstellungsfehler (-) *nm*
favour *n* Gefallen (-) *nm* **to do sb a favour** jemandem einen Gefallen tun
favourable *adj* **favourable balance of payments** günstige Zahlungsbilanz *nf* **favourable balance of trade** günstige Handelsbilanz *nf* **favourable exchange** günstiger Umtausch *nm* **favourable price** günstiger Preis (-e) *nm* **favourable terms** günstige Bedingungen *nfpl*
fax 1. *n* Fax (-e) *nm* 2. *vb* faxen *vb*
feasibility *n* Durchführbarkeit *nf* **feasibility study** Durchführbarkeitsstudie (-n) *nf*
feasible *adj* durchführbar *adj*
federal *adj* Bundes- *cpd*

federation *n* Bund (Bünde) *nm*
fee *n* Gebühr (-en) *nf* **to charge a fee** eine Gebühr berechnen **to pay a fee** eine Gebühr zahlen
feedback *n* Rückmeldung *nf* **to give feedback** Rückmeldung geben
fiat *n* **fiat money** Papiergeld ohne Deckung *nn*
fictitious *adj* **fictitious assets** fiktiver Vermögenswert *nm* **fictitious purchase** Scheinkauf (-e) *nm* **fictitious sale** Scheinverkauf *nm*
fidelity *n* **fidelity bond** Kautionsverpflichtung (-e) *nf* **fidelity insurance** Garantieversicherung *nf*
fiduciary *adj* **fiduciary bond** Kautionsverpflichtung *nf* **fiduciary issue** ungedeckte Notenausgabe *nf*
field *n* **field investigation** Umfrage (-n) *nf* **field manager** Außendienstleiter (-) *nm* **field personnel** Mitarbeiter im Außendienst *nmpl* **field research** Feldforschung *nf* **field test** Bewährung *nf* **field work** Außendienstarbeit *nf*
FIFO (first in first out) *abbr* Fifo-Methode (-n) *nf*
file 1. *n* Akte (-n) *nf* 2. *vb* ablegen *vb*
filing *n* **filing cabinet** Aktenschrank (-änke) *nm* **filing system** Ablagesystem (-e) *nn*
final *adj* **final accounts** Endabrechnung *nf* **final demand** letzte Mahnung (-en) *nf* **final entry** letzte Eintragung *nf* **final invoice** Schlußrechnung (-en) *nf* **final offer** endgültiges Angebot (-e) *nn* **final products** Enderzeugnisse *nnpl* **final settlement** Abschlußzahlung (-en) *nf* **final utility** Grenznutzen *nm*
finance 1. *n* Finanzwesen *nn* **Finance Act** Finanzgesetz (-e) *nn* **finance bill** Finanzwechsel (-) *nm* **finance company** Finanzierungsgesellschaft (-en) *nf* 2. *vb* finanzieren *vb*
financial *adj* finanziell *adj* **financial accounting** Finanzbuchhaltung *nf* **financial assets** finanzielle Aktiva *npl* **financial balance** Bilanz *nf* **financial company** Finanzierungsgesellschaft (-en) *nf* **financial consultancy** Finanzberatung *nf* **financial consultant** Finanzberater (-) *nm* **financial control** Finanzkontrolle *nf* **financial crisis** Finanzkrise (-n) *nf* **financial difficulty** finanzielle Schwierigkeit (-en) *nf* **financial exposure** finanzielles Engagement *nn* **financial incentive** finanzieller Anreiz (-e) *nm* **financial institution** Finanzinstitut (-e) *nn* **financial**

investment Finanzinvestition *nf* **financial loan** Darlehen (-) *nn* **financial management** Finanzmanagement *nn* **financial market** Finanzmarkt (-märkte) *nm* **financial measures** finanzielle Maßnahmen *nfpl* **financial operation** Finanzgeschäft (-e) *nn* **financial planning** Finanzplanung *nf* **financial policy** Finanzpolitik *nf* **financial report** Finanzbericht (-e) *nm* **financial resources** Finanzmittel *nnpl* **financial risk** finanzielles Risiko (-iken) *nn* **financial situation** Finanzlage *nf* **financial stability** finanzielle Stabilität *nf* **financial statement** Jahresabschluß (-üsse) *nm* **financial strategy** Finanzstrategie (-n) *nf* **financial structure** Finanzstruktur *nf* **financial year** Geschäftsjahr *nn*
financier *n* Finanzier (-s) *nm*
financing *n* Finanzierung *nf* **financing surplus** Finanzüberschuß (-üsse) *nm*
fine *adj* **fine rate of interest** günstiger Zinssatz *nm*
finished *adj* **finished goods** Fertigerzeugnisse *nnpl* **finished stock** Fertigwarenlager (-) *nn* **finished turnover** Umschlaghäufigkeit des Warenbestandes *nf*
fire* *vb* entlassen *vb*
firm *adj* fest *adj* **firm offer** festes Angebot (-e) *nn* **firm price** Festpreis (-e) *nm*
first *adj* **first bill of exchange** Primawechsel (-) *nm* **first class** erste Klasse *nf* **first-class paper** erstklassiger Wechsel (-) *nm* **first customer** erster Kunde (-n) *nm* **first-hand** erster Hand **first mortgage** erste Hypothek *nf* **first-rate** (investment) erstklassig *adj*
fiscal *adj* **fiscal agent** Hauptzahlungsagent (-en) *nm* **fiscal balance** Geschäftsbilanz *nf* **fiscal charges** steuerliche Belastung *nf* **fiscal measures** Finanzmaßnahmen *nfpl* **fiscal policy** Finanzpolitik *nf* **fiscal receipt** Steuerbeleg (-e) *nm* **fiscal year** Geschäftsjahr *nn* **fiscal year end (fye)** Geschäftsjahresende *nn* **fiscal zoning** Steuerklassifizierung *nf*
fix *vb* **to fix the price** den Preis festsetzen
fixed *adj* **fixed assets** Anlagevermögen *nn* **fixed asset turnover** Umsatz des Anlagevermögens *nm* **fixed budget** feststehendes Budget *nn* **fixed charges** feste Belastung (-en) *nf* **fixed costs** Fixkosten *npl* **fixed credit** Festsatzkredit (-e) *nm* **fixed income** festes Einkommen *nn* **fixed interest** Festzins (-e) *nm* **fixed liabilities** langfristige

Verbindlichkeiten *nfpl* **fixed price** Festpreis (-e) *nm*
fixture *n* **fixtures and fittings** Anschlüsse und unbewegliches Inventar *npl*
flat *adj* **flat bond** Anleihe ohne Zinseinschluß (-n) *nf* **flat market** umsatzloser Markt (-märkte) *nm* **flat rate** Einheitstarif (-e) *nm* **flat-rate income tax** einheitlicher Einkommenssteuersatz (-sätze) *nm* **flat-rate tariff** Einheitstarif (-e) *nm*
flexibility *n* (of prices) Flexibilität *nf*
flexible *adj* **flexible budget** flexibles Budget (-s) *nn* **flexible exchange rate** flexibler Wechselkurs (-e) *nm* **flexible price** flexibler Preis (-e) *nm*
flexitime, flextime (US) *n* gleitende Arbeitszeit *nf*
flight *n* (in plane) Flug (-üge) *nm* **flight capital** Fluchtkapital *nn* **to book a flight** einen Flug buchen
float *vb* (currency) floaten *vb*, freigeben *vb*
floating *adj* **floating assets** Umlaufkapital *nn* **floating exchange rate** veränderlicher Wechselkurs (-e) *nm* **floating rate interest** veränderlicher Zinssatz (-sätze) *nm*
floor *n* **floor broker** Börsenmakler (-) *nm* **shopfloor** Verkaufsfläche (-n) *nf*, Werkstatt (-stätte) *nf*
flotation *n* Kapitalaufnahme durch Emission von Aktien *nf*
flow *n* **cash flow** Cashflow *nm* **flow chart** Flußdiagramm (-e) *nn* **flow line production** Reihenfertigung *nf* **flow of income** Einkommenszufluß *nm* **flow production** Reihenfertigung *nf*
fluctuate *vb* schwanken *vb*
fluctuation *n* Schwankung (-en) *nf* **fluctuation in sales** Absatzschwankungen *nfpl*
fluid *adj* flüssig *adj* **fluid market** veränderlicher Markt (-Märkte) *nm*
FOB (free on board) *abbr* frei an Bord
for *prep* **for sale** zu verkaufen
forced *adj* **forced currency** Zwangswährung (-en) *nf*
forecast 1. *n* Prognose (-n) *nf* 2. *vb* vorhersehen *vb*
forecasting *n* Vorhersage *nf*
foreclose *vb* kündigen *vb*
foreclosure *n* Wettbewerbsausschluß *nm*
foreign *adj* ausländisch *adj* **foreign aid** Auslandshilfe *nf* **foreign aid programme** Auslandshilfsprogramm *nn* **foreign bank** Auslandsbank (-en) *nf* **foreign company** Auslandsunternehmen (-) *nn* **foreign competition** Auslandskonkurrenz *nf* **for-**

eign currency Fremdwährung (-en) nf
foreign exchange Devisen nfpl foreign
exchange dealer Devisenhändler (-) nm
foreign exchange market Devisenmarkt
(-märkte) nm foreign currency holdings
Auslandsgelder nnpl foreign investment
Auslandsinvestitionen nfpl foreign loan
Auslandskredit (-e) nm foreign travel
Auslandsreise (-n) nf
foreman n Vorarbeiter (-) nm
forestall vb vorbeugen vb
forestalling adj forestalling policy pro-
duktionsorientierte Wirtschaftspolitik nf
forfeit 1. n Kaduzierung nf (shares)
Aktienkaduzierung nf 2. vb verlieren vb,
verwirken vb
forfeiture n Kaduzierung nf
forgery n Fälschung nf
form n (document) Formular (-e) nn
formal adj formell adj formal agreement
Abkommen nn formal contract offizieller
Vertrag (-äge) nm
formality n customs formalities
Zollformalitäten nfpl to observe formalities die Formalitäten beachten
formation n (of company) Gründung (-en)
nf capital formation Kapitalbildung nf
forward 1. adj forward contract Terminkontrakt (-e) nm forward cover
Terminsicherung nf forward market Terminmarkt (-märkte) nm forward transaction Termingeschäft (-e) nn 2. vb
befördern vb
forwarder n Spediteur (-e) nm
forwarding n Expedition nf forwarding
agency Spedition (-en) nf forwarding
agent Spediteur (-e) nm forwarding
charges Versandgebühren nfpl forwarding note Frachtbrief (-e) nm
found vb to found a company ein Unternehmen gründen
founder n Gründer (-) nm
fraction n Bruchteil (-e) nm
fractional adj Bruch- cpd fractional money Scheidemünzen nfpl fractional shares vorgeschriebene
Mindestreserven nfpl
franc n Belgian franc Belgischer Franken
(-) nm French franc Französischer Franken (-) nm Swiss franc Schweizer Franken (-) nm
franchise 1. adj franchise outlet franchisierter Ortshändler (-) nm 2. n Konzession (-en) nf 3. vb franchisieren vb
franchisee n Franchisenehmer (-) nm
franchising n Franchising nn

franchisor n Franchisegeber (-) nm
franco adj frei adj franco domicile frei
Haus franco price frei Preis franco zone
frei Zone
frank vb frankieren vb
franked adj frankiert adj franked income
Dividendenerträge nach Steuern nmpl
franking n franking machine Frankierma-
schine (-n) nf
fraud n Betrug nm
fraudulent adj betrügerisch adj
free adj free agent unabhängige Handelsvertretung (-en) nf free alongside
ship (FAS) Frei Längsseite Schiff free
competition Wettbewerbsfreiheit nf free
delivery Lieferung frei Bestimmungsort nf
duty free zollfrei adj free economy freie
Wirtschaft nf free entry Eintritt frei nm
free goods zollfreie Waren nfpl free
market freier Markt (Märkte) nm free
market economy freie Marktwirtschaft
(-en) nf free movement of goods freier
Warenverkehr nm free of charge
kostenlos adj free of freight ohne
Frachtgebühr free of tax steuerfrei adj
free on board (FOB) frei Schiff free on
quay frei Kai free port frei Hafen free
trade freier Handel nm free trade area
Freihandelszone (-n) nf
freedom n freedom of choice freie Wahl nf
Freefone (R) (GB) n Telephongebühr bar
bezahlt nf
freelance adj freiberuflich adj
freelancer (GB) n Freiberufliche/r nmf
Freepost (R) (GB) n Postgebühr bar
bezahlt nf
freeze 1. n (prices, wages) Stopp (-s) nm
2. vb (prices, wages) einen Lohnstopp
durchführen
freight n Frachtgut nn freight forwarder
Spediteur (-e) nm freight traffic
Frachtverkehr nm
freighter n Befrachter (-) nm
frequency n Frequenz nf
friendly adj freundlich adj Friendly Society Hilfskasse nf
fringe adj fringe benefits
Lohnnebenleistungen nfpl fringe market
Nebenmarkt (-märkte) nm
frontier n Grenze (-n) nf
fronting n Rückversicherung nf
frozen adj frozen assets eingefrorene
Guthaben nnpl frozen credits eingefrorener Kredit nm
FT Index (Financial Times Index) n Index
der Financial Times nm

full *adj* **full cost** Vollkosten *npl* **full liability** volle Haftung *nf* **full payment** volle Zahlung (-en) *nf*
full-time *adj/adv* Vollzeit- *cpd* **full-time worker** Vollzeitkraft (-kräfte) *nf*
function *n* (role) Funktion *nf*
functional *adj* **functional analysis** Funktionsanalyse *nf* **functional organization** Berufsverband (-bände) *nm*
fund 1. *n* Fonds *nm* **2.** *vb* finanzieren *vb*
funded *adj* **funded debt** fundierte Schulden *nfpl*
funding *n* Finanzierung *nf* **funding bonds** Umschuldungsanleihe *nf*
funds *npl* Kapital *nn* **funds flow** gesamtwirtschaftliche Finanzierung *nf* **funds surplus** außerordentliche Reservefonds *nm*
furlough (US) 1. *n* Urlaub *nm* **2.** *vb* Urlaub machen
future *adj* **future commodity** Warentermingeschäft *nn* **future delivery** Terminlieferung *nf* **future goods** Terminware *nf*
futures *npl* Termingeschäfte *nnpl* **futures contract** Terminkontrakt (-e) *nm* **futures exchange** Markt für Termingeschäfte *nm* **futures market** Terminkontraktmarkt *nm* **futures marketing** Terminkontraktmarketing *nn* **futures price** Terminkontraktpreis (-e) *nm* **futures trading** Terminhandel *nm*
fye (fiscal year end) *abbr* Geschäftsjahresende *nn*
gain 1. *n* Gewinn *nm* **capital gain** Kapitalgewinn *nm* **capital gains tax** Kapitalgewinnsteuer *nf* **gain in value** Wertgewinn (-e) *nm* **gain sharing** Gewinnbeteiligung *nf* **2.** *vb* gewinnen *vb*
gainful *adj* **gainful employment** Erwerbstätigkeit *nf*
galloping *adj* galoppierend *adj* **galloping inflation** galoppierende Inflation *nf*
Gallup *n* **Gallup poll (R)** Meinungsumfrage (-n) *nf*
gap *n* Lücke (-n) *nf* **trade gap** Handelsbilanzdefizit (-e) *nn*
gas *n* **natural gas** Erdgas *nn*
GATT (General Agreement on Tariffs and Trade) *abbr* GATT *nn*
gazump *vb* an einen Höherbietenden verkaufen
GDP (Gross Domestic Product) *abbr* Bruttoinlandsprodukt *nn*
general *adj* **general accounting** Buchhaltung *nf* **general agencies (US)**

Generalvertretungen *nfpl* **general agent** Generalvertreter (-) *nm* **general average** Durchschnitt *nm* **general election** Bundestagswahl (-en) *nf* **general management** allgemeine Verwaltung *nf* **general manager** Manager (-) *nm* **general partner** Vollhafter (-) *nm* **general partnership** allgemeine Personengesellschaft (-en) *nf* **general strike** Generalstreik (-s) *nm*
generate *vb* **to generate income** Einkommen erwirtschaften
generation *n* **income generation** Einkommenserwirtschaften *nn*
generosity *n* Großzügigkeit *nf*
gentleman *n* **gentleman's agreement** Gentlemen's Agreement (-s) *nn*, mündliche Absprache (-n) *nf*
gilt-edged *adj* erstklassig *adj* **gilt-edged market** Markt für Staatspapiere (Märkte) *nm* **gilt-edged security** Staatspapier (-e) *nn*
gilts *npl* Staatspapiere *nnpl*
giveaway *n* Schleuderpreis (-e) *nm*
global *adj* global *adj* **global economy** Weltwirtschaft *nf* **global market** Weltmarkt (-märkte) *nm* **global marketing** weltweites Marketing *nn*
globalization *n* Globalisierung *nf*
GMT (Greenwich Mean Time) *abbr* Greenwich Mean Time
gnome *n* **the Gnomes of Zurich** die Züricher Gnomen *nmpl*
GNP (Gross National Product) *abbr* Bruttosozialprodukt *nn*
go-slow *n* (strike) Bummelstreik (-s) *nm*
going *adj* gängig *adj* **going concern** arbeitendes Unternehmen (-) *nn*
gold *n* Gold *nn* **gold bullion** Barrengold *nn* **gold coin** Goldmünze (*n*) *nf* **gold market** Goldmarkt (-märkte) *nm* **gold reserves** Goldreserven *nfpl* **gold standard** Goldstandard *nm*
golden *adj* **golden handcuffs** Vergünstigungen *nfpl* **golden handshake** hohe Abfindung (-en) *nf* **golden hello** Einstandsgeld *nn* **golden parachute** großzügige Abfindung (-en) *nf*
goods *npl* Waren *nfpl* **bulk goods** Massengüter *nnpl* **domestic goods** Haushaltswaren *nfpl* **export goods** Exportartikel *nmpl* **import goods** Importartikel *nmpl* **goods on approval** Waren auf Probe *nfpl* **goods in process** Transitgüter *nnpl* **goods in progress** Transitwaren *nfpl* **goods on consignment**

Konsignationswaren *nfpl* **goods transport** Güterverkehr *nm*
goodwill *n* Goodwill *nm*
govern *vb* regieren *vb*
government *n* Regierung (-en) *nf* **government body** Regierungsausschuß (-üsse) *nm* **government bond** Staatsanleihe (-n) *nf* **government enterprise** Regierungsunternehmen (-) *nn* **government loan** Staatsanleihe (-n) *nf* **government policy** Regierungspolitik *nf* **government sector** Regierungssektor (-en) *nm* **government security** Staatspapiere *nnpl* **government subsidy** Regierungszuschuß (-üsse) *nm*
graduate 1. *n* (of university) Graduierte/ r *nmf* **2.** *vb* graduieren *vb*
grant 1. *n* (of a patent) Erteilung *nf* **regional grant** regionale Subvention *nf* **2.** *vb* gewähren *vb*
graphics *npl* **computer graphics** Computergrafik *nf*
gratuity *n* Trinkgeld (-er) *nn*
green *adj* **Green Card** Aufenthaltserlaubnis (-sse) *nf* **green currency** grüne Dollarwährung *nf* **green pound** grünes Pfund *nn*
Greenwich *n* **Greenwich Mean Time (GMT)** Greenwich Mean Time *nf*
grievance *n* Beschwerdepunkt (-e) *nm*
gross *adj* brutto *adj* **gross amount** Bruttosumme *nf* **gross domestic product (GDP)** Bruttoinlandsprodukt *nn* **gross interest** Bruttozins *nm* **gross investment** Bruttoinvestition *nf* **gross loss** Bruttoverlust (-e) *nm* **gross margin** Bruttospanne (-n) *nf* **gross national product (GNP)** Bruttosozialprodukt *nn* **gross negligence** grobe Fahrlässigkeit *nf* **gross output** Bruttoproduktion *nf* **gross sales** Bruttoumsatz *nm* **gross weight** Bruttogewicht *nn*
group *n* Gruppe (-n) *nf* **group insurance** Gruppenversicherung *nf* **group of countries** Länderblock (-s) *nm* **group travel** Gruppenreise *nf*
growth *n* Wachstum *nn* **annual growth rate** jährliche Wachstumsrate (-n) *nf* **economic growth** Wirtschaftswachstum *nn* **export-led growth** durch Export bedingtes Wachstum *nn* **market growth** Marktwachstum *nn* **growth rate** Wachstumsrate (-n) *nf* **sales growth** Verkaufssteigerung *nf* **growth strategy** Wachstumsstrategie (-n) *nf*

guarantee *n* Garantie (-n) *nf* **quality guarantee** Qualitätsgarantie (-n) *nf*
guarantor *n* Garantiegeber (-) *nm*
guest *n* **guest worker** Gastarbeiter (-) *nm*
guild *n* Verein (-e) *nm*
guilder *n* Gulden (-) *nm*
h *abbr* (hour) St. (Stunde) *abbr*
half *n* Hälfte (-n) *nf* **half-an-hour** eine halbe Stunde *nf* **half-board** Halbpension *nf* **half-pay** Halblohn *nm* **half-price** halber Preis *nm* **to reduce sth by half** um die Hälfte reduzieren **half-year** Halbjahr (-e) *nn*
hall *n* **exhibition hall** Ausstellungshalle (-n) *nf*
hallmark *n* Feingehaltsstempel (-) *nm*
halt *vb* (inflation) stoppen *vb*
halve *vb* halbieren *vb*
hand *n* **in hand** noch nicht fertiggestellt **to hand** zur Hand
hand over *vb* überreichen *vb*
handbook *n* Handbuch (-bücher) *nn*
handle *vb* (deal) handeln mit *vb* (money) verwalten *vb* umgehen mit *vb* **handle with care** Vorsicht - zerbrechlich!
handling *n* **handling charges** Ladekosten *npl* **data handling** Datenverarbeitung *nf*
handmade *adj* handgearbeitet *adj*
handshake *n* Händedruck (-ücke) *nm*
handwritten *adj* handgeschrieben *adj*
handy *adj* praktisch *adj*
hang on *vb* (wait) warten *vb* (on telephone) am Apparat bleiben *vb*
hang together *vb* (argument) zusammenhängen *vb*
hang up *vb* (telephone) aufhängen *vb*
harbour *n* Hafen (Häfen) *nm* **harbour authorities** Hafenbehörden *nfpl* **harbour dues** Hafengeld *nn* **harbour facilities** Hafenanlagen *nfpl* **harbour fees** Hafengebühren *nfpl*
hard *adj* **hard bargain** harte Forderungen *nfpl* **hard cash** Bargeld *nn* **hard currency** harte Währung (-en) *nf* **hard disk** Festplatte (-n) *nf* **hard-earned** schwer verdient **hard-hit** schwer betroffen **hard-line** harte Linie *nf* **hard loan** hartes Darlehen (-) *nn* **hard news/ information** konkrete Information *nf* **hard price** fester Preis *nm* **hard sell** aggressive Verkaufsmethode *nf* **the hard facts** die Tatsachen *nfpl* **hard-working** fleißig *adj*
hardware *n* **computer hardware** Computerhardware *nf*

haul *n* **long-haul** Langstrecken- *cpd* **short-haul** Kurzstrecken- *cpd*
haulage, freight (US) *n* **road haulage** Beförderung *nf* **haulage company** Kraftverkehrsunternehmen (-) *nn*, Spedition (-en) *nf*
haulier *n* Transportunternehmen (-) *nn*
hazard *n* Gefahr (-en) *nf* **natural hazard** natürliche Gefahr *nf* **occupational hazard** Berufsrisiko (-iken) *nn*
hazardous *adj* gefährlich *adj*
head 1. *adj* **head accountant** Chefbuchhalter (-) *nm* **head office** Hauptverwaltung (-en) *nf* 2. *n* **at the head of** an der Spitze von **head of department** Abteilungsleiter (-) *nm* **head of government** Regierungschef (-s) *nm* **per head** pro Kopf **to be head of** führen 3. *vb* (department) leiten *vb*
head for *vb* zugehen auf *vb*
headed *adj* **headed notepaper** Papier mit Briefkopf *nn*
heading *n* Überschrift (-en) *nf*
headquarters *n* Hauptsitz *nm*
headway *n* **to make headway** vorankommen *vb*
health *n* **health benefits** Kassenleistungen *nfpl* **health care industry** Gesundheitswesen *nn* **health hazard** Gesundheitsgefahr (-en) *nf* **industrial health** Arbeitshygiene *nf* **health insurance** Krankenversicherung *nf* **Ministry of Health** Gesundheitsministerium (-ien) *nn*
healthy *adj* **finances** solide *adj*
heavy *adj* **heavy-duty** strapazierfähig *adj* **heavy goods vehicle** Lastkraftwagen (-) *nm* **heavy industry** Schwerindustrie *nf* **heavy trading** hohe(n) Umsätze *npl* **heavy user** Dauerbenutzer ( ) *nm*
hedge *n* **hedge against inflation** Inflationssicherung *nf* **hedge clause** (US) Schutzklausel (-n) *nf*
hidden *adj* **hidden assets** verstecktes Vermögen *nn* **hidden defect** versteckter Fehler (-) *nm*
hierarchy *n* (corporate) Hierarchie (-n) *nf* **data hierarchy** Datenhierarchie *nf* **hierarchy of needs** Bedürfnishierarchie (-n) *nf*
high *adj* **high-class** erstklassig *adj* **high finance** Hochfinanz *nf* **high-grade** hochwertig *adj* **high-income** mit hohem Einkommen **high-level** Spitzen- *cpd* **high-powered** einflußreich *adj* **high-priced** teuer *adj* **high-ranking** von hohem Rang **high-risk** risikoreich *adj* **high sea-**

son Hochsaison (-s) *nf* **hi-tech** Hochtechnologie- *cpd*
higher *adj* **higher bid** höheres Angebot (-e) *nn*
hire 1. *n* Mieten *nn* **hire charges** Mietkosten *npl* **hire contract** Mietvertrag (-äge) *nm* **for hire** zu vermieten **hire purchase** Teilzahlungskauf *nm* 2. *vb* (person) mieten *vb*
history *n* **employment/work history** Berufserfahrung *nf*
hit *vb* **hit-or-miss** ungenau *adj*, nachlässig *adj* **to hit the headlines** Schlagzeilen machen **to hit the market** einschlagen *vb* **to be hard hit by** von etwas schwer betroffen sein
HO (head office) *abbr* Hauptverwaltung (-en) *nf*
hoard *vb* horten *vb*
hold *vb* **to hold a meeting** eine Sitzung abhalten **hold area** Wartezone (-n) *nf* **to hold sth as security** etwas als Sicherheit halten **to hold sb liable** jemanden haftbar machen für **on hold** (on phone) warten **hold queue, hold line** (US) Warteschlange (-n) *nf* **to hold sb responsible** jemanden für etwas verantwortlich halten/machen
hold back *vb* (not release) zurückhalten *vb*
hold on *vb* (on phone) warten *vb*
hold over *vb* (to next period) verschieben *vb*
hold up *vb* (delay) aufhalten *vb* (withstand scrutiny) verzögern *vb*
holder *n* Inhaber (-) *nm* **joint holder** Mitinhaber (-) *nm* **licence holder** Lizenzinhaber (-) *nm* **office holder** amtierend *adj* **policy holder** Versicherte/r *nmf*
holding *n* Beteiligung (-en) *nf* **holding company** Holding-Gesellschaft (-en) *nf* **foreign exchange holdings** Devisenbestände *nmpl* **majority/minority holding** Mehrheitsbeteiligung/Minderheitsbeteiligung *nf* **to have holdings** eine Beteiligung besitzen
holdup *n* Verzögerung (-en) *nf*
holiday, vacation (US) *n* **bank holiday** (GB) öffentlicher Feiertag (-e) *nm* **on holiday, on vacation** (US) auf Urlaub **holiday pay** Urlaubsgeld *nn* **tax holiday** Steuerfreijahre *nnpl*
home *n* **home address** Heimatanschrift *nf* **home buyer** Eigenheimerwerber (-) *nm* **home country** Heimat *nf* **home delivery** Lieferung frei Haus *nf* **home industry** Inlandsindustrie (-n) *nf* **home loan** Hypothek (-en) *nf* **home market** Binnen-

markt (-märkte) *nm* **home owner** Hausbesitzer (-) *nm* **home sales** Inlandsverkäufe *nmpl* **home service** Zustelldienst *nm* **home shopping** Home-Shopping *nn* **honorary** *adj* ehrenamtlich *adj* **horizontal** *adj* **horizontal analysis** horizontale Analyse *nf* **horizontal integration** horizontale Integration *nf* **host** *n* Gastgeber (-) *nm* **host country** Gastland (-länder) *nn* **hot** *adj* **hot line** heißer Draht *nm* **hot money** heißes Geld *nn* **hot seat** Schleudersitz *nm* **to be in hot demand** Verkaufsschlager sein **hotel** *n* Hotel (-s) *nn* **hotel accommodation** Hotelunterkunft *nf* **hotel chain** Hotelkette (-n) *nf* **five-star hotel** Hotel mit 5 Sternen (-s) *nn* **hotel industry/trade** Hotelindustrie *nf* **hotel management** Hotelverwaltung *nf* **to run a hotel** ein Hotelgeschäft betreiben **hour** *n* **after hours** nach Betriebsschluß **business hours** Geschäftsstunden *nfpl* **busy hours (US)** Spitzenzeiten *nfpl* **fixed hours** festgesetzte Arbeitszeit (-en) *nf* **office hours** Geschäftsstunden *nfpl* **per hour** pro Stunde **per hour output** Produktion pro Stunde *nf* **hourly** *adj* stündlich *adj* **hourly-paid work** nach Stunden bezahlte Arbeit *nf* **hourly rate** Stundenlohn (-öhne) *nm* **hourly workers** Stundenlohnarbeiter *npl* **house** *n* **clearing house** Clearingstelle (-n) *nf* **house duty (US)** Haussteuer (-n) *nf* **house journal/magazine** Firmenzeitschrift (-en) *nf* **mail-order house** Versandhaus (-häuser) *nn* **packing house (US)** Konservenfabrik *nf* **house prices** Hauspreise *nmpl* **publishing house** Verlag (-e) *nm* **house sale** Hausverkauf (-äufe) *nm* **house telephone** Haustelefon (-e) *nn* **household** *n* Haushalt (-e) *nm* **household expenditure** Haushaltsausgaben *nfpl* **household goods** Haushaltswaren *nfpl* **household survey** Haushaltumfrage (-n) *nf* **householder** *n* Hausinhaber (-) *nm* **housewares (US)** *npl* Haushaltswaren *nfpl* **housing** *n* **housing estate, tenement (US)** Wohnsiedlung (-en) *nf* **housing industry** Wohnungsbauindustrie *nf* **housing project** Wohnungsbauprojekt (-e) *nn* **housing scheme** Wohnungsbauprogramm (-e) *nn*

hull *n* Schiffskörper (-) *nm* **hull insurance** Schiffskörperversicherung *nf* **human** *adj* **human relations** Personalbeziehungen *nfpl* **human resource management (HRM)** Personalmanagement *nn* **human resources** Personal *nn*, Arbeitskräfte *nfpl* **hundred** *adj* **one hundred per cent** hundert Prozent **hydroelectricity** *n* durch Wasserkraft erzeugte Energie **hype** *n* übertriebene Werbung *nf* **hyperinflation** *n* übermäßige Inflation *nf* **hypermarket** *n* Verbrauchergroßmarkt (-märkte) *nm* **hypothesis** *n* Hypothese (-n) *nf* **idle** *adj* ungenutzt *adj* **idle capacity** freie Kapazität *nf* **illegal** *adj* illegal *adj* **implication** *n* **this will have implications for our sales** das hat Folgen für unseren Absatz **import** 1. *n* Import *nm*, Einfuhr *nf* **import agent** Importagent (-en) *nm* **import barrier** Importschranke (-n) *nf* **import control** Importkontrolle (-n) *nf* **import department** Importabteilung (-en) *nf* **import duty** Einfuhrzoll *nm* **import licence** Einfuhrlizenz (-en) *nf* **import office** Importamt (-ämter) *nn* **import quota** Einfuhrquote (-n) *nf* **import restrictions** Einfuhrbeschränkungen *nfpl* **import surplus** Einfuhrüberschuß (-üsse) *nm* 2. *vb* importieren *vb* **importation** *n* Import *nm* **importer** *n* Importeur (-e) *nm* **importing** *adj* **importing country** Importland (-länder) *nn* **impose** *vb* **to impose a tax** eine Steuer auferlegen **to impose restrictions** Beschränkungen auferlegen **imposition** *n* (of tax) Belastung *nf* **impound** *vb* beschlagnahmen *vb* **imprint** *n* **to take an imprint** (credit card) einen Abdruck machen, abdrucken **improve** *vb* verbessern *vb* **we must improve our performance** wir müssen unsere Leistung verbessern **inadequate** *adj* unzureichend *adj* **incentive** *n* Anreiz (-e) *nm* **incidental** *adj* **incidental expenses** Nebenkosten *npl* **include** *vb* **our price includes delivery** Lieferung ist im Preis enthalten **taxes are included** Steuern sind im Preis enthalten **inclusive** *adj* **inclusive of tax and delivery**

costs einschließlich Steuern und Lieferkosten **the prices quoted are inclusive** die angegebenen Preise sind Gesamtpreise **income** n Einkommen nn **gross income** Bruttoeinkommen nn **net income** Nettoeinkommen nn **private income** Privateinkommen nn **income tax** Einkommensteuer (-n) nf **inconvenience** n Unannehmlichkeit nf **inconvenient** adj ungelegen adj **increase 1.** n **increase in the cost of living** Erhöhung der Lebenshaltungskosten **price increase** Preiserhöhung nf **wage increase** Lohnerhöhung (-en) nf **2.** vb (prices, taxes) erhöhen vb **indebted** adj verpflichtet adj **indemnify** vb entschädigen vb **indemnity** n Schadenersatz nm **indemnity insurance** Schadenersatzversicherung nf **index** n Index (-e) nm **cost of living index** Lebenshaltungskostenindex (-e) nm **growth index** Wachstumsindex (-e) nm **price index** Preisindex (-e) nm **share index** Aktienindex (-e) nm **indicate** vb hinweisen auf vb **indication** n Hinweis (-e) nm **indirect** adj indirekt adj **indirect cost** indirekte Kosten npl **indirect expenses** indirekte Kosten npl **indirect tax** indirekte Steuer (-n) nf **industrial** adj industriell adj **industrial accident** Arbeitsunfall (-fälle) nm **industrial arbitration** Schiedsgerichtsverfahren (-) nn **industrial democracy** Mitbestimmung nf **industrial dispute** Arbeitskampf (-kämpfe) nm **industrial expansion** industrielle Ausweitung nf **industrial region** Industriegebiet (-e) nn **industrial relations** industrielle Arbeitsbeziehungen nfpl **industrial tribunal** Arbeitsgericht (-e) nn **industrial union** Industriegewerkschaft (-en) nf **industry** n Industrie (-n) nf **inefficient** adj ineffizient adj **inferior** adj (goods) (von) minderer Qualität, minderwertig adj **inflation** n Inflation nf **rate of inflation** Inflationsrate (-n) nf **inflationary** adj inflationär adj **inflationary gap** Inflationslücke (-n) nf **inflationary spiral** Inflationsspirale (-n) nf **inform** vb informieren vb **information** n Information (-en) nf **information desk** Informationsschalter (-) nm **information management**

Marktforschung nf **information office** Informationsbüro (-s) nn **information processing** Datenverarbeitung nf **information retrieval** Informationswiedergewinnung nf **information storage** Datenspeicherung nf **information systems** Informationssysteme nnpl **information technology (IT)** Informationstechnologie (-n) nf **infrastructure** n Infrastruktur (-en) nf **inherit** vb erben vb **inheritance** n Erbe (-n) nn **inheritance laws** Erbschaftsgesetze nnpl **inhouse** adj **inhouse training** n betriebliche Ausbildung nf **injunction** n gerichtliche Verfügung (-en) nf **to take out an injunction** eine gerichtliche Verfügung erwirken **inland** adj Inlands- cpd **the Inland Revenue, the Internal Revenue Service (IRS)** (US) Finanzamt (-ämter) nn **insider** n Insider (-) nm **insider dealing, insider trading** (US) Insidergeschäfte nnpl **insist on** vb bestehen auf (dat) vb **insolvency** n Zahlungsunfähigkeit nf **insolvent** adj zahlungsunfähig adj **inspect** vb besichtigen vb, prüfen vb **inspection** n (customs) (Zoll-)Kontrolle (-n) nf **inspector** n Inspektor (-en) nm **customs inspector** Zollinspektor (-en) nm **instability** n Instabilität nf **install(l)** vb installieren vb **installation** n Installation nf **instalment, installment** (US) n Rate (-n) nf **institute** n Institut (-e) nn **institution** n Anstalt (-en) nf **credit institution** Kreditanstalt (-en) nf **instruction** n Anweisung (-en) nf **instruction book** Bedienungsanleitung (-en) nf **instruction sheet** Bedienungsanleitung (-en) nf **to follow instructions** Anweisungen befolgen **insurable** adj **insurable risk** Versicherungsrisiko (-iken) nn **insurance** n Versicherung nf **insurance agent** Versicherungsvertreter (-) nm **insurance broker** Versicherungsmakler (-) nm **car insurance** Autoversicherung nf **insurance certificate** Versicherungspolice (-n) nf **insurance company** Versicherungsgesellschaft (-en) nf **comprehensive insurance** Vollkaskoversicherung nf **insurance contract** Versicherungsvertrag (-äge) nm **fire insurance**

Brandversicherung *nf* **insurance fund** Versicherungsfonds (-) *nm* **National Insurance (GB)** Sozialversicherung *nf* **insurance policy** Versicherungspolice (-n) *nf* **insurance premium** Versicherungsprämie (-n) *nf* **insurance representative** Versicherungsvertreter (-) *nm* **insurance salesperson** Versicherungsvertreter (-) *nm* **third party insurance** Haftpflichtversicherung *nf* **to take out insurance** eine Versicherung abschließen **insurance underwriter** Versicherungsträger (-) *nm* **unemployment insurance** Arbeitslosenversicherung *nf*
insure *vb* versichern *vb*
intangible *adj* **intangible asset** immaterielle Aktiva *npl*
intensive *adj* intensiv *adj* **capital-intensive** kapitalintensiv *adj* **labour-intensive** arbeitsintensiv *adj*
interest *n* Zinsen *nmpl* **interest-bearing** zinstragend *adj* **interest-free** zinslos *adj* **interest period** Zinsperiode (-n) *nf* **interest rate** Zinskurs (-e) *nm* **to bear interest** Zinsen tragen **to charge interest** Zinsen berechnen **to pay interest** Zinsen zahlen
interface *n* Schnittstelle (-n) *nf*
interim *adj* vorläufig *adj*
intermediary *adj* vermittelnd *adj*, Zwischen- *cpd*
internal *adj* **internal audit** innerbetriebliche Revision *nf* **internal auditor** innerbetrieblicher Prüfer (-) *nm* **the Internal Revenue Service (IRS) (US)** Finanzamt (-ämter) *nn*
international *adj* international *adj* **international agreement** internationales Abkommen (-) *nn* **international competition** internationale Konkurrenz *nf* **International Date Line** Datumsgrenze (-n) *nf* **international organization** Weltunternehmen (-) *nn* **international trade** Welthandel *nm*
intervene *vb* intervenieren *vb*
intervention *n* Intervention (-en) *nf* **state intervention** staatliche Intervention *nf*
interview 1. *n* Vorstellungsgespräch (-e) *nn* **to attend for interview** sich vorstellen *vr* **to hold an interview** ein Vorstellungsgespräch führen **to invite sb to interview** zum Vorstellungsgespräch einladen **2.** *vb* ein Vorstellungsgespräch mit jemandem führen *vb*
introduce *vb* (product) ein Produkt auf dem Markt bringen *vb*

inventory *n* Inventar (-e) *nn* **inventory control** Bestandskontrolle *nf*
invest *vb* (money) investieren *vb*
investment *n* Investition (-en) *nf* **investment adviser** Anlageberater (-) *nm* **investment portfolio** Effektenportefeuille (-s) *nn* **investment programme, investment program** (US) Investitionsprogramm (-e) *nn* **investment strategy** Investitionsstrategie (-n) *nf*
investor *n* Investor (-en) *nm*
invisible *adj* **invisible exports** unsichtbare Exporte *nmpl* **invisible imports** unsichtbare Importe *nmpl*
invitation *n* Einladung (-en) *nf*
invite *vb* einladen *vb*
invoice *n* Rechnung (-en) *nf* **duplicate invoice** Rechnungsduplikat (-e) *nn* **to issue an invoice** eine Rechnung ausstellen **to settle an invoice** eine Rechnung begleichen
irrecoverable *adj* (loss) uneinbringlicher Verlust (-e) *nm*
irrevocable *adj* unwiderruflich *adj* **irrevocable letter of credit** unwiderrufliches Akkreditiv (-e) *nn*
issue 1. *n* **bank of issue** Notenbank (-en) *nf* **share issue, stock issue** (US) Aktienemission (-en) *nf* **2.** *vb* (cheques,shares, tickets, notes) ausgeben *vb* (policy) ausstellen *vb* **to issue sb with sth** etwas an jemanden ausgeben *vb*
issuing *adj* **issuing bank** Notenbank (-en) *nf*
item *n* Artikel (-) *nm*
itemize *vb* aufgliedern *vb*
itemized *adj* **itemized account** spezifizierte Rechnung (-en) *nf*
itinerary *n* (Reise)Route (-n) *nf*
jackpot *n* Hauptgewinn (-) *nm*
jingle *n* **advertising jingle** Werbespruch (-üche) *nm*
job *n* **job analysis** Arbeitsanalyse (-n) *nf* **job creation** Arbeitsbeschaffung *nf* **job description** Stellenbeschreibung (-en) *nf* **job offer** Stellenangebot (-e) *nn* **job rotation** Stellenrotation *nf* **job satisfaction** Arbeitsfreude *nf* **job shop** Arbeitsamt (-ämter) *nn*
jobber *n* Jobber (-) *nm*
Jobcentre (GB) *n* Arbeitsamt (-ämter) *nn*
jobless *adj* arbeitslos *adj* **the jobless** die Arbeitslosen *npl*
joint *adj* gemeinsam *adj* **joint account** Gemeinschaftskonto (-konten) *nn* **joint obligation** gemeinsame Verpflichtung *nf*

joint ownership Mitbesitz *nm* joint responsibility gemeinsame Verantwortung *nf*
joint-stock company Aktiengesellschaft (-en) *nf* joint venture Gemeinschaftsunternehmen (-) *nn*
jointly *adv* gemeinsam *adv*
journal *n* Tagebuch (-bücher) *nn*
journalism *n* Journalismus *nm*
judicial *adj* gerichtlich *adj*
junior *adj* untergeordnet *adj*
junk *n* junk bond Junk Bond (-s) *nm*
jurisdiction *n* Zuständigkeitsbereich *nm*
juror *n* Geschworene/r *nmf*
jury *n* die Geschworenen *npl*
K *abbr* (1000) K *abbr*
keen *adj* (competition) scharf *adj* (price) extrem niedrig *adj*
keep *vb* (goods) führen *vb* to keep an appointment einen Termin einhalten to keep the books die Bücher halten/führen to keep the business running das Geschäft führen
keep back *vb* (money) Geld zurückhalten
keep down *vb* (prices) Preise niedrig halten
keep up with *vb* (events) sich auf dem laufenden halten *vr*
key *adj* key currency Schlüsselwährung (-en) *nf* key industry Schlüsselindustrie (-n) *nf* key person Schlüsselkraft (-kräfte) *nf*, Hauptperson (-en) *nf* key question Schlüsselfrage (-n) *nf*
key in *vb* eingeben *vb*
keyboard *n* Tastatur (-en) *nf*
keynote *adj* keynote speech programmatische Rede (-n) *nf*
keyword *n* (computer) Stichwort (-wörter) *nn*
kill *vb* to kill a project ein Projekt streichen
kilowatt *n* Kilowatt (-) *nn*
kind 1. *adj* nett *adj* would you be so kind as to... würden Sie bitte so nett sein... 2. *n* Sorte (-n) *nf*
king-size(d) *adj* riesengroß *adj*
kiosk *n* (phone) Kabine (-n) *nf*
kit *n* (equipment) Ausrüstung *nf*
kite *n* kite mark (GB) Gütezeichen (-) *nn*
knock *vb* (disparage) schlagen *vb*
knock down *vb* (price) herabsetzen *vb*
knock off* *vb* (finish work) Arbeit einstellen *vb*
knock-for-knock *adj* gegenseitige Aufrechnung *nf* knock-for-knock agreement Regreßverzichtsvereinbarung (-en) *nf*

knock-on *adj* knock-on effect Folgewirkung (-en) *nf*
knockdown *adj* knockdown price niedrigster Preis (-e) *nm*
know-how *n* Know-how *nn*
knowledge *n* Wissen *nn* knowledge base Wissensbasis (-basen) *nf* it is common knowledge es ist allgemein bekannt, daß... to have a thorough knowledge of sth etwas gut kennen to have a working knowledge of sth vertraut sein mit to my knowledge soviel ich weiß
knowledgeable *adj* kenntnisreich *adj*
known *adj* known facts die anerkannten Tatsachen *nfpl*
krona *n* (Swedish) Krone (-n) *nf*
krone *n* (Danish, Norwegian) Krone (-n) *nf*
kudos *n* Ansehen *nn*
kWh *abbr* KwS (Kilowattstunde) *abbr*
label 1. *n* Etikett (-e) *nn* 2. *vb* etikettieren *vb*
labour, labor (US) *n* Arbeit *nf* labour costs Arbeitskosten *npl* labour dispute Arbeitskampf (-kämpfe) *nm* labour-intensive arbeitsintensiv *adj* labour law Arbeitsrecht (-e) *nn* labour market Arbeitsmarkt *nm* labour relations Arbeitsbeziehungen *nfpl*
labourer *n* ungelernter Arbeiter (-) *nm*
lack *n* Mangel (Mängel) *nm* lack of investment Investitionsmangel *nm*
land *n* land purchase Grundstückskauf *nm* land reform Bodenrechtsreform (-en) *nf* land register Grundbuch *nn* land tax Grundsteuer (-n) *nf* land tribunal Enteignungsausschuß (-üsse) *nm*
landlord *n* Wirt (-e) *nm*
landowner *n* Grundbesitzer (-) *nm*
language *n* Sprache (-n) *nf* language specialist Sprachexperte (-n) *nm*
large *adj* large-scale groß angelegt
launch 1. *n* product launch Produkteinführung (-en) *nf* 2. *vb* (product) einführen *vb*
law *n* Gesetz (-e) *nn* business law Handelsrecht *nn* civil law Zivilrecht *nn* criminal law Strafrecht *nn* international law internationales Recht *nn* law of diminishing returns Gesetz des abnehmenden Ertrags *nn* public law öffentliches Recht *nn*
lawsuit *n* Prozeß (-sse) *nm*
lay off *vb* (workers) entlassen *vb*
LBO (leveraged buy-out) *abbr* Leveraged Buyout (-s) *nm*
leader *n* market leader Marktführer (-) *nm*

leadership n Führung nf
leading adj führend adj, Haupt- cpd
leading product Hauptprodukt (-e) nn
lease vb (ver)mieten vb
leasehold n Pachtbesitz nm
leaseholder n Pächter (-) nm
leave 1. n Urlaub nm leave of absence
Beurlaubung nf sick leave
Genesungsurlaub nm to take leave sich
beurlauben lassen vr to take leave of sb
von jemandem Abschied nehmen 2.
vb abfahren vb (resign from) zurücktreten
von vb
ledger n Hauptbuch (-bücher) nn bought
ledger Wareneinkaufsbuch (-bücher) nn
ledger entry Hauptbucheintragung nf
left adj left luggage
Gepäckaufbewahrung nf left-luggage
locker Schließfach (-fächer) nn left-luggage office Gepäckaufbewahrung nf
legacy n Erbschaft (-en) nf
legal adj gesetzlich adj legal tender
gesetzliches Zahlungsmittel (-) nn to
take legal action Klage erheben (gegen
jemanden)
legislate vb Gesetze erlassen
legislation n Gesetzgebung nf to introduce legislation ein Gesetz einführen
lend vb leihen vb
lender n Kreditgeber (-) nm
lessee n Leasingnehmer (-) nm
lessor n Leasinggeber (-) nm
let vb (property) (ver)mieten vb
letter n letter of application Bewerbungsschreiben (-) nn letter of credit
Akkreditiv (-e) nn letter of introduction
Empfehlungsschreiben (-) nn
letterhead n Briefkopf (-köpfe) nm
level n Niveau (-s) nn level of employment Beschäftigtenstand nm level of
inflation Inflationsrate (-n) nf level of
prices Preisniveau (-s) nn
levy vb (tax) erheben vb
liability n Haftung nf current liabilities
Verbindlichkeiten nfpl fixed liability
langfristige Verbindlichkeiten nfpl limited liability beschränkte Haftung nf
liable adj haftbar adj liable for damages
schadenersatzpflichtig adj liable for tax
steuerpflichtig adj
libel n (schriftliche) Verleumdung nf
licence n Lizenz (-en) nf licence fee
Lizenzgebühr (-en) nf
license vb genehmigen vb
licensee n Konzessionsinhaber (-) nm
licensor n Lizenzgeber (-) nm

life n life assurance/insurance
Lebensversicherung nf life member Mitglied auf Lebenszeit (-er) nn
LIFO (last in first out) abbr Lifo-Methode
(-n) nf
limit n Grenze (-n) nf credit limit Kreditlinie (-n) nf
limited adj begrenzt adj limited capital
begrenztes Kapital nn limited company
Gesellschaft mit Haftungsbeschränkung
(-en) nf limited liability beschränkte
Haftung nf limited partnership Kommanditgesellschaft (-en) nf
line n above the line zum ordentlichen
Haushalt gehörig assembly line Montageband (-bänder) nn below the line nicht
zum ordentlichen Haushalt gehörig line
management Fachgebietsleitung nf line
manager Fachgebietsleiter (-) nm line of
business Sparte (-n) nf product line
Sortiment (-e) nn
liquid adj liquide adj liquid assets liquide
Mittel nnpl liquid capital liquides
Kapital nn
liquidate vb liquidieren vb
liquidation n Liquidation (-en) nf liquidation value Liquidationswert nm
liquidity n Liquidität nf
list 1. n Liste (-n) nf list price Listenpreis
(-e) nm 2. vb verzeichnen vb,
registrieren vb
listed adj listed share, listed stock (US)
börsennotierte Aktie (-n) nf
litigant n streitende Partei (-en) nf
litigate vb einen Prozeß führen
litigation n Rechtsstreit (-e) nm
load 1. n Ladung (-en) nf, Belastung (-en)
nf 2. vb laden vb
loan n Kredit (-e) nm loan agreement
Kreditvertrag (-äge) nm bank loan Bankkredit (-e) nm bridging loan, bridge loan
(US) Überbrückungskredit (-e) nm personal loan Personalkredit (-e) nm to
grant a loan einen Kredit gewähren to
request a loan einen Kredit beantragen
local adj örtlich adj local taxes örtliche
Steuern nfpl
location n Standort (-e) nm
lockout n (of strikers) Aussperrung (-en) nf
logistics npl Logistik nf
Lombard Rate n Lombardsatz nm
long n long capital langfristiges Kapital nn
long credit langfristiger Kredit nm long
deposit langfristige Einlage nf long-distance Langstrecken- long-range
Langstrecken- cpd long-term

langfristig adj long-term planning langfristige Planung nf
lose vb (custom) verlieren vb
loss n Verlust (-e) nm financial loss finanzieller Verlust (-e) nm gross loss Bruttoverlust (-e) nm loss leader Lokkartikel (-) nm net loss Nettoverlust (-e) nm loss of earnings Verdienstausfall (-fälle) nm loss of job Arbeitsplatzverlust (-e) nm to minimise losses Verluste minimieren
lost-property adj lost-property office Fundbüro (-s) nn
lot n (at auction) Partie (-n) nf
low adj (price) niedrig adj
lower vb (price, interest rate) herabsetzen vb
lucrative adj lukrativ adj
luggage n Gepäck nn excess luggage Übergewicht nn luggage insurance Reisegepäckversicherung nf
lump n lump sum settlement Pauschalentschädigung nf
luxury adj luxury goods Luxusartikel nmpl luxury tax Luxussteuer (-n) nf
machine 1. n Maschine (-n) nf 2. vb bearbeiten vb
machinery n Maschinerie nf machinery of government Regierungsapparat nm
macroeconomics npl Makrowirtschaft(slehre) nf
made adj hergestellt adj made in France in Frankreich hergestellt
magazine n (journal) Zeitschrift (-en) nf
magnate n Magnat (-en) nm
magnetic adj magnetisch adj magnetic tape (DP) Magnetband (-bänder) nn
mail order n Versandhandel nm
mailing n mailing list Adressenkartei (-en) nf
main adj Haupt- cpd main office Hauptverwaltung (-en) nf main supplier Hauptlieferant (-en) nm
mainframe n (DP) Großrechner (-) nm
maintenance n Unterhaltung nf, Wartung nf maintenance costs Unterhaltungskosten npl
major adj führend adj
majority n Mehrheit (-en) nf majority holding Mehrheitsbeteiligung nf in the majority meistens
make vb to make a fortune ein Riesengeschäft machen to make a living sich seinen Lebensunterhalt verdienen to make money Geld verdienen
malingerer n Simulant (-en) nm

mall n shopping mall Einkaufszentrum (-en) nn
malpractice n Berufsvergehen (-) nn
man-made adj künstlich adj
manage vb führen vb, leiten vb
management n Management nn business management Geschäftsleitung nf management buy-out Management Buyout (-s) nn management by objectives zielgesteuerte Unternehmensführung nf management consultant Unternehmensberater (-) nm financial management Finanzmanagement nn middle management mittleres Management nn personnel management Personal-Management nn top management Unternehmensspitze nf management training Management-Ausbildung nf
manager n Manager (-) nm
manpower n Personalbestand nm
manual adj manual worker (manueller) Arbeiter (-) nm
manufacture 1. n Herstellung nf 2. vb herstellen vb
manufacturer n Hersteller (-) nm
margin n (Handels-)Spanne (-n) nf profit margin Gewinnspanne (-n) nf
marginal adj Grenz- cpd marginal cost Grenzkosten npl marginal revenue Grenzertrag nm
marine 1. adj See- cpd marine engineering Schiffsmaschinenbau nm marine insurance Seeversicherung nf 2. n merchant marine Handelsmarine nf
mark n Deutschmark deutsche Mark (DM) nf
mark down vb (price) herabsetzen vb
mark up vb erhöhen vb
markdown n Herabsetzung nf
market 1. n Markt (Märkte) nm market analysis Marktanalyse (-n) nf bear market Baissemarkt nm black market schwarzer Markt nm bond market Bondmarkt nm bull market Haussemarkt nm buyer's market Käufermarkt nm capital market Kapitalmarkt nm Common Market Gemeinsamer Markt nm domestic market Binnenmarkt nm down-market (product) von niedriger Qualität market economy Marktwirtschaft (-en) nf falling market fallender Markt nm firm market fester Markt nm market forces Marktkräfte nfpl foreign market Außenmarkt nm futures market Terminkontraktmarkt nm labour market Arbeitsmarkt nm market leader Marktführer (-) nm money market

Geldmarkt *nm* **market opportunity** Marktgelegenheit (-en) *nf* **market price** Marktwert (-e) *nm* **property market (GB)/ real estate market (US)** Immobilienmarkt *nm* **market research** Marktforschung *nf* **retail market** Einzelhandelsmarkt *nm* **market segmentation** Marktsegmentierung *nf* **seller's market** Verkäufermarkt *nm* **market share** Marktanteil (-e) *nm* **stock market** (Aktien)Börse (-n) *nf* **the bottom has fallen out of the market** der Markt erreichte seinen Tiefststand *nm* **to play the market** an der Börse spekulieren **upmarket** (product) von guter Qualität **market value** Marktwert (-e) *nm* **wholesale market** Großhandelsmarkt *nm* **2.** *vb* verkaufen *vb*, vermarkten *vb*

marketable *adj* absetzbar *adj*

marketing *n* Marketing *nn* **marketing consultant** Vertriebsberater (-) *nm*, Marketingberater (-) *nm* **marketing department** Marketingabteilung (-en) *nf*

marketing director Vertriebsleiter (-) *nm*

markup *n* Erhöhung *nf*

mart *n* (Finanz)Markt (Märkte) *nm*

mass *adj* **mass marketing** Massenabsatz *nm* **mass media** Massenmedien *npl* **mass production** Massenfertigung *nf* **mass unemployment** Massenarbeitslosigkeit *nf*

material *adj* **1. material needs** materielle(n) Bedürfnisse **2.** *npl* Material *nn* **building materials** Baumaterial *nn* **raw materials** Rohstoffe *nmpl*

maternity *n* **maternity leave** Schwangerschaftsurlaub *nm*

matrix *n* Matrix (-izen) *nf*

mature *vb* (business, economy) fällig werden *vb*

maximise *vb* maximieren *vb*

maximum *adj* **maximum price** Höchstpreis (-e) *nm*

MBA (Master of Business Administration) *abbr* MBA *abbr*

mean 1. *adj* (average) durchschnittlich *adj* **2.** *n* (average) Durchschnitt (-e) *nm*

means *npl* Mittel *nnpl* **financial means** Finanzmittel *npl* **to live beyond one's means** über seine Verhältnisse leben *vb* **we do not have the means to...** wir sind nicht in der Lage...

measure 1. *n* Maßnahme (-n) *nf* **financial measure** finanzielle Maßnahme (-n) *nf* **safety measure** Sicherheitsmaßnahme (-n) *nf* **2.** *vb* messen *vb*

mechanical *adj* mechanisch *adj* **mechanical engineering** Maschinenbau *nm*

media *npl* Medien *npl*

median *adj* mittler *adj*, Mittel- *cpd*

mediate *vb* vermitteln *vb*

mediation *n* Vermittlung *nf*

mediator *n* Vermittler (-) *nm*

medical *adj* ärztlich *adj* **medical insurance** Krankenversicherung *nf*

medium 1. *adj* mittler *adj*, Mittel- *cpd* **medium-sized firm** mittelgroßes Unternehmen (-) *nn* **medium term** mittelfristig *adj* **2.** *n* **advertising medium** Werbemittel (-) *nn*

meet *vb* treffen *vb*

meeting *n* Sitzung (-en) *nf* **board meeting** Vorstandssitzung (-en) *nf* **business meeting** Geschäftssitzung (-en) *nf* **to hold a meeting** eine Sitzung abhalten

megabyte *n* Megabyte *nn*

member *n* Mitglied (-er) *nn* **Member of Parliament (MP) (GB)** Bundestagsabgeordnete/r *nmf* **Member of the European Parliament (MEP)** Abgeordnete/r des Europaparlaments *nmf*

memo *n* Mitteilung (-en) *nf*

memorandum *n* Mitteilung (-en) *nf*

memory *n* (DP) Speicher (-) *nm* **memory capacity** Speicherkapazität *nf*

mercantile *adj* Handels- *cpd*

merchandise *vb* vertreiben *vb*

merchandizer *n* Händler (-) *nm*

merchandizing *n* Vertrieb *nm*

merchant *n* Handelsvertreter (-) *nm* **merchant bank** Handelsbank (-en) *nf* **merchant navy, merchant marine (US)** Handelsmarine *nf* **merchant ship** Handelsschiff (-e) *nn*

merge *vb* fusionieren *vb*

merger *n* Fusion (-en) *nf*

merit *n* **merit payment** Leistungszulage (-n) *nf*

message *n* Mitteilung (-en) *nf*

messenger *n* Bote (-n) *nm*

metal *n* Metall (-e) *nn*

meter *n* Meter (-) *nmn*

method *n* **method of payment** Zahlungsmethode (-n) *nf* **production method** Produktionsmethode (-n) *nf*

metre, meter (US) *n* Meter (-) *nmn* **cubic metre** Kubikmeter *nmn* **square metre** Quadratmeter (-) *nmn*

metric *adj* metrisch *adj*

metrication *n* Umstellung auf das metrische Maßsystem *nf*

metropolis *n* Metropole (-n) *nf*

microchip n Mikrochip (-s) nn
microcomputer n Mikrocomputer (-) nm
microeconomics n Mikroökonomik nf,
Betriebswirtschaft nf
microfiche n Mikrofiche (-s) nm
microprocessor n Mikroprozessor (-en)
nm
middle adj **middle management** mittleres
Management nn **middle manager** mittlerer Manager (-) nm
middleman n Zwischenhändler (-) nm
migrant n **migrant worker** Gastarbeiter (-)
nm
mile n Meile (-n) nf **nautical mile** Seemeile
(-n) nf
mileage n Meilenzahl nf
million n Million (-en) nf
millionaire n Millionär (-e) nm
mine n Mine (-n) nf **coal mine** Kohlengrube (-n) nf
mineral n Mineral (-ien) nn
minimal adj minimal adj
minimum adj **index-linked minimum
wage** indexgekoppelter Mindestlohn
(-löhne) nm **minimum lending rate**
Mindestzins (-en) nm
mining n Bergbau nm **mining industry**
Bergbau nm
minister n Minister (-) nm
ministry n Ministerium (-ien) nn **Ministry
of Transport** Verkehrsministerium (-ien)
nn
minor adj unbedeutend adj
minority n Minderheit (-) nf **minority
holding** Minderheitsbeteiligung nf **in the
minority** in der Minderheit
mint 1. n Münzanstalt (-en) nf 2. vb
prägen vb **he/she mints money** er/sie
macht einen Haufen Geld
minutes npl **the minutes of the meeting**
Protokoll nn
misappropriation n Veruntreuung nf
miscalculation n Rechenfehler (-) nm,
Fehlkalkulation (-en) nf
misconduct n (bad management)
Berufsvergehen nn
mishandling n falsche Behandlung nf
mismanagement n Mißmanagement nn
mistake n Fehler (-) nm **to make a mistake**
einen Fehler machen
mix n **marketing mix** Marketing-Mix n
product mix Produktmix nm
mixed adj **mixed economy** Mischwirtschaft (-en) nf
mode n (method) Art nf
model n (person) Modell (-e) nn

modem n Modem (-s) nm
moderate 1. adj gemäßigt adj 2. vb
mäßigen vb
moderation n Mäßigung nf
modern adj modern adj
modernization n Modernisierung nf
modernize vb modernisieren vb
module n Modul (-e) nn
monetarism n Monetarismus nm
monetary adj monetär adj **European
Monetary System (EMS)** Europäisches
Währungssystem nn **International
Monetary Fund (IMF)** Internationaler
Währungsfonds nm **monetary policy**
Finanzpolitik nf
money n **dear money** teures Geld nn
money market Geldmarkt (-märkte) nm
money order Zahlungsanweisung (en) nf
public money öffentliches Geld nn
money supply Geldangebot nn **to raise
money** Mittel aufbringen **money trader**
Geldhändler (-) nm
moneymaking adj (profitable)
gewinnbringend adj
monopoly n Monopol (-e) nn **Monopolies
and Mergers Commission**
Monopolkommission nf, (Germany) Bundeskartellamt (-ämter) nn
monthly adj monatlich adj
moonlight* vb schwarz arbeiten vb
moor vb festmachen vb
mooring n Anlegeplatz (-plätze) nm
mooring rights Anlegerecht nn
mortgage n Hypothek (-en) nf **mortgage
deed** Hypothekenvertrag (-äge) nm
mortgage loan Hypothekendarlehen (-)
nn
mortgagee n Hypothekengläubiger (-) nm
mortgagor n Hypothekenschuldner (-) nm
motor n **motor industry** Autoindustrie nf
multilateral adj multilateral adj
multinational adj multinational adj **multinational corporation** multinationales
Unternehmen (-) nn
multiple adj mehrfach adj **multiple store**
Filialgeschäft (-e) nn
multiply vb vermehren vb
multipurpose adj Vielzweck- cpd
municipal adj **municipal bonds**
Kommunalanleihen nfpl
mutual adj gegenseitig adj **mutual fund
(US)** offener Investmentfonds nm
mutually adv gegenseitig adv
N/A (not applicable) abbr nicht zutreffend
name 1. n **brand name** Markenname (-n)
nm **by name** mit Namen **full name** voller

Name *nm* in the name of im Namen...
registered trade name eingetragener Firmenname (-n) *nm* 2. *vb* nennen *vb*,
ernennen *vb*
named *adj* named person der/die genannte...
narrow *adj* narrow margin kleine Spanne
(-n) *nf* narrow market begrenzter Markt
(-märkte) *nm*
nation *n* Nation (-en) *nf* the United
Nations die Vereinten Nationen *nfpl*
national *adj* national debt Staatsschuld *nf*
national income Volkseinkommen *nn*
national insurance (GB)
Sozialversicherung *nf* national interest
nationales Interesse *nn* National Bureau
of Economic Research (US) Institut für
Wirtschaftsforschung *nn*
nationality *n* Staatsangehörigkeit *nf*
nationalization *n* Verstaatlichung *nf*
nationalize *vb* verstaatlichen *vb*
nationalized *adj* nationalized industry
verstaatlichte Industrie (-n) *nf*
nationwide *adj* landesweit *adj*
natural *adj* natural rate of increase natürliche Zuwachsrate (-n) *nf* natural resources Bodenschätze *nmpl*
necessary *adj* erforderlich *adj* necessary
qualifications erforderliche
Qualifikationen *nfpl*
necessity *n* (goods) Notwendigkeit *nf*
need *n* needs assessment
Bedarfserfassung *nf* needs of industry
industrielle Bedürfnisse *nnpl* to be in
need brauchen (dringend) *vb*
negative *adj* negative cash flow
Einnahmeunterdeckung *nf* negative
feedback negative Rückmeldung *nf*
neglect *n* Vernachlässigung *nf* neglect
clause Freizeichnungsklausel für Fahrlässigkeit (-n) *nf*
negligence *n* Fahrlässigkeit *nf* negligence
clause Fahrlässigkeitsklausel (-n) *nf*
contributory negligence mitwirkendes
Verschulden *nn* gross negligence grobe
Fahrlässigkeit *nf*
negligent *adj* fahrlässig *adj*
negotiable *adj* begebbar *adj* negotiable
bill durch Indossament übertragbarer
Wechsel (-) *nm* negotiable cheque begebbarer Scheck (-s) *nm*
negotiate *vb* verhandeln (über) *vb*
negotiated *adj* negotiated price vereinbarter Preis (-e) *nm*
negotiating *adj* negotiating session Sit-

zungsperiode (-n) *nf* negotiating skills
Verhandlungsgeschick *nn*
negotiation *n* Verhandlung (-en) *nf* by
negotiation durch Verhandlung to begin
negotiations Verhandlungen beginnen
under negotiation unter Verhandlung
wage negotiations
Lohnverhandlungen *nfpl*
negotiator *n* Verhandlungsführer (-) *nm*
net, nett 1. *adj* netto net amount
Nettobetrag (-äge) *nm* net assets
Nettovermögen *nn* net cost
Nettokosten *npl* net earnings
Nettoverdienst *nm* net interest
Nettozinsen *nmpl* net investment
Nettoinvestition *nf* net loss Reinverlust
(-e) *nm* net price Nettopreis (-e) *nm* net
proceeds Auszahlung *nf* net profit
Reingewinn *nm* net result Endergebnis
(-sse) *nn* net sales Nettoauftragseingang
(-änge) *nm* net saving
Nettoersparnisse *nfpl* terms strictly net
zahlbar sofort ohne Abzug net wage
Nettolohn (-öhne) *nm* net weight
Nettogewicht *nn* 2. *vb* einbringen *vb*
network 1. *n* banking network Banknetz
(-e) *nn* computer network Computernetz
(-e) *nn* distribution network Verteilernetz
(-e) *nn* 2. *vb* ausstrahlen (im
Netzbereich) *vb*
neutral *adj* neutral *adj*
new *adj* new account neues Konto (-ten)
nn new business Neugeschäft *nn* new
product neues Produkt (-e) *nn* new
technology neue Technologie (-n) *nf*
newly *adv* newly-appointed neu
angestellt newly-industrialised neu industrialisiert
news *n* Nachrichten *nfpl* news agency
Nachrichtenagentur (-en) *nf* bad news
schlechte Nachrichten *nfpl* news bulletin
Bulletin (-s) *nn* news coverage aktuelle
Berichterstattung *nf* financial news finanzielle Nachrichten *nfpl* good news
gute Nachrichten *nfpl*
newsdealer (US) *n* Nachrichtenagentur
(-en) *nf*
newsletter *n* Mitteilungsblatt (-blätter) *nn*
newspaper *n* Zeitung (-en) *nf* newspaper
advertisement Zeitungsanzeige (-n) *nf*
daily newspaper Tageszeitung (-en) *nf*
newspaper report Zeitungsbericht (-e)
nm
nil *n* Null *nn* nil profit Nullgewinn (-e) *nm*
no *det* no agents wanted wir brauchen
keine Agenten no-claims bonus

Schadensfreiheitsrabatt *nm* **of no commercial value** ohne Marktwert
nominal *adj* nominell *adj* **nominal amount** Nominalbetrag (-äge) *nm* **nominal assets** Nominalvermögen *nn* **nominal damages** nomineller Schadenersatz *nm* **nominal inflation** Nominalinflation *nf* **nominal price** Nennwert (-e) *nm* **nominal value** Nennwert (-e) *nm*
nominate *vb* vorschlagen *vb* **nominate sb to a board/committee** ernennen (als Mitglied des/der...)
nomination *n* Nominierung (-en) *nf*, Ernennung (-en) *nf*
nominee *n* Kandidat (-en) *nm* **nominee shareholder** vorgeschobener Aktionär (-en) *nm*
non-acceptance *n* Annahmeverweigerung *nf*
non-attendance *n* Abwesenheit *nf*
non-completion *n* Nichtabschluß (-üsse) *nm*
non-contributory *adj* beitragsfreies Programm (-e) *nn*
non-convertible *adj* nicht konvertierbar *adj*
non-delivery *n* Nichtlieferung *nf*
non-discriminatory *adj* nichtdiskriminierend *adj*
non-essential *adj* unnötig *adj*, verzichtbar *adj*
non-interest-bearing *adj* zinsfrei *adj*
non-intervention *n* Nichteingreifen *nn*
non-negotiable *adj* nichtbegebbar *adj*
non-payment *n* Nichtzahlung *nf*
non-profitmaking *adj* nicht erwerbswirtschaftlich *adj*
non-returnable *adj* Einweg- *cpd*
non-stop *adj* nonstop *adj*
non-transferable *adj* nicht übertragbar *adj*
norm *n* Norm (-en) *nf*
normal *adj* **normal trading hours** allgemeine Geschäftsstunden *nfpl*
not *adv* **not applicable** nicht zutreffend *adj* **not available** nicht verfügbar *adj* **not dated** undatiert *adj*
notary *n* Notar (-en) *nm*
note *n* **advice note** Gutschriftsanzeige (-n) *nf* **cover note** Deckungsbestätigung (-en) *nf* **credit note** Gutschriftsanzeige (-n) *nf* **debit note** Belastungsanzeige (-n) *nf* **delivery note** Lieferschein (-e) *nm* **dispatch note** Versandanzeige (-n) *nf* **open note (US)** offener Kredit *nm* **to compare notes** Notizen vergleichen **to make a note of sth** sich etwas notieren
noteworthy *adj* beachtenswert *adj*

notice *n* **advance notice** (An)Kündigung (-en) *nf* **at short notice** kurzfristig **final notice** letzte Mahnung *nf* **notice period** Kündigungsfrist (-en) *nf* **term of notice** Kündigungsfrist (-en) *nf* **to come to the notice of sb** erfahren **to give notice of sth** etwas bekanntgeben **to take notice** merken *vb* **until further notice** bis auf weiteres
notification *n* Benachrichtigung *nf*
notify *vb* benachrichtigen *vb*
null *adj* **null and void** null und nichtig
number *n* **account number** Kontonummer *nf* **opposite number** Pendant *nn* **order number** Bestellnummer (-n) *nf* **serial number** Seriennummer (-n) *nf* **telephone number** Telefonnummer (-n) *nf* **wrong number** (phone) falsche Nummer (-n) *nf*
numeracy *n* Rechnen *nn*
numerate *adj* rechenkundig *adj*
numeric *adj* **alpha-numeric** numerisches Alphabet *nn* **numeric character** Ziffer (-n) *nf*
numerical *adj* **numerical analysis** Zahlenanalyse *nf*
NYSE (New York Stock Exchange) *abbr* New Yorker Börse
object *vb* protestieren *vb*
objection *n* Einwand (-wände) *nm* **to make/raise an objection** Einwände erheben gegen
objective *n* Ziel (-e) *nn* **to reach an objective** das Ziel erreichen
obligation *n* Verpflichtung (-en) *nf* **to meet one's obligations** seinen Verpflichtungen nachkommen
obligatory *adj* obligatorisch *adj*
oblige *vb* **to be obliged to do sth** verpflichtet sein, etwas zu tun
observation *n* **under observation** unter Beobachtung
observe *vb* **observe the rules** die Regeln einhalten
obsolescence *n* Veralten *nn* **built-in obsolescence** geplanter Verschleiß *nm*
obsolete *adj* veraltet *adj*
obtain *vb* bekommen *vb* **to obtain credit** Kredit aufnehmen
occupant *n* Bewohner (-) *nm*
occupation *n* Beruf (-e) *nm*
occupational *adj* **occupational disease** Berufskrankheit (-en) *nf* **occupational hazard** Berufsrisiko (-iken) *nn*
occupier *n* Inhaber (-) *nm*
occupy *vb* (premises) bewohnen *vb*

off-the-job *adj* **off-the-job training** außerbetriebliche Weiterbildung *nf*
offence, offense (US) *n* Vergehen (-) *nn*
offer *n* **firm offer** festes Angebot *nn* **offer in writing** schriftliches Angebot *nn* **offer subject to confirmation** Angebot vorbehaltlich der Bestätigung (-e) *nn* **offer valid until...** Angebot gilt bis... *nn*
offeree *n* Empfänger eines Angebots *nm*
offeror *n* Anbieter (-) *nm*
office *n* Büro (-s) *nn* **office equipment** Büroeinrichtung (-en) *nf* **office hours** Geschäftsstunden *nfpl* **office management** Büroverwaltung *nf* **office staff** Büropersonal *nn* **to hold office** im Amt sein **to resign from office** zurücktreten *vb*
official *n* Beamte/r *nmf* **official strike** offizieller Streik (-s) *nm*
offshore *adj* **offshore company** Offshore-Gesellschaft (-en) *nf*
oil *n* **oil industry** Erdölindustrie *nf* **oil state** ölproduzierender Staat (-en) *nm*
oilfield *n* Ölfeld (-er) *nn*
oligopoly *n* Oligopolie (-n) *nf*
ombudsman *n* Ombudsmann (-männer) *nm*
on-line *adj* on-line *adj*
on-the-job *adj* **on-the-job training** betriebliche Weiterbildung *nf*
onus *n* **the onus is on us to...** es liegt an uns...zu...
open 1. *adj* offen *adj* **open cheque** Barscheck (-s) *nm* **open credit** Blankokredit *nm* **open market** freier Markt (Märkte) *nm* **open shop** Firma, die nicht gewerkschaftsgebunden ist **2.** *vb* **to open an account** ein Konto eröffnen **open up** *vb* (market) den Markt erschließen
opening *adj* **opening price** Eröffnungskurs (-e) *nm* **opening times** Öffnungszeiten *nfpl*
operate *vb* **to operate a business** ein Geschäft führen
operating *adj* **operating expenditure** Betriebsausgaben *nfpl* **operating expenses** Betriebskosten *npl* **operating income** Betriebseinkommen *nn* **operating profit** Betriebsergebnis *nn* **operating statement** Betriebsbilanz (-en) *nf*
operation *n* (of business) Betrieb *nm*, Verwaltung *nf* (of machine) Unterhaltung *nf*
operator *n* Betreiber (-) *nm*
opportunity *n* Gelegenheit (-en) *nf* **market opportunities**

Marktgelegenheiten *nfpl* **to seize an opportunity** die Gelegenheit ergreifen
option *n* Option (-en) *nf* **share option, stock option** (US) Aktienbezugsrecht (-e) *nn* **options market** Optionsmarkt (-märkte) *nm* **option to buy** Kaufoption *nf* **option to cancel** Stornierungsoption (-en) *nf*
optional *adj* freiwillig *adj*
order *n* **order book** Auftragsbuch (-bücher) *nn* **order form** Bestellformular (-e) *nn* **order number** Bestellnummer (-n) *nf* **pay to the order of...** zahlbar an **to cancel an order** eine Bestellung widerrufen **to place an order** einen Auftrag erteilen
ordinary *adj* gewöhnlich *adj* **ordinary general meeting** gewöhnliche Sitzung *nf* **ordinary share, ordinary stock** (US) Stammaktie (-n) *nf*
organization *n* Organisation (-en) *nf*, Unternehmen (-) *nn*
organize *vb* organisieren *vb*
organized *adj* **organized labour** (trade unions) Gewerkschaftsmitglieder *nnpl*
origin *n* (of a product) Ursprung (-ünge) *nm* **country of origin** Herkunftsland (-länder) *nn* **statement of origin** Ursprungsangabe (-n) *nf*
original *adj* **original cost** Selbstkosten *npl*
outbid *vb* überbieten *vb*
outcome *n* Ergebnis (-sse) *nn*
outgoings *npl* Ausgänge *nmpl*
outlay *n* **capital outlay** Kapitalkosten *npl*
outlet *n* **market outlet** Absatzgebiet (-e) *nn* **sales outlet** Verkaufsstelle (-n) *nf*
outlook *n* **business outlook** Geschäftsaussichten *nfpl*
output *n* Output *nm*, Produktion *nf* **to increase output** die Produktion steigern
outstanding *adj* ausstehend *adj* **outstanding amount** aussehender Betrag (-äge) *nm* **outstanding debt** Außenstände *npl* **outstanding stock** Aktien im Publikumsbesitz *npl*
overcharge *vb* jemandem zu viel berechnen
overdraft *n* Überziehung *nf* **to request an overdraft** einen Überziehungskredit beantragen
overdraw *vb* überziehen *vb*
overdrawn *adj* **overdrawn account** überzogenes Konto (Konten) *nn*
overdue *adj* überfällig *adj*
overhead *adj* **overhead costs** Gemeinkosten *npl*

overheads *npl* allgemeine
Geschäftskosten *npl*
overheating *n* (of economy) Überheizen *nn*
overload *vb* überladen *vb*
overlook *vb* übersehen *vb*
overman *vb* eine zu große Belegschaft
haben
overmanned *adj* (mit einer zu großen
Belegschaft)
overmanning *n* (excess staff) zu große
Belegschaft
overnight *adj* **overnight delivery** Lieferung bis Morgen *nf*
overpay *vb* überzahlen *vb*
overpayment *n* Überzahlung *nf*
overpopulation *n* Überbevölkerung *nf*
overproduce *vb* überproduzieren *vb*
overproduction *n* Überproduktion *nf*
overseas *adj* Übersee- *cpd* **overseas market** Überseemarkt (-märkte) *nm* **overseas
territory** Überseegebiet (-e) *nn* **overseas
trade** Überseehandel *nm*
oversell *vb* überverkaufen *vb*
oversight *n* Versehen (-) *nn* **due to an
oversight** aus Versehen
oversold *adj* überverkauft *adj*
oversubscribed *adj* überzeichnet *adj*
oversupply *vb* Überangebot *nn*
overtime *n* Überstunden *nfpl*
overvalue *vb* überbewerten *vb*
overworked *adj* überarbeitet *adj*
owe *vb* schulden *vb*
own *vb* besitzen *vb*
owner *n* Besitzer (-) *nm*
owner-occupier *n* Besitzer im eigenen
Haus (-) *nm*
ownership *n* Eigentum *nn*
pack *vb* packen *vb*
package *n* Paket (-e) *nn* **package deal**
Verhandlungspaket (-e) *nn* **package tour**
Pauschalreise (-n) *nf*
packaging *n* Verpackung *nf*
packet *n* Paket (-e) *nn*
paid *adj* bezahlt *adj* **paid holiday** bezahlter
Urlaub *nm*
paid-up *adj* **paid-up capital** voll eingezahltes Kapital *nn*
pallet *n* Palette (-n) *nf*
palletized *adj* palettisiert *adj* **palletized
freight** palettisierte Fracht *nf*
paper *n* **commercial paper**
Wertpapiere *nnpl* **paper loss** nicht realisierter Kursverlust (-e) *nm* **paper profit**
nicht realisierter Kursgewinn (-e) *nm*
paperwork *n* Schreibarbeit (-en) *nf*

par *n* **above par** über pari **below par** unter
pari
parent *n* **parent company** Muttergesellschaft (-en) *nf*
parity *n* Parität *nf*
part *n* (of a machine) Teil (-e) *nn* **part
payment** Teilzahlung (-en) *nf* **part shipment** Teillieferung (-en) *nf* **spare part** (for
machine) Ersatzteil (-e) *nn*
part-time *adj* Teilzeit- *cpd*
participation *n* **worker participation**
Mitbestimmung *nf*
partner *n* Partner (-) *nm* **sleeping partner**
stiller Gesellschafter (-) *nm*
partnership *n* Personengesellschaft (-en)
nf **trading partnership** Handelsgesellschaft (-en) *nf*
passenger *n* Passagier (-e) *nm*
patent *n* Patent (-e) *nn*
patented *adj* patentrechtlich geschützt *adj*
patronage *n* Kundschaft *nf*
pattern *n* **spending patterns**
Ausgabenstruktur *nf*
pay 1. *n* (salary, wages) Lohn (-öhne) *nm*
equal pay gleicher Lohn *nm* **pay rise**
Gehaltserhöhung (-en) *nf* **severance pay**
Abfindungszahlung (-en) *nf* **unemployment pay** Arbeitslosengeld *nn* 2. *vb* **to
pay an invoice** eine Rechnung begleichen
to pay by credit card mit Kreditkarte
zahlen **to pay for a service** für einen
Dienst zahlen **to pay in advance** im
voraus zahlen **to pay in cash** bar zahlen
payable *adj* **accounts payable**
Verbindlichkeiten *nfpl*
payee *n* Zahlungsempfänger (-) *nm*
payer *n* **prompt payer** prompter Zahler (-)
nm **slow payer** säumiger Zahler (-) *nm*
payload *n* (of vehicle) Ladung *nf*
payment *n* Zahlung (-en) *nf* **down payment** Anzahlung *nf*
payola (US) *n* Auszahlung (-en) *nf*
payroll *n* Lohnliste (-n) *nf*, Gehaltsliste (-n)
nf **to be on the payroll** auf der Lohnliste
sein
peak *n* Spitze (-n) *nf* **peak demand**
Spitzennachfrage *nf* **peak period** Spitzenzeit (-en) *nf*
pecuniary *adj* **for pecuniary gain** um Geld
zu verdienen
peddle *vb* feilbieten *vb*
peg *vb* (prices) festsetzen *vb* **the HK dollar
is pegged to the US dollar** der HK-Dollar
hängt an dem US-Dollar
penetration *n* **market penetration**
Markteindringen *nn*

pension n Rente (-n) **nf pension fund**
Rentenfonds **nm retirement pension**
Altersrente (-n) **nf pension scheme** Pensionsplan (-äne) **nm**
per prep pro prep **per annum** pro Jahr
per capita pro Kopf **per cent** Prozent **nn**
percentage n Prozentsatz (-ätze) **nm percentage of profit** Prozentsatz des
Gewinns **nm**
performance n (behaviour) Leistung **nf**
performance appraisal
Leistungsbewertung **nf performance-related bonus** Leistungsprämie (-n) **nf**
period n **cooling-off period** Karenzzeit **nf**
period of grace Karenzzeit **nf**
peripheral adj Rand- cpd
perishable adj leicht verderblich adj **perishable goods** leicht verderbliche
Güter **nnpl**
perk n Nebenleistung (-en) **nf**
permanent adj **permanent employment**
Dauerbeschäftigung **nf**
permit n Lizenz **nf building permit** Baugenehmigung (-en) **nf**
perquisite n (formal) Nebenleistung (-en)
nf
person n **third person** Dritte/r **nmf**
personal adj persönlich adj
personnel n Personal **nn personnel department** Personalabteilung (-en) **nf**
personnel management Personal-
Management **nn**
peseta n Peseta (-s) **nf**
petrodollar n Öldollar **nm**
petroleum n **petroleum industry**
Ölindustrie **nf**
pharmaceutical adj **pharmaceutical industry** Pharmazieindustrie **nf**
phoney* adj gefälscht adj **phoney* company** Schwindelunternehmen (-) **nn**
photocopier n Kopiergerät (-e) **nn**
photocopy 1. n Fotokopie (-n) **nf** 2. vb
fotokopieren vb
pick up vb (improve) sich erholen vb
picket n (strike) Streikposten (-) **nm**
piecework n Akkordarbeit **nf**
pig iron n Roheisen **nn**
pilferage n Diebstahl **nm**
pilot n **pilot plant** Pilotanlage (-n) **nf pilot scheme** Pilotprojekt **nn**
pipeline n Pipeline (-s) **nf**
piracy n (at sea) Piraterie **nf software piracy** Softwarepiraterie **nf**
place vb **to place an order** eine Bestellung
erteilen
plan 1. n Plan (-äne) **nm economic plan**

Wirtschaftsplan (-äne) **nm plan of campaign** Werbeplan (-pläne) **nm to make plans** Pläne machen 2. vb planen vb
planned adj **planned economy** Planwirtschaft (-en) **nf planned obsolescence**
geplanter Verschleiß **nm**
planning n Planung **nf regional planning**
Gebietsplanung **nf**
plant n (machinery) Anlage (-n) **nf plant hire** Anlagenvermietung **nf plant manager** Betriebsleiter (-) **nm**
plastics npl **plastics industry**
Plastikindustrie **nf**
pledge n Versprechen (-) **nn**
plenary adj (assembly, session) Plenarcpd
plough back, plow back, to (US) vb (profits) Gewinne reinvestieren
point n Punkt (-e) **nm point of sale**
Verkaufspunkt (-e) **nm**
policy n **insurance policy** Versicherungspolice (-n) **nf pricing policy** Preispolitik **nf**
political adj politisch adj
politics npl Politik **nf**
port n Hafen (Häfen) **nm**
portable adj tragbar adj
portfolio n Portefeuille (-n) **nn investment portfolio** Effektenportefeuille (-s) **nn**
post 1. n (job) Stelle (-n) **nf post office**
Postamt (-ämter) **nn** 2. vb einwerfen vb
postal adj **postal services**
Postdienste **nmpl**
postdate vb vordatieren vb
poste restante n postlagernd adj
poster n (advertising) Plakat (-e) **nn**
postpone vb aufschieben vb
potential n **sales potential**
Verkaufspotential **nn**
pound n (weight) Pfund **nn pound sterling** Pfund Sterling **nn**
power n Macht **nf power of attorney**
Vollmacht **nf**
preference n Vorzug **nm community preference** Vorzugszollsystem in EU **nn**
preferential adj Vorzugs- cpd
premises npl Räumlichkeiten **nfpl office premises** Bürogebäude **nn**
premium n Prämie (-n) **nf at a premium**
hoch im Kurs
prepayment n Vorauszahlung (-en) **nf**
president n (of company) Aufsichtsratsvorsitzende/r **nmf**
press n **press baron** Pressezar (-en) **nm**
press conference Pressekonferenz (-en)
nf
price n Preis (-e) **nm market price** letzter

Kurs *nm* **stock exchange prices**
Kurse *nmpl* **threshold price** Höchstpreis
(-e) *nm*
pricing *adj* **pricing policy**
Preisbildungspolitik *nf*
primary *adj* **primary industry** Grundstoffindustrie (-n) *nf*
prime *adj* **prime lending rate** Prime Rate *nf*
priority *n* Priorität *nf*
private *adj* **private sector** Privatbereich
(-e) *nm*
privatization *n* Privatisierung *nf*
privatize *vb* privatisieren *vb*
pro 1. *n* **pros and cons** Für und Wider *nn*
2. *prep* **pro rata** anteilig
probate *n* gerichtliche
Testamentsbestätigung *nf*
proceeds *npl* Erlös *nm*
process 1. *n* Verfahren (-) *nn* **2.** *vb*
bearbeiten *vb*
produce 1. *n* Agrarerzeugnisse *nfpl* **2.** *vb*
produzieren *vb*
producer *n* Produzent (-en) *nm*
product *n* Produkt (-e) *nn* **primary product**
Rohstoff (-e) *nm*
production *n* Produktion *nf* **production
line** Fertigungsstraße (-n) *nf*
productive *adj* produktiv *adj*
productivity *n* Produktivität *nf* **productivity gains** Produktivitätssteigerung *nf*
profession *n* Beruf (-e) *nm* **the professions**
die gehobenen Berufe *nmpl*
profit *n* Gewinn *nm* **profit and loss**
Gewinn und Verlust *nm/nm* **profit margin**
Gewinnspanne (-n) *nf* **net profit**
Reingewinn *nm* **operating profit**
Betriebsergebnis *nn* **profit-sharing
scheme** Gewinnbeteiligung *nf* **to make a
profit** einen Gewinn machen
profitability *n* Rentabilität *nf*
profiteer *vb* Preise treiben
program *n* Programm (-e) *nn*
programmer *n* Programmierer (-) *nm*
programming *n* Programmieren *nn*
progress 1. *n* Fortschritt (-e) *nm* **2.** *vb*
(research, project) Fortschritte machen
project *n* Projekt (-e) *nn*
promissory *adj* **promissory note** Solawechsel (-) *nm*
promote *vb* (person) befördern *vb* (product) werben für
promotion *n* (of product) Werbung *nf* (of
person) Beförderung *nf*
promotional *adj* Werbe- *cpd* **promotional
budget** Werbeetat (-s) *nm*
prompt *adj* unverzüglich *adj*

property *n* Besitz *nm* **property company**
Immobiliengesellschaft (-en) *nf* **property
developer** Bauträger (-) *nm* **private property** Privateigentum *nn*
proprietary *adj* Marken- *cpd* **proprietary
brand** Markenartikel *nm*
proprietor *n* Inhaber (-) *nm*
prospect *n* **future prospects** die
Aussichten *nfpl*
prospectus *n* Prospekt (-e) *nm*
prosperous *adj* florierend *adj*
protectionism *n* Protektionismus *nm*
protectionist *adj* protektionistisch *adj*
provide *vb* (supply) versorgen *vb*
provision *n* (stipulation) Versorgung *nf*
proxy *n* (power) Vollmacht *nf*
public *adj* öffentlich *adj* **public company**
Publikumsgesellschaft (-en) *nf* **public
funds** Staatsanleihen *npl* **public relations**
Öffentlichkeitsarbeit *nf* **public sector**
öffentlich *adj* **public service**
Staatsdienst *nm*
publicity *n* Publizität *nf*
publishing *n* Verlagswesen *nn* **desk-top
publishing** DTP *nn*, Desk-Top-
Publishing *nn*
purchase 1. *n* Kauf (-äufe) *nm* **purchase
price** Kaufpreis (-e) *nm* **2.** *vb* kaufen *vb*
purchasing *n* **purchasing power**
Kaufkraft *nf*
pyramid *n* **pyramid scheme** mehrmaliger
Erwerb der gleichen Aktie **pyramid selling** Vertrieb nach dem
Schneeballprinzip *nm*
qualification *n* Qualifikation *nf* **academic
qualification** Qualifikation *nf* **educational
qualification** Qualifikation (-en) *nf* **professional qualification** berufliche
Qualifikation *nf*
qualified *adj* **qualified acceptance** eingeschränktes Akzept **qualified personnel**
qualifizierte Arbeitskräfte
qualitative *adj* qualitativ *adj*
quality *n* Qualität *nf* **quality control** Qualitätskontrolle (-n) *nf* **quality report** Qualitätsbericht (-e) *nm* **quality standard**
Qualitätsnorm (-en) *nf*
quantitative *adj* quantitativ *adj*
quantity *n* Quantität *nf* **quantity discount**
Mengenrabatt *nm* **quantity theory of
money** Quantitätstheorie des Geldes
quarter *n* (of year) Viertel (-) *nn*
quarterly *adj* vierteljährlich *adj* **quarterly
interest** Vierteljahreszinsen *nmpl* **quarterly trade accounts** vierteljährliche
Kundenkonten *npl*

quasi-contract *n* Quasi-Vertrag (-äge) *nm*
quasi-income *n* Quasi-Einkommen *nn*
quay *n* Kai (-s) *nm*
quayage *n* Kaigebühren *nfpl*
questionnaire *n* Fragebogendesign *nn*
  market research questionnaire Marktforschungsfragebogen (-) *nm*
queue *n* Schlange (-n) *nf*
quick *adj* **quick assets** flüssige Mittel *nnpl*
quiet *adj* **quiet market** ruhiger Markt
  (Märkte) *nm*
quit *vb* (resign) zurücktreten *vb*
quittance *n* Schuldenerlaß *nm*
quorate *adj* (meeting) beschlußfähig *adj*
quorum *n* Quorum (-a) *nn* **quorum of
  creditors** Gläubigerquorum (-a) *nn*
quota *n* Quote (-n) *nf* **quota agreement**
  Produktionskartell (-e) *nn* **quota buying**
  Quotenkauf *nm* **import quota** Einfuhrquote (-n) *nf* **sales quota** Absatzquote
  (-n) *nf* **quota sampling**
  Quotenauswahlverfahren *nn* **quota system** Quotensystem (-e) *nn*
quotation *n* (price) Preisangabe (-n) *nf*
quoted *adj* **quoted company** börsennotiertes Unternehmen (-) *nn* **quoted investment** börsennotierte
  Wertpapiere *nnpl* **quoted shares, quoted
  stocks** (US) börsennotierte Aktien *nfpl*
racket *n* Schwindelgeschäft (-e) *nn*
racketeer *n* Gauner (-) *nm*
racketeering *n* Gaunereien *nfpl*
rag *n* **the rag trade** (informal)
  Kleiderbranche *nf*
rail *n* **by rail** per Bahn
railway, railroad (US) *n* Eisenbahn (-en) *nf*
raise *vb* (price, interest rate) erhöhen *vb*
  (capital, loan) aufbringen *vb*
RAM (random access memory) *abbr* (DP)
  RAM *abbr*
random *adj* **at random** willkürlich *adj*
  random selection Stichprobe *nf*
range *n* (of products) Reihe (-n) *nf*
rate *n* **base rate** Basiszins (-en) *nm* **rate of
  exchange** Wechselkurs (-e) *nm* **rate of
  expansion** Wachstumsrate *nf* **rate of
  growth** Wachtumsrate (-n) *nf* **rate of
  inflation** Inflationsrate (-n) *nf* **rate of
  interest** Zinskurs (-e) *nm*, Zinssatz
  (-sätze) *nm* **rate of investment** Investitionsrate (-n) *nf* **rate of return** Rendite *nf*
  rates (tax) Kommunalsteuern *nfpl*
ratification *n* Ratifizierung *nf*
ratify *vb* ratifizieren *vb*
ratio *n* Verhältnis (-sse) *nn*
rationale *n* Gründe *nmpl*

rationalization *n* Rationalisierung *nf* **rationalization measures**
  Rationalisierungsmaßnahmen *nfpl*
rationalize *vb* rationalisieren *vb*
raw *adj* (unprocessed) roh *adj*
re *prep* Betreff *nm*
re-elect *vb* wieder wählen *vb*
re-election *n* Wiederwahl (-en) *nf*
ready *adj* **ready for despatch**
  versandbereit *adj*
real *adj* **real estate** Immobilien *npl* **real
  price** effektiver Preis (-e) *nm* **real time**
  Echtzeit *nf* **real value** Realwert (-e) *nm*
  real wages Effektivlohn (-löhne) *nm*
realization *n* **realization of assets** Flüssigmachung von Vermögenswerten *nf*
realize *vb* (profit) erkennen *vb*
reallocate *vb* (funds) erneut zuteilen *vb*
reallocation *n* (of funds) Umschichten *nn*
realtor (US) *n* Immobilienmakler (-) *nm*
reappoint *vb* wiederernennen *vb*
reappointment *n* Wiederernennung (-en)
  nf
reasonable *adj* (price) vernünftig *adj*
rebate *n* Rabatt (-e) *nm* **to grant a rebate**
  einen Rabatt gewähren
receipt *n* **to acknowledge receipt** den
  Empfang bestätigen **to issue a receipt**
  eine Quittung geben
receive *vb* erhalten *vb*
receiver, administrator (US) *n* (bankruptcy) Konkursverwalter (-) *nm*
recession *n* Rezession (-en) *nf*
recipient *n* Empfänger (-) *nm*
reciprocal *adj* gegenseitig *adj*
reclaimable *adj* (materials) nutzbar *adj*
recommend *vb* empfehlen *vb*
recommendation *n* Empfehlung (-en) *nf*
recompense *n* Entschädigung (-en) *nf*
record *n* Urkunde (-n) *nf* **according to our
  records** gemäß unseren Aufzeichnungen
recover *vb* **to recover money from sb**
  Geld einziehen von
recovery *n* (of debt) Einziehung (-en) *nf*
  (economic) Erholung *nf*
recruit *vb* einstellen *vb*
recruitment *n* Einstellung (-en) *nf* **recruitment campaign** Einstellungskampagne (-n) *nf*
recyclable *adj* recycelbar *adj*
recycle *vb* wiederverwerten *vb*
red *adj* rot *adj* **red tape** Amtsschimmel *nm*
  to be in the red Verluste haben
redeem *vb* einlösen *vb*, amortisieren *vb*
redeemable *adj* amortisierbar *adj* **re-**

deemable bond Amortisationsschuld (-en) *nf*
redemption *n* Amortisierung *nf* **redemption fund** Amortisationsfonds (-) *nm*
redirect *vb* (mail) nachschicken *vb*
reduce *vb* (prices) reduzieren *vb* (taxes) ermäßigen *vb*
reduced *adj* vermindert *adj* **at a greatly reduced price** zu einem stark herabgesetzten Preis
reduction *n* Ermäßigung (-en) *nf*
redundancy *n* Arbeitslosigkeit *nf*
redundant *adj* arbeitslos *adj* **to make sb redundant** entlassen *vb*
refer *vb* **we refer to our letter of...** wir beziehen uns auf unser Schreiben vom... **we refer you to our head office** wir verweisen Sie an unser Hauptbüro
referee *n* Referenz (-en) *nf* **to act as referee** (Herr X ist bereit,) als Referenz zu dienen
reference *n* Empfehlung (-en) *nf* **credit reference** Kreditauskunft (-ünfte) *nf* **reference number** Geschäftszeichen (-) *nn* **to take up a reference** den Auskunftgeber anschreiben **with reference to** mit Bezug auf
referendum *n* Plebiszit (-e) *nn*
reflation *n* expansive Konjunkturpolitik *nf*
reflationary *adj* expansiv *adj*
reform *n* Reform (-en) *nf* **currency reform** Währungsreform (-en) *nf*
refund 1. *n* Rückerstattung (-en) *nf* 2. *vb* zurückzahlen *vb*
refundable *adj* rückvergütbar *adj*
refurbish *vb* renovieren *vb*
refurbishment *n* Renovierung (-en) *nf*
refusal *n* Ablehnung (-en) *nf*
refuse *vb* **to refuse a claim** einen Anspruch ablehnen **to refuse goods** die Warenannahme verweigern **to refuse payment** die Zahlung verweigern
regard *n* **with regard to...** in bezug auf
regarding *prep* bezüglich *prep*
regional *adj* regional *adj* **regional office** Regionalbüro (-s) *nn*
register *n* Verzeichnis (-sse) *nn*
registered *adj* eingetragen *adj* **registered bond** Namensschuldverschreibung (-en) *nf* **registered capital** Grundkapital *nn* **registered company** handelsgerichtlich eingetragene Gesellschaft (-en) *nf* **registered letter** eingeschriebener Brief (-e) *nm* **registered mail** Einschreibpost (-) *nf* **registered office** Hauptniederlassung (-en) *nf* **registered share** Namensaktie

(-n) *nf* **registered trademark** eingetragenes Warenzeichen (-) *nn*
regret *vb* **we regret to inform you that...** wir bedauern, Ihnen mitzuteilen, daß...
regular *adj* regulär *adj* **regular customer** Stammkunde (-n) *nm*
regulation *n* Vorschrift (-en) *nf* **according to the regulations** vorschriftsgemäß *adj*
reimburse *vb* rückvergüten *vb*
reimbursement *n* Rückvergütung (-en) *nf*
reimport *vb* wieder einführen *vb*
reimportation *n* Wiedereinfuhr *nf*
reinsurance *n* Rückversicherung *nf*
reinsure *vb* rückversichern *vb*
reject *vb* (goods) ablehnen *vb*
relation *n* **business relations** Geschäftsbeziehungen *nfpl* **industrial relations** Beziehungen zwischen Arbeitgebern und Gewerkschaften *npl*
relationship *n* **working relationship** Arbeitsverhältnis (-sse) *nn*
relax *vb* (restrictions) lockern *vb*
relevant *adj* entsprechend *adj*
reliability *n* Zuverlässigkeit *nf*
reliable *adj* verläßlich *adj*
relocate *vb* den Sitz verlegen *vb*
relocation *n* Umsiedlung (-en) *nf*
remaining *adj* (sum) verbleibend *adj*
reminder *n* Mahnung (-en) *nf*
remittance *n* Überweisung (-en) *nf* **remittance advice** Überweisungsanzeige (-n) *nf*
remunerate *vb* vergüten *vb*
remuneration *n* Vergütung (-en) *nf*
renew *vb* (policy, contract) erneuern *vb*
renewable *adj* erneuerbar *adj*
rent 1. *n* Miete (-n) *nf* 2. *vb* (house, office) mieten *vb*
rental *n* Miete (-n) *nf*
repair 1. *n* **costs of repair** Reparaturkosten *npl* 2. *vb* reparieren *vb*
reparation *n* Wiederherstellung (-en) *nf*
repatriation *n* Repatriierung (-en) *nf*
repay *vb* zurückzahlen *vb*
repayment *n* (of loan) Rückzahlung (-en) *nf*
repeat *adj* **repeat order** Nachbestellung (-en) *nf*
replace *vb* ersetzen *vb*
replacement *n* (person) Ersatzperson (-en) *nf*
reply *n* **in reply to your letter of...** in Antwort auf Ihr Schreiben vom...
report *n* Bericht (-e) *nm* **annual report** Jahresbericht (-e) *nm* **to draw up a report** einen Bericht verfassen **to submit/present a report** einen Bericht vorlegen
repossess *vb* wieder in Besitz nehmen

repossession n Wiederbesitznahme (-n) nf

representative n Vertreter (-) nm **area representative** Gebietsvertreter (-) nm **sales representative** Handelsvertreter (-) nm

repudiate vb (contract) zurückweisen vb

reputation n Ruf nm **to enjoy a good reputation** einen guten Ruf haben

request n Bitte (-n) nf **request for payment** Zahlungsaufforderung (-en) nf

requirement n Bedarf nm **in accordance with your requirements** Ihren Anforderungen entsprechend **it is a requirement of the contract that...** vertragsgemäß wird verlangt, daß...

resale n Weiterverkauf nm

rescind vb widerrufen vb

research n Forschung nf **research and development (R&D)** Forschung und Entwicklung nf/nf **market research** Marktforschung nf

reservation n Reservierung (-en) nf **to make a reservation** eine Reservierung vornehmen

reserve 1. adj **reserve currency** Reservewährung (-en) nf **reserve stock** Vorratslager (-) nn 2. n **currency reserve** Währungsreserve (-n) nf **to hold sth in reserve** auf Lager haben 3. vb reservieren vb

residual adj restlich adj

resign vb zurücktreten vb

resignation n Rücktritt (-e) nm **to hand in one's resignation** seinen Rücktritt erklären

resolution n (decision) Beschluß (-üsse) nm **to make a resolution** einen Beschluß fassen

resolve vb (sort out) lösen **to resolve to do sth** beschließen vb

resort to vb (have recourse) sich auf etwas verlegen

resources npl Mittel nnpl

respect n **in respect of...** hinsichtlich (gen)

response n **in response to...** als Antwort auf

responsibility n **to take responsibility for sth** die Verantwortung übernehmen

responsible adj verantwortlich adj

restrict vb beschränken vb

restriction n Beschränkung (-en) nf **to impose restrictions on** Beschränkungen auferlegen

restrictive adj beschränkend adj **restric-**

tive practices Wettbewerbsbeschränkung nf

restructure vb umstrukturieren vb

retail adj **retail outlet** Einzelhandelsgeschäft (-e) nn **retail price** Ladenpreis (-e) nm **retail sales tax** Einzelverkaufssteuer nf **retail trade** Einzelhandel nm

retain vb behalten. vb

retention n Beibehaltung nf **retention of title** Eigentumsvorbehalt nm

retire vb in den Ruhestand treten vb

retirement n Ruhestand nm **to take early retirement** in Frührente gehen

retrain vb umschulen vb

retraining n Umschulung nf **retraining programme, retraining program** (US) Umschulungsprogramm (-e) nn

return n Rückgabe nf **in return** dafür adv **return on capital** Kapitalverzinsung nf **return on equity** Eigenkapitalrendite nf **return on investment** Ertrag des investierten Kapitals **return on sales** Gewinnspanne (-n) nf **returns** Ertrag nm

returnable adj (deposit) rückgabepflichtig adj

revaluation n (currency) Aufwertung (-en) nf

revalue vb (currency) aufwerten vb

revenue n Einnahmen nfpl

reverse vb umkehren vb

revert vb zurückkehren vb

revert to vb zurückkommen auf vb

revise vb revidieren vb

revocable adj **revocable letter of credit** widerrufliches Akkreditiv (-e) nn

revoke vb (offer) rückgängig machen vb (licence) zurücknehmen vb

right n Recht (-e) nn **right of recourse** Rückgriffsrecht nn **right of way** Vorfahrtsrecht nn **the right to do sth** das Recht haben, etwas zu tun **the right to sth** das Recht auf etwas nn

rights npl **rights issue** Bezugsrechtsangebot (-e) nn **sole rights** alleiniges Recht nn

rise, raise (US) 1. n (in earnings, unemployment) Anstieg (-e) nm (in bank rate) Steigerung nf (in inflation) Zunahme (-n) nf 2. vb steigen vb

risk n Risiko (-iken) nn **all-risks insurance** globale Risikoversicherung nf **risk analysis** Risikoanalyse (-n) nf **risk assessment** Risikoeinschätzung (-en) nf **at the buyer's risk** vom Käufer übernommenes Risiko nn **risk capital** Risikokapital nn

risk management Absicherung von Risiken *nf* **the policy covers the following risks...** die Police bietet folgenden Versicherungsschutz
road *n* Straße (-nn) *nf* **by road** per Spedition **road haulage** Spedition *nf* **road haulage company** Spedition (-en) *nf* **road traffic** Straßenverkehr *nm* **road transport** Straßengüterverkehr *nm*
Rome *n* Rom *nn* **the Treaty of Rome** Vertrag von Rom *nm*
room *n* Raum (-äume) *nm* **room for manoeuvre** Spielraum *nm*
royal *adj* **the Royal Mint (GB)** Britische Münzanstalt *nf*
RSVP (répondez s'il vous plaît) *abbr* U.A.w.g. (Um Antwort wird gebeten) *abbr*
run *vb* (manage) betreiben *vb*
run down *vb* (stocks) Vorräte abbauen
run low *vb* (stocks) einen geringen Vorrat haben
running *n* Betrieb *nm* **running costs** laufende Kosten *npl*
rush *adj* **rush hour** Stoßzeit (-en) *nf* **rush job** eiliger Auftrag (-äge) *nm* **rush order** Eilauftrag (-äge) *nm*
sack, fire* (US) *vb* entlassen *vb*
safe *adj* sicher *adj*
safety *n* Sicherheit *nf* **safety officer** Sicherheitsbeauftragte/r *nmf*
salary *n* Gehalt (-älter) *nn* **salary scale** Gehaltsskala (-en) *nf*
sale *n* Verkauf (-äufe) *nm* **closing-down sale, closing-out sale** (US) Räumungsverkauf (-äufe) *nm* **sales campaign** Verkaufskampagne (-n) *nf* **sales conference** Verkaufskonferenz (-en) *nf* **sales department** Verkaufsabteilung (-en) *nf* **export sales** Auslandsabsatz *nm* **sales figures** Verkaufsziffern *nfpl* **sales forecast** Absatzprognose (-n) *nf* **home sales** Inlandsabsatz *nm* **sales ledger** Warenausgangsbuch (-bücher) *nn* **sales management** Verkaufsleitung *nf*
salesperson *n* Verkäufer (-) *nm*
salvage *vb* retten *vb*
sample 1. *n* Muster (-) *nn* 2. *vb* probieren *vb*
sampling *n* Probe *nf*
sanction *n* **trade sanctions** Handelssanktionen *nfpl*
savings *npl* Einsparungen *nfpl,* Ersparnisse *nfpl* **savings bank** Sparkasse *nf*
scab* *n* Streikbrecher (-) *nm*
scale *n* Skala (-en) *nf*

scarcity *n* Knappheit (-en) *nf*
schedule 1. *n* Zeitplan (-pläne) *nm* 2. *vb* planen *vb*
scheme *n* **pension scheme** Pensionsplan (-pläne) *nm* **recovery scheme** Bergungsplan (-pläne) *nm*
scrap *n* (metal) Altmetall *nn*
scrip *n* Interimsschein (-e) *nm*
SDRs (special drawing rights) *abbr* Sonderziehungsrechte *nnpl*
sea *n* **by sea** auf dem Seeweg, per Schiff **sea freight** Seefracht *nf*
seal 1. *n* Siegel (-) *nn* 2. *vb* versiegeln *vb*
sealed *adj* **sealed bid** Submissionsgeld im versiegelten Umschlag *nn*
season *n* Jahreszeit (-en) *nf* **high season** Hochsaison (-s) *nf* **low season** Nebensaison (-s) *nf*
seasonal *adj* jahreszeitlich bedingt *adj*
SEC (Securities and Exchange Commission) (GB) *abbr* Börsenaufsichtsrat *nm*
secondary *adj* sekundär *adj* **secondary industry** verarbeitende Industrie (-n) *nf* **secondary market** Nebenmarkt (-märkte)
secondment *n* Abordnung (-en) *nf*
secretary *n* Sekretär/in (-en/innen) *nm/nf* **executive secretary** Geschäftsführer (-) *nm*
sector *n* Sektor (-en) *nm* **primary sector** Grundstoffindustrie *nf* **secondary sector** Fertigungsindustrie *nf* **tertiary sector** Dienstleistungsindustrie *nf*
secure *adj* sicher *adj*
secured *adj* gesichert *adj* **secured loan** gesicherter Kredit (-e) *nm*
securities *npl* Wertpapiere *nnpl* **gilt-edged securities** mündelssichere Wertpapiere *nnpl* **listed securities** amtlich notierte Werte *nmpl* **unlisted securities** nicht notierte Werte *nmpl*
security *n* Sicherheit *nf* **Social Security (GB)** Sozialversicherung *nf*
self-assessment *n* Selbsteinschätzung *nf*
self-employed *adj* freiberuflich *adj*
self-financing *adj* Eigenfinanzierung *nf*
self-management *n* Selbstverwaltung *nf*
self-sufficient *adj* autark *adj*
sell 1. *n* **hard sell** aggressive Verkaufstaktik *nf* **soft sell** weiche Verkaufstaktik *nf* 2. *vb* verkaufen *vb* **to sell sth at auction** versteigern *vb* **to sell sth in bulk** im Großhandel verkaufen *vb* **to sell sth on credit** verkaufen *vb* **to sell sth retail** im Einzelhandel verkaufen *vb* **this article sells well**

diese Ware verkauft sich gut **to sell sth
wholesale** im Großhandel verkaufen *vb*
sell off *vb* abverkaufen *vb*
sell up *vb* (Besitz) verkaufen *vb*
seller *n* Verkäufer (-) *nm*
semi-skilled *adj* angelernt *adj*
send *vb* senden *vb*
send back *vb* zurücksenden *vb*
sendee *n* Empfänger (-) *nm*
sender *n* Absender (-) *nm*
senior *adj* höher *adj* **senior management**
Geschäftsleitung *nf*
seniority *n* höhere Position *nf*
service *n* Dienstleistung *nf* **after-sales
service** Kundendienst *nm* **civil service**
öffentlicher Dienst *nm* **service included**
inklusive Bedienung **service industry**
Dienstleistungsindustrie *nf* **National
Health Service (GB)** britischer staatlicher
Gesundheitsdienst *nm*
set up *vb* (company) einrichten *vb*,
gründen *vb*
settle *vb* (dispute) beilegen *vb* (account)
erledigen *vb*
severance *n* Lösen *nn* **severance pay**
Abfindung (-en) *nf*
shady* *adj* (dealings) dunkel *adj*
share 1. *n* Aktie (-n) *nf* **a share in the
profits** Gewinnbeteiligung *nf* **market
share** Aktienmarkt (-märkte) *nm* **ordinary
share** Stammaktie (-n) *nf* **2.** *vb* teilen *vb*
to share the responsibilities gemeinsam
die Verantwortung tragen
shareholder *n* Aktionär (-en) *nm*
shark* *n* Geschäftshai (-e) *nm*
sharp *adj* scharf *adj* **sharp practice** unsaubere Geschäfte *nnpl*
shift *n* Schicht (-en) *nf* **the three-shift
system** dreischichtiger Betriebsplan
(-pläne) *nm* **shift work** Schichtarbeit *nf*
shipbuilding *n* Schiffbau *nm*
shipment *n* (consignment) Versand *nm*
shipper *n* Spediteur (-e) *nm*
shipping *n* Verladung *nf* **shipping agent**
Spediteur (-e) *nm* **shipping broker**
Schiffsmakler (-) *nm* **shipping line**
Schiffahrtslinie (-n) *nf*
shipyard *n* Schiffswerft (-en) *nf*
shirker* *n* Drückeberger (-) *nm*
shoddy* *adj* minderwertig *adj*
shop *n* Laden (-äden) *nm* **shop assistant**
Verkäufer (-) *nm* **closed shop** gewerkschaftspflichtiger Betrieb (-e) *nm* **shop
steward** Gewerkschaftsverteter (-) *nm* **to
shut up shop** (informal) den Laden

schließen, das Geschäft aufgeben **to talk
shop** (informal) fachsimpeln *vb*
shopping *n* Einkauf *nm* **shopping centre**
Einkaufszentrum (-en) *nn*
short *adj* kurz *adj* **short delivery** Teillieferung (-en) *nf* **to be on short time** kurz
arbeiten *vb*
shortage *n* Mangel (Mängel) *nm*
show *n* (exhibition) Ausstellung (-en) *nf*
showroom *n* Schauraum (-räume) *nm*
shredder *n* Reißwolf (-wölfe) *nm*
shrink *vb* schrumpfen *vb*
shrinkage *n* Rückgang (-gänge) *nm* **stock
shrinkage** Lagerverlust (-e) *nm*
shutdown *n* Stillegung (-en) *nf*
shuttle *n* Pendelverkehr *nm*
**SIB (Securities and Investment Board)
(GB)** *abbr* Amt für Anlagen und
Wertpapiere *nn*
sick *adj* krank *adj* **sick leave**
Krankenurlaub *nm*
sickness *n* Krankheit (-en) *nf* **sickness
benefit** Krankengeld (-er) *nn*
sight *n* Sicht *nf* **sight draft** Sichtwechsel
(-) *nm*
sign *vb* unterschreiben *vb*
signatory *n* Unterzeichner (-) *nm*
signature *n* Unterschrift (-en) *nf*
silent *adj* still *adj* **silent partner** stiller
Teilhaber (-) *nm*
sinking *adj* **sinking fund** Ablösungsfonds
(-) *nm*
sit-in *n* (strike) Sitzstreik (-s) *nm*
size *n* Größe (-n) *nf*
skill *n* Fertigkeit (-en) *nf*
skilled *adj* (worker) gelernter Arbeiter *nm*
slackness *n* (laxity) Nachlässigkeit *nf*
sliding *adj* gleitend *adj* **sliding scale**
gleitender (Lohn)Tarif (-e) *nm*
slogan *n* Slogan (-s) *nm*
slow down *vb* verlangsamen *vb*
slowdown *n* Verlangsamung *nf*
slump 1. *n* Preissturz (-ürze) *nm* **2.** *vb*
fallen *vb*
slush *adj* **slush fund** Schmiergeldfonds (-)
nm
small *adj* klein *adj* **small ads**
Kleinanzeigen *nfpl* **small scale**
begrenzt *adj*
smuggle *vb* schmuggeln *vb*
society *n* **building society** Bausparkasse
(-n) *nf* **consumer society** Verbrauchergesellschaft (-en) *nf*
socio-economic *adj* sozioökonomisch *adj*
socio-economic categories sozialwirtschaftliche Begriffe *nmpl*

software *n* Software *nf* **software package** Softwarepaket (-e) *nn*
sole *adj* **sole agent** Alleinvertreter (-) *nm*
solicitor, lawyer (US) *n* Anwalt (-älte) *nm*
solvency *n* Zahlungsfähigkeit *nf*
solvent *adj* zahlungsfähig *adj*
source *n* Quelle (-n) *nf*
sourcing *n* Beschaffung *nf*
specialist *n* Fachmann (Fachleute) *nm*
speciality *n* Spezialität (-en) *nf*
specialize *vb* spezialisieren *vb*
specification *n* Angabe (-en) *nf*
specify *vb* angeben *vb*
speculate *vb* spekulieren *vb*
speculator *n* Spekulant (-en) *nm*
spend *vb* ausgeben *vb*
spending *n* Ausgaben *nfpl*
spendthrift *adj* verschwenderisch *adj*
sphere *n* **sphere of activity** Wirkungskreis (-e) *nm*, Tätigkeitsfeld (-er) *nn*
spin-off *n* Nebenprodukt (-e) *nn*
split 1. *adj* **split division** nicht einstimmige Abstimmung *nf* 2. *vb* teilen *vb*, spalten *vb*
spoilage *n* Schadenhaftigkeit *nf*
spoils *npl* Ausbeute *nf*
spokesperson *n* Sprecher (-) *nm*
sponsor *n* Förderer (-) *nm*
sponsorship *n* Förderung (-en) *nf*
spot *adj* **spot cash** sofortige Bezahlung *nf* **spot market** Spotmarkt (-märkte) *nm* **spot price** Kassapreis (-e) *nm* **spot rate** Kassakurs (-e) *nm*
spread *vb* (payments) ausbreiten *vb*
spreadsheet *n* Tabellenkalkulation (-en) *nf*
squander *vb* verschwenden *vb*
squeeze 1. *n* **credit squeeze** Kreditbeschränkung (-en) *nf* 2. *vb* (spending) drücken *vb*
stable *adj* (economy) stabil *adj*
staff *n* Belegschaft *nf*
staffing *n* Stellenbesetzung *nf*
stage *n* **in stages** stufenweise *adv*
staged *adj* **staged payments** Ratenzahlungen *nfpl*
stagger *vb* (holidays) staffeln *vb*
stagnation *n* Stagnierung *nf*
stake *n* Anteil (-e) *nm*
stakeholder *n* Anteilseigner (-) *nm*
stalemate *n* Patt *nn*
standard 1. *adj* Standard- *cpd* **standard agreement** Modellvertrag (-äge) *nm* 2. *n* **gold standard** Goldstandard *nm* **standard of living** Lebensstandard (-s) *nm*
standardization *n* Vereinheitlichung *nf*
standardize *vb* vereinheitlichen *vb*

standing *adj* **standing charges** laufende Unkosten *npl* **standing order** Dauerauftrag (-äge) *nm*
staple *adj* **staple commodities** Hauptprodukte *nnpl*
start-up *n* Beginn *nm* **start-up capital** Startkapital *nn*
state *n* **state-owned enterprise** verstaatlichter Betrieb (-e) *nm*
statement *n* **bank statement** Kontoauszug (-üge) *nm*
statistics *npl* Statistik *nf*
status *n* **financial status** Finanzlage (-n) *nf* **status quo** Status quo *nm*
statute *n* Statut (-e) *nn*
steel *n* Stahl (-e) *nm* **steel industry** Stahlindustrie (-n) *nf*
sterling *n* englisches Pfund *nn* **sterling area** Sterlinggebiet *nn* **sterling balance** Pfundguthaben (-) *nn* **pound sterling** Pfund Sterling (-) *nn*
stock, inventory (US) *n* (goods) Lager (-) *nn* **stock control** Lagerkontrolle *nf* **stock exchange** Börse (-n) *nf* **in stock** auf Lager **stock market** Wertpapiermarkt (-märkte) *nm* **out of stock** ausverkauft **stocks and shares** Aktien und Obligationen *npl*
stockbroker *n* Börsenmakler (-) *nm*
stockholder *n* Anteilseigner (-) *nm*
stocktaking *n* Inventur *nf*
stoppage *n* (strike) Stillegung (-en) *nf*
storage *n* **storage capacity** Lagervermögen *nn* **cold storage plant** Kühlhaus (-häuser) *nn*
store *n* (shop) Geschäft (-e) *nn* **chain store** Kettenladen (-läden) *nm* **department store** Warenhaus (-häuser) *nn*
stowage *n* Laderaum *nm*
strategic *adj* strategisch *adj*
strategy *n* Strategie (-n) *nf*
stress *n* **executive stress** Führungsstress *nm*
strike 1. *n* Streik (-s) *nm* **strike action** Streikmaßnahmen *nfpl* **strike ballot** Streikabstimmung (-en) *nf* **wildcat strike** wilder Streik (-s) *nm* 2. *vb* streiken *vb*
strikebreaker *n* Streikbrecher (-) *nm*
striker *n* Streikende/r *nmf*
subcontract *vb* weitervergeben an *vb*
subcontractor *n* Subunternehmer *nm*
subordinate *n* Untergeordnete/r *nmf*
subscribe *vb* abonnieren *vb*
subsidiary *n* Tochtergesellschaft (-en) *nf*
subsidize *vb* subventionieren *vb*
subsidy *n* Subvention (-en) *nf* **state subsidy** öffentlicher Zuschuß (-üsse) *nm*

suburbs *npl* Vororte *nmpl* **outer suburbs**
Außenbezirke *nmpl*
supermarket *n* Supermarkt (-märkte) *nm*
supertanker *n* Riesentanker (-) *nm*
supertax *n* Zusatzsteuer (-n) *nf*
supervisor *n* Aufseher (-) *nm*
supervisory *n* aufsichtsführend *adj*
supervisory board Aufsichtsrat (-räte) *nm*
supplementary *adj* ergänzend *adj*
supplier *n* Lieferant (-en) *nm*
supply 1. *n* Lieferung (-en) *nf*, Bestand
(-ände) *nm* **supply and demand** Angebot
und Nachfrage *nn/nf* 2. *vb* liefern *vb*
surface *n* **surface mail** Post auf dem
Landweg/Seeweg *nf*
surplus *n* Überschuß (-üsse) *nm* **budget
surplus** Haushaltsüberschuß (-üsse) *nm*
trade surplus Handelsüberschuß (-üsse)
nm
surtax *n* Steuerzuschlag (-äge) *nm*
survey *n* **market research survey** Marktforschungsstudie (-n) *nf*
swap 1. *n* Tausch (-e) *nm* 2. *vb*
tauschen *vb*
sweetener* *n* (bribe) Schmiergeld (-er) *nn*
swindle* *n* Schwindel (-) *nm*
swindler* *n* Schwindler (-) *nm*
switchboard *n* Telefonzentrale (-n) *nf*
switchboard operator Telefonist (-en) *nm*
syndicate *n* Syndikat (-e) *nn*
synergy *n* Synergie (-n) *nf*
synthesis *n* Synthese (-n) *nf*
synthetic *adj* synthetisch *adj*
system *n* System (-e) *nn* **expert system**
Expertensystem (-e) *nn* **systems analyst**
Systemanalytiker (-) *nm*
table *vb* (motion, paper) einbringen *vb*
tabulate *vb* (data) tabellarisieren *vb*
tabulated *adj* tabellarisch *adj* **tabulated
data** tabellarische Datenaufstellung *nf*
tacit *adj* stillschweigend *adj* **by tacit
agreement** aufgrund einer stillschwei-
genden Vereinbarung
tactic *n* Taktik *nf* **delaying tactics**
Verzögerungstaktik *nf* **selling tactics**
Verkaufsmethoden *nfpl*
tailor *vb* (adapt) anpassen *vb*
take *vb* **to take legal action** gerichtlich
vorgehen *vb* **to take notes** Notizen
machen *vb* **to take part in** teilnehmen an
(+dat) *vb* **to take the chair** den Vorsitz
übernehmen *vb* **to take the lead** die
Führung übernehmen **to take one's time**
Zeit nehmen
take over *vb* (company) übernehmen *vb*
takeover *n* Übernahme (-n) *nf*

takeup *n* Inanspruchnahme *nf*
takings *npl* Einkünfte *nfpl*
talk 1. *n* Gespräch (-e) *nn* **sales talk**
Verkaufsgespräch *nn* 2. *vb* **to talk
business** etwas Geschäftliches besprechen
tally 1. *n* Rechnung (-en) *nf* 2. *vb*
übereinstimmen *vb*
tally up *vb* zusammenrechnen *vb*
tally with *vb* übereinstimmen mit
tangible *adj* **tangible asset** Sachanlage
(-n) *nf*
tap *vb* anzapfen *vb* **to tap a market** einen
Markt erschließen **to tap resources**
Geldmittel flüssig machen
target *n* Ziel (-e) *nn* **target date** Stichtag
(-e) *nm* **target market** Zielmarkt
(-märkte) *nm* **production target** Produktionsziel (-e) *nn* **sales target** Verkaufsziel
(-e) *nn* **to set a target** ein Ziel setzen
targeted *adj* **targeted campaign** gezielte
Aktion *nf*
tariff *n* Tarif (-e) *nm* **tariff barrier** Zollschranke (-n) *nf* **tariff negotiations**
Zollverhandlungen *nfpl* **tariff quota**
Zollkontingent (-e) *nn* **tariff reform** Zollreform (-en) *nf* **to raise tariffs** Zölle
erhöhen *vb*
task *n* Aufgabe (-n) *nf* **task management**
Aufgabenverteilung *nf*
tax *n* Steuer (-n) *nf* **after tax** nach Abzug
der Steuern **tax allowance** Steuervergünstigung (-en) *nf* **before tax** vor Abzug
der Steuern **capital gains tax** Kapitalzuwachssteuer (-n) *nf* **tax claim**
Steuerforderung *nf* **tax-deductible** steuerlich absetzbar *adj* **direct tax** direkte
Steuer (-n) *nf* **tax-free** steuerfrei *adj*
income tax Einkommensteuer (-n) *nf*
indirect tax indirekte Steuer (-n) *nf* **tax
liability** Steuerpflicht (-en) *nf* **tax rate**
Steuersatz (-sätze) *nm* **to levy taxes**
Steuern einheben *vb* **value-added tax,
sales tax** (US) Mehrwertsteuer (-n) *nf* **tax
year** Finanzjahr (-e) *nn*
taxable *adj* **taxable income**
Steuereinkommen *nn*
taxation *n* Besteuerung *nf* **corporate
taxation** Firmenbesteuerung *nf*
taxpayer *n* Steuerzahler *nm*
team *n* Team (-s) *nn* **research team**
Forschungsteam (-s) *nn*
technical *adj* **technical director** technischer Direktor (-) *nm*
technician *n* Techniker (-) *nm*

technique n **sales technique** Verkaufsmethode (-n) nf
technology n Technologie (-n) nf **information technology** Informationstechnik nf **technology transfer** Technologietransfer nm
telebanking n Telefonbankdienst (-e) nm
telecommunications npl Fernmeldewesen nn
telecopier n Fernkopierer (-) nm
telefax n Fax nn
telephone n Telefon (-e) nn **telephone box, telephone booth** (US) Telefonzelle (-n) nf **telephone call** Anruf (-e) nm **telephone directory** Telefonbuch (-bücher) nn **telephone number** Telefonnummer (-n) nf
teleprocessing n Datenfernübertragung nf
telesales npl Telefonverkauf nm
televise vb im Fernsehen bringen vb
teleworking n Heimarbeit am Computer
telex 1. n Fernschreiber (-) nm 2. vb (message) eine Mitteilung per Telex schicken
teller n Schalterbeamte (-n) nm
temporary adj provisorisch adj **temporary employment** befristete Stellung (-en) nf
tenant n Mieter (-) nm
tend vb tendieren vb **to tend toward** anstreben vb
tendency n Tendenz (-en) nf **market tendencies** Markttrend (-s) nm
tender n Angebot (-e) nn **tender offer** Übernahmeangebot (-e) nn **tender price** Angebotspreis (-e) nm **sale by tender** Verkauf aufgrund einer Ausschreibung (-äufe) nm **to lodge a tender** ein Angebot einreichen **to put sth out for tender** ausschreiben vb
tenderer n Angebotsteller (-) nm
tendering n Ausschreibung nf
tentative adj **tentative offer** unverbindliches Angebot (-e) nn **tentative plan** vorläufiger Plan (-äne) nm
tenure n Amtszeit nf
term n **at term** zum festgesetzten Termin **long term** langfristig adj **medium term** mittelfristig adj **term of office** Amtszeit (-en) nf **terms and conditions** Bedingungen nfpl **short term** kurzfristig adj **terms of reference** Aufgabenbereich nm **terms of trade** Austauschrelationen nfpl
terminal 1. adj Abschluß- cpd, End- cpd **terminal bonus** Endprämie nf **terminal market** Terminalmarkt (-märkte) nm 2. n

air terminal Flughafenterminal (-e) nm **computer terminal** Computerterminal (-e) nn
termination n Beendigung (-en) nf **termination date** Verfalltag (-e) nm **termination of employment** Beendigung des Dienstverhältnisses (-en) nf
tertiary adj **tertiary industry** Dienstleistungsbereich (-e) nm
test n **test case** Musterfall (-fälle) nm **test data** Testdaten nnpl **to put sth to the test** auf die Probe stellen vb **to stand the test** die Probe bestehen
test-market vb Testmarkt (-märkte) nm
testimonial n Referenz (-en) nf
textile n Textil (-ien) nn **textile industry** Textilidustrie (-n) nf
theory n **in theory** theoretisch adj
third adj dritte/r adj **third party** dritte Person (-en) nf **third-party insurance** Haftpflichtversicherung nf **the Third World** Dritte Welt nf
thirty adj dreißig adj **Thirty-Share Index (GB)** Dreißig-Aktien-Index nm
thrash out vb (agreement, policy) ausdiskutieren vb
three adj drei adj **three-way split** Dreiteilung (-en) nf
threshold n **tax threshold** Steuerschwelle (-n) nf
thrive vb florieren vb
through prep durch prep **to get through to sb** (phone) durchkommen zu jemandem vb **to put sb through (to sb)** (phone) verbinden mit vb
tick over vb (ganz) normal laufen vb
ticket n Fahrkarte (-n) nf, Flugkarte (-n) nf **ticket agency** Verkaufsstelle (-n) nf **ticket office** Fahrkartenschalter (-) nm, Kasse (-n) nf **price ticket** Preisetikett (-e) nn **return ticket, round-trip ticket** (US) Rückfahrkarte (-n) nf **season ticket** Zeitkarte (-n) nf, Jahreskarte (-n) nf **single/one-way ticket** (rail/flight) einfache Fahrkarte (-n) nf
tide over vb ausreichen vb
tie up vb (capital) festmachen vb
tied adj **tied loan** zweckgebundene Anleihe (-n) nf
tier n Rang (-änge) nm **two-tier system** zweistufiges Verwaltungssystem (-e) nn
tight adj eng adj **to be on a tight budget** ein knapp bemessenes Budget haben
time n Zeit (-en) nf **time and a half** 50% Lohnzuschlag nm **double time** 100% Lohnzuschlag (-äge) nm **time frame**

Zeitraum (-räume) *nm* **lead time** Einführungszeit (-en) *nf* **time limit** Zeitbeschränkung (-en) *nf* **time management** Zeiteinteilung *nf*
time-consuming *adj* zeitraubend *adj*
time-saving *adj* zeitsparend *adj*
timescale *n* Zeitmaßstab (-stäbe) *nm*
timeshare *n* Wohnung auf Timesharing-Basis (-en) *nf*
timetable *n* Fahrplan (-äne) *nm*, Stundenplan (-äne) *nm*
timing *n* Terminierung *nf*
tip *n* (suggestion) Hinweis (-e) *nm* **market tip** Börsentip (-s) *nm*
title *n* (to goods) Titel (-) *nm* **title deed** Eigentumsurkunde (-n) *nf*
token *n* **token payment** Teilzahlung (-en) *nf* **token strike** Warnstreik (-s) *nm*
toll *n* Abgabe (-n) *nf*
ton *n* Tonne (-n) *nf* **metric ton** metrische Tonne (-n) *nf*
tone *n* **dialling tone, dial tone** (US) (phone) Amtszeichen (-) *nn*
tonnage *n* Tonnage *nf* **bill of tonnage** Meßbrief (-e) *nm* **gross tonnage** Bruttotonnage *nf* **net tonnage** Nettotonnage *nf*
top *adj* **top management** Führungsspitze (-n) *nf* **top prices** Höchstpreise *nmpl* **top priority** höchste Dringlichkeit *nf*
top-level *adj* Spitzen- *cpd*
top-of-the-range *adj* Spitzenqualität *nf*
total 1. *adj* total *adj* **total sales** Gesamtumsatz *nm* 2. *n* Gesamtsumme (-n) *nf* **the grand total** Gesamtsumme (-n) *nf*
tough *adj* **tough competition** harte Konkurrenz *nf*
tour *n* **tour of duty** Amtsperiode (-n) *nf*
tourism *n* Tourismus *nm*
tourist *n* Tourist (-en) *nm* **the tourist trade** Fremdenverkehrsbranche *nf*
town *n* Stadt (-ädte) *nf* **town centre** Stadtmitte (-n) *nf* **town council** Gemeinderat (-räte) *nm* **town hall** Rathaus (-häuser) *nn* **town planning** Stadtplanung *nf*
TQM (Total Quality Management) *abbr* Total Quality Management *nn*
track *n* Spur (-en) *nf*, Schiene (-n) *nf* **track record** bisherige Erfolge *nmpl* **to be on the right track** auf dem richtigen Weg sein
trade 1. *adj* **trade agreement** Handelsabkommen (-) *nn* **trade balance** Handelsbilanz (-en) *nf* **trade barrier**

Handelsschranke (-n) *nf* **trade cycle** Konjunkturzyklus (-klen) *nm* **trade directory** Firmenverzeichnis (-sse) *nn* **trade fair** Messe (-n) *nf* **trade figures** Handelsziffern *nfpl* **trade name** Handelsbezeichnung (-en) *nf* **trade price** Großhandelspreis (-e) *nm* **trade restrictions** Handelsbeschränkungen *nfpl* **trade secret** Branchengeheimnis (-sse) *nn* **trade talks** Handelsgespräche *nnpl* **Trade Descriptions Act** Warenkennzeichnungsgesetz (-e) *nn* **Trades Union Congress** Dachorganisation der britischen Gewerkschaften *nf* **trade union** Gewerkschaft (-en) *nf* 2. *n* Handel *nm*, Gewerbe *nn* **balance of trade** Handelsbilanz (-en) *nf* **by trade** von Beruf **fair trade** Preisbindung *nf* **foreign trade** Außenhandel *nm* **retail trade** Einzelhandel *nm* **to be in the trade** (informal) in der Branche sein *vb* 3. *vb* handeln *vb* **to trade as** (name) geschäftlich tätig sein als... *vb* **to trade with sb** handeln mit *vb*
trademark *n* Warenzeichen (-) *nn* **registered trademark** eingetragenes Warenzeichen (-) *nn*
trader *n* Händler (-) *nm*
trading *adj* **trading area** Verkaufsgebiet (-e) *nn* **trading capital** Betriebskapital *nn* **trading company** Handelsgesellschaft (-en) *nf* **trading estate** Industriesiedlung (-en) *nf*, Industriegelände (-) *nn* **trading loss** Betriebsverlust (-e) *nm* **trading margin** Handelsspanne (-n) *nf* **trading nation** Handelsnation (-en) *nf* **trading partner** Handelspartner (-) *nm* **trading standards** Handelsnormen *nfpl* **Trading Standards Office (US)** Handelsnormenausschuß *nm* **trading year** Geschäftsjahr (-e) *nn*
traffic *n* **air traffic** Luftverkehr *nm* **rail traffic** Schienenverkehr *nm* **road traffic** Straßenverkehr *nm* **sea traffic** Schiffsverkehr *nm*
train 1. *n* **goods train, freight train** (US) Güterzug (-üge) *nm* **passenger train** Personenzug (-üge) *nm* 2. *vb* (staff) ausbilden *vb*
trainee *n* Auszubildende/r *nmf* **trainee manager** Nachwuchsführungskraft (-äfte) *nf*
training *n* Ausbildung *nf* **advanced training** Fortbildung *nf* **training centre** Ausbildungszentrum (-en) *nn* **training**

course Ausbildungslehrgang (-gänge) *nm*
transaction *n* Transaktion (-en) *nf* **cash transaction** Kassegeschäft (-e) *nn* **transaction management** Transaktionsverwaltung *nf*
transcribe *vb* übertragen *vb*
transfer 1. *adj* **transfer desk** (transport) Transitschalter (-) *nm* **transfer duty** Umschreibungsgebühr (-en) *nf* **transfer lounge** (transport) Transitraum (-räume) *nm* **transfer payments** Übernahmezahlung (-en) *nf* **transfer price** Tageskurs (-e) *nm* **transfer tax** Kapitalverkehrssteuer (-n) *nf* **transfer technology** Transfertechnik *nf* 2. *n* Transfer (-s) *nm* **bank transfer** Banküberweisung (-en) *nf* **capital transfer** Kapitaltransferierung *nf* **credit transfer** bargeldlose Überweisung (-en) *nf* 3. *vb* (call) ein R-Gespräch vornehmen *vb* (ownership) überschreiben *vb* (transport) umsteigen *vb*
transferable *adj* übertragbar *adj*
transit *n* Durchreise *nf* **transit goods** Transitgüter *npl* **in transit** unterwegs **lost in transit** auf dem Transport verlorengegangen **transit lounge** (transport) Warteraum für Transitpassagiere (-räume) *nm* **transit passenger** (transport) Durchreisende/r *nmf*
transmit *vb* senden *vb*
transnational *adj* überstaatlich *adj*
transport *n* Transport *nm* **transport agent** Spediteur (-e) *nm* **air transport** Lufttransport *nm* **transport company** Verkehrsbetrieb (-e) *nm* **public transport** öffentlicher Verkehr *nm* **rail transport** Bahntransport *nm* **road transport** Straßentransport *nm*
transportation *n* Versand *nm*
transship *vb* umladen *vb*
travel *n* **travel agency** Reisebüro (-s) *nn* **air travel** Flugreisen *nfpl* **business travel** Geschäftsreisen *nfpl* **travel insurance** Reiseversicherung *nf*
traveller, traveler (US) *n* Reisende/r *nmf*
traveller's cheque, traveler's check (US) Reisescheck (-s) *nm*
travelling, traveling (US) *n* Reisen *nn* **travelling expenses, travel expenses** (US) Reisespesen *npl*
treasurer *n* **treasurer check (US)** Schatzanweisung *nf* **company treasurer** Finanzdirektor (-en) *nmf*
treasury *n* **Treasury bill** Schatzanweisung (-en) *nf* **the Treasury** britisches Finanz-

ministerium (-ien) *nn* **the Treasury Department (US)** US-Finanzministerium *nn*
treaty *n* Vertrag (-äge) *nm* **commercial treaty** Handelsabkommen (-) *nn* **to make a treaty** einen Vertrag abschließen
trend *n* Trend (-s) *nm* **trend analysis** Trendanalyse (-n) *nf* **current trend** aktueller Trend (-s) *nm* **economic trend** Konjunkturverlauf *nm* **market trend** Markttrend (-s) *nm* **price trend** Preisentwicklung (-en) *nf* **to buck a trend** der Konjunkturentwicklung entgegenhandeln **to set a trend** richtungsweisend sein *vb*
trial *n* **trial and error** Ausprobieren *nn* **trial offer** Probeangebot (-e) *nn* **trial period** Probezeit *nf* **to carry out trials** Tests durchführen
tribunal *n* **industrial tribunal** Arbeitsgericht (-e) *nn*
trim *vb* (investment) kürzen *vb* (workforce) abbauen *vb*
trimming *n* Kürzung *nf* **cost trimming** Kosteneinsparung *nf*
trip *n* **business trip** Geschäftsreise (-n) *nf* **round trip** Rundfahrt (-en) *nf*
triplicate *n* dreifache Ausführung *nf* **in triplicate** in dreifacher Ausführung
trust *n* Vertrauen *nn* **trust agreement** Treuhandvertrag (-äge) *nm* **trust company** Trust (-s) *nm* **trust estate** Treuhandvermögen (-) *nn* **trust fund** Treuhandmittel *nnpl* **investment trust** Kapitalanlagegesellschaft *nf* **to hold sth in trust** treuhänderisch verwalten **to set up a trust** eine Stiftung errichten **to supply sth on trust** auf Kredit liefern *vb* **unit trust** Kapitalanlagegesellschaft (-en) *nf*
trustee *n* Treuhänder (-) *nm* **trustee department** (bank) Sparkasse (-n) *nf*
trusteeship *n* Treuhandschaft *nf*
try out *vb* probieren *vb*
turn *vb* (market) ändern *vb*
turn down *vb* (offer) ablehnen *vb*
turn on *vb* (machine) einschalten *vb*
turn out *vb* (end) sich herausstellen *vb*
turn over *vb* wenden *vb*
turnabout *n* Umkehr *nf*
turning *adj* **turning point** Wendepunkt (-e) *nm*
turnover *n* Umsatz (-ätze) *nm* **capital turnover** Kapitalumschlag *nm* **turnover rate** Umsatzrate (-n) *nf* **turnover ratio** Umsatzquote (-n) *nf* **turnover tax** Umsatzsteuer (-n) *nf*

twenty-four adj **twenty-four-hour service** Dienst rund um die Uhr nm
two adj zwei adj **two-speed** Zweigang-cpd **two-tier** zweistufig adj **two-way** zweibahnig adj
tycoon n Großindustrielle/r nmf
type 1. n **bold type** Fettschrift nf, fett gedruckt adj **italic type** Kursivdruck nm **large type** Großgedrucktes nn **small type** Kleingedrucktes nn **2.** vb tippen vb
typewriter n Schreibmaschine (-n) nf
typing n Tippen nn **typing error** Tippfehler (-) nm
typist n Typist/in (-en/-innen) nm/nf
ultimo adj letzte/r adj
unanimous adj einstimmig adj
uncleared adj (customs) unabgefertigt adj (cheque) noch nicht verrechnet adj
unconditional adj bedingungslos adj
unconfirmed adj unbestätigt adj
undeclared adj (goods) nicht deklariert adj
undercapitalized adj unterkapitalisiert adj
undercharge vb zu wenig berechnen vb
undercut vb unterbieten vb
underdeveloped adj **underdeveloped country** Entwicklungsland (-länder) nn
underemployed adj unterbeschäftigt adj
underinsured adj zu niedrig versichert
underpay vb unterbezahlen vb
underpayment n Unterbezahlung (-en) nf
undersell vb verschleudern vb
understanding n Vereinbarung nf
undersubscribed adj unpopulär adj
undertake vb unternehmen vb
undertaking n Unternehmen (-) nn
undervalue vb unterbewerten vb
underwrite vb (risk) Versicherung unter Risikoverteilung übernehmen
underwriter n Unterzeichner (-), Versicherungsagent (-en)
undischarged adj (bankrupt) nicht rehabilitiert adj
unearned adj **unearned income** Einkünfte aus Kapitalvermögen npl
unemployed adj arbeitslos adj
unemployment n Arbeitslosigkeit nf **unemployment benefit** Arbeitslosenunterstützung nf **unemployment insurance** Arbeitslosenversicherung nf **level of unemployment** Arbeitslosenziffer (-n) nf **rate of unemployment** Arbeitslosenrate (-n) nf
unexpected adj unerwartet adj
unfair adj **unfair dismissal** ungerechtfertigte Kündigung (-en) nf

unforeseen adj **unforeseen circumstances** unvorhergesehene Umstände nmpl
unification n Vereinigung nf
unilateral adj (contract) einseitig bindend adj
uninsurable adj nicht versicherungsfähig adj
union n Verband (-bände) nm, Gewerkschaft (-en) nf **union membership** Gewerkschaftsmitgliedschaft nf **union representative** Gewerkschaftsvertreter (-) nm **trade union, labor union** (US) Gewerkschaft (-en) nf
unit n Einheit (-en) nf **unit cost** Stückkosten npl **unit of production** Produktionseinheit (-en) nf **unit price** Stückpreis (-e) nm **unit trust** Kapitalanlagegesellschaft (-en) nf
united adj vereint adj **the United Nations** die Vereinten Nationen nfpl
unlimited adj unbeschränkt adj **unlimited company** Gesellschaft mit unbeschränkter Haftung (-en) nf **unlimited credit** Blankokredit (-e) nm **unlimited liability** unbeschränkte Haftung nf
unload vb entladen vb
unmarketable adj unverkäuflich adj
unofficial adj inoffiziell adj **unofficial strike** wilder Streik (-s) nm
unpack vb auspacken vb
unpaid adj unbezahlt adj **unpaid balance** Restschuld (-en) nf **unpaid bill** unbezahlter Wechsel (-) nm **unpaid cheque** unbezahlter Scheck (-s) nm
unprofessional adj unfachkaufmännisch adj
unprofitable adj unprofitabel adj
unsaleable adj unverkäuflich adj
unsatisfactory adj unzureichend adj
unsecured adj ungesichert adj **unsecured bond** ungesicherter Schuldschein (-e) nm **unsecured credit** offener Kredit nm
unskilled adj ungelernt adj **unskilled worker** Hilfsarbeiter (-) nm
unsold adj unverkauft adj
unsolicited adj freiwillig adj **unsolicited offer** unverbindliches Angebot (-e) nn
up-to-date adj aktuell adj **to bring sth up-to-date** etwas auf den neuesten Stand bringen
update vb (records) auf den neuesten Stand bringen vb
upgrade vb befördern vb
upswing n Aufschwung (-ünge) nm
upturn n Aufschwung (-ünge) nm
upward adj Aufwärts- cpd aufwärts adv

upward trend Aufwärtsentwicklung (-en) nf
urban adj städtisch adj **urban renewal** Stadterneuerung nf **urban sprawl** Stadtausbreitung nf
urgency n Dringlichkeit nf **a matter of urgency** dringende Angelegenheit (-en) nf
urgent adj dringend adj
urgently adv dringlich adv
usage n Brauch nm, Praxis nf **intensive usage** intensive Anwendung nf
use n verwenden vb, benützen vb **to make use of sth** Gebrauch machen von
user-friendly adj benutzerfreundlich adj
usury n Wucher nm
utility n Nutzen nm **marginal utility** Grenznutzen nm **public utility** Versorgungsbetrieb (-e) nm
utilization n Verwendung nf
utilize vb verwenden vb
vacancy n freie Stelle (-n) nf
vacant adj leer adj
valid adj gültig adj
validate vb anerkennen vb
validity n Gültigkeit nf
valuable adj wertvoll adj
valuation n Wertung (-en) nf
value n Wert (-e) nm **face value** Nennwert (-e) nm **market value** Marktwert (-e) nm **to gain value** an Wert zunehmen **to get value for one's money** preiswert kaufen **to lose value** an Wert verlieren
variable adj veränderlich adj **variable costs** veränderliche Kosten npl **variable rate** veränderlicher Kurs (-e) nm
variance n **budget variance** Budgetabweichung (-en) nm
VAT (value added tax) abbr Mehrwertsteuer (-n) nf, MwSt abbr
vendee n Käufer (-) nm
vending machine n Automat (-en) nm
vendor n Verkäufer (-) nm **vendor capital** Verkaufskapital nn **joint vendor** Mitverkäufer (-) nm
verbatim adv wörtlich adj
vertical n vertikal adj, senkrecht adj **vertical integration** Vertikalintegration nf
vested adj übertragen vb **vested interests** finanzielle Beteiligung nf **vested rights** erworbene Rechte nnpl
veto 1. n Einspruch (-sprüche) nm 2. vb Einspruch einlegen gegen
viability n Leistungsfähigkeit nf
video n Video (-s) nn, Videofilm (-s) nm, Videorekorder (-) nm **video facilities** Videogeräte nnpl

viewer n Zuschauer (-) nm
VIP (very important person) n VIP (-s) nm, prominente Persönlichkeit (-en) nf
visa n Visum (-en) nn
visible adj sichtbar adj **visible exports** Warenausfuhr nf
visit 1. n Besuch (-e) nm 2. vb besuchen vb
visitor n Besucher (-) nm
visual adj visuell adj **visual display unit (VDU)** Sichtgerät (-e) nn **visual telephone** Sichtfernsprecher (-) nm
vocational adj Berufs- cpd
volatile adj (prices) unbeständig adj
volume n Volumen nn **volume discount** Mengenrabatt (-e) nm **trading volume** Handelsvolumen nn
voluntary adj freiwillig adj **to go into voluntary liquidation** in freiwillige Liquidation treten **voluntary wage restraint** freiwillige Lohnbegrenzung nf
vote 1. n Stimme (-n) nf **vote of no confidence** Mißtrauensantrag (-äge) nm **vote of thanks** Dankadresse (-n) nf 2. vb abstimmen vb
voting adj Abstimmung nf **voting right** Stimmrecht nn
voucher n Gutschein (-e) nm
wage 1. adj **wage demand** Lohnforderung (-en) nf **wage earner** Verdiener (-) nm **wage increase** Lohnerhöhung (-en) nf **wage negotiations** Lohnverhandlungen nfpl **wage packet, salary package** (US) Lohntüte (-n) nf **wage policy** Lohnpolitik nf **wage restraint** Verhinderung von Lohnsteigerungen nf **wage rise** Lohnerhöhung (-en) nf **wage(s) agreement** Tarifabkommen (-) nn **wage(s) bill** Lohnetat nm **wage scale** Lohntarif (-e) nm **wage(s) claim** Lohnanspruch (-sprüche) nm **wage(s) freeze** Lohnstopp (-s) nm **wage(s) settlement** Tarifabkommen (-) nn 2. n Lohn (-öhne) nm **average wage** Durchschnittslohn (-löhne) nm **minimum wage** Mindestlohn (-löhne) nm **net(t) wage** Nettolohn (-löhne) nm **real wage** Reallohn (-löhne) nm **starting wage** Anfangslohn (-löhne) nm 3. vb führen vb **to wage a campaign** eine Kampagne führen
waiting n Warten nn **waiting list** Warteliste (-n) nf
waive vb verzichten (auf) vb
waiver n Verzicht nm **waiver clause** Verzichtsleistungsklausel (-n) nf

wall *n* Mauer (-n) *nf* tariff wall Zollmauer (-n) *nf* to go to the wall in Konkurs gehen *vb* Wall Street (US) Wallstreet *nf* war *n* Krieg (-e) *nm* price war Preiskampf (-kämpfe) *nm* trade war Wirtschaftskrieg (-e) *nm*

warehouse *n* Lagerhaus (-häuser) *nn* bonded warehouse Transitlager (-) *nn* warehousing *n* Lagerhaltung *nf*

wares *npl* Waren *nfpl*

warn *vb* warnen *vb* to warn sb against doing sth jemandem von einer Sache abraten

warning *n* Warnung (-en) *nf* due warning rechtzeitiger Bescheid *nm* warning sign Alarmzeichen (-) *nn* without warning unerwartet *adj*

warrant 1. *n* Vollmacht *nf* warrant for payment Zahlungsanweisung (-en) *nf* 2. *vb* bestätigen *vb*, garantieren *vb*

warranty *n* Garantie (-n) *nf*, Berechtigung (-en) *nf* under warranty unter Garantie

wastage *n* Verschleiß *nm* wastage rate Verlustquote (-n) *nf*

waste 1. *adj* waste products Abfallprodukte *nnpl* 2. *n* Verschwendung *nf* industrial waste Industriemüll *nm* waste of time Zeitvergeudung *nf* to go to waste verkümmern *vb*, ungenutzt sein 3. *vb* verschwenden *vb*

wasting *adj* wasting asset kurzlebiges Wirtschaftsgut (-güter) *nn*

watch *vb* beobachten *vb* to watch developments Entwicklungen verfolgen

watchdog *n* (fig.) Wachthund (-e) *nm* watchdog committee Überwachungsausschuß (-üsse) *nm*

water down *vb* verdünnen *vb*, verwässern *vb*

watered *adj* verwässert *adj* watered capital verwässertes Aktienkapital *nn* watered stock verwässertes Aktienkapital *nn*

watertight *adj* (fig.) stichhaltig *adj*

wave *n* (of mergers, takeovers) Welle (-n) *nf*

wavelength *n* Wellenlänge (-n) *nf* to be on the same wavelength auf derselben Wellenlänge sein

weaken *vb* (market) schwächer werden *vb*

wealth *n* Reichtum *nm*, Vermögen *nn* national wealth Volksvermögen *nn* wealth tax Vermögenssteuer (-n) *nf*

week *n* Woche (-n) *nf* twice a week zweimal wöchentlich *adj* working week Arbeitswoche (-n) *nf*

weekly *adj* wöchentlich *adj* weekly wages Wochenlöhne *npl*

weigh *vb* abwägen *vb*, abwiegen *vb* to weigh the pros and cons das Für und Wider abwägen

weight *n* Gewicht *nn* dead weight Eigengewicht *nn* excess weight Mehrgewicht *nn*, Übergewicht *nn* gross weight Bruttogewicht *nn* net(t) weight Nettogewicht *nn* weights and measures Maße und Gewichte *npl*

weighted *adj* beeinflußt *adj*, verfälscht *adj* weighted average Bewertungsdurchschnitt (-e) *nm* weighted index Bewertungsindex (-en) *nm*

weighting *n* Zulage *nf*

weighty *adj* gewichtig *adj*

welfare 1. *adj* welfare benefits Sozialhilfeleistung *nf* welfare state Wohlfahrtsstaat (-en) *nm* 2. *n* Wohl *nn*

well-advised *adj* gut beraten *adj*

well-informed *adj* wohl informiert *adj*

well-known *adj* bekannt *adj*

well-made *adj* solide *adj*, von guter Qualität *adj*

well-paid *adj* gutbezahlt *adj*

well-tried *adj* wohlerprobt *adj*, bewährt *adj*

WEU (Western European Union) *abbr* Westeuropäische Union *nf*

white *adj* white-collar worker Angestellte/r *nmf*

wholesale *n* Großhandel *nm* at/by wholesale im Großhandel, en gros wholesale price Großhandelspreis (-e) *nm* wholesale trade Großhandel *nm*

wholesaler *n* Großhändler (-) *nm*

wholly *adv* vollständig *adj* wholly-owned subsidiary hundertprozentige Tochtergesellschaft (-en) *nf*

wide-ranging *adj* weit *adj*, breit *adj*

will *n* Testament (-e) *nn*

win *vb* gewinnen *vb* win customers Kunden gewinnen to win support Unterstützung finden

wind up *vb* beendigen *vb*

windfall *n* unerwarteter Glücksfall (-fälle) *nm* windfall profit unerwarteter Gewinn (-e) *nm*

winding-up *n* Liquidation *nf* winding-up arrangements Liquidationsmaßnahmen *nfpl* winding-up order Konkursbeschluß (-üsse) *nm*

window *n* Fenster (-) *nn* window of opportunity Chance (-n) *nf*, Gelegenheit (-en) *nf*

withdraw vb zurückziehen vb **to withdraw an offer** ein Angebot zurückziehen **withdrawal** n Zurückziehen nn **withdrawal of funds** Abhebungen nfpl **withhold** vb vorenthalten vb **to withhold a document** eine Urkunde nicht herausgeben **withstand** vb standhalten vb **witness** 1. n Zeuge (-n) nm 2. vb bezeugen vb **to witness a signature** beglaubigen vb **word** n Wort nn **word processing** Textverarbeitung nf **word processor** Textverarbeitungsgerät (-e) nn **to give one's word** versprechen vb **to keep one's word** sein Wort halten **wording** n Wortlaut nm **work** 1. adj **work experience** Berufserfahrung nf **work permit** Arbeitsgenehmigung (-en) nf **work schedule** Arbeitsplan (-pläne) nm **work sharing** Arbeitsteilung nf **work study** Zeitstudie (-n) nf 2. n Arbeit nf **casual work** Gelegenheitsarbeit nf **day off work** freier Tag (-e) nm **day's work** Tagewerk nn **factory work** Fabrikarbeit nf **office work** Bürotätigkeit nf **to be in work** berufstätig sein vb **to be out of work** arbeitslos sein vb **to look for work** Arbeit suchen 3. vb arbeiten vb **to work to rule** Dienst nach Vorschrift machen **to work unsocial hours** außerhalb der normalen Arbeitszeit arbeiten vb
workable adj durchführbar adj
workaholic n Arbeitswütige/r nmf
workday (US) n Arbeitstag (-e) nm
worker n Arbeiter (-) nm **casual worker** Gelegenheitsarbeiter (-) nm **clerical worker** Bürokraft (-kräfte) nf **workerdirector** Arbeiterdirektor (-en) nm **manual worker** manueller Arbeiter (-) nm **worker participation** Mitbestimmung nf **skilled worker** Facharbeiter (-) nm **unskilled worker** Hilfsarbeiter (-) nm
workforce n Belegschaft nf
working adj berufstätig adj, funktionierend adj **working agreement** Absprache (-n) nf **working area** Arbeitsbereich (-e) nm **working capital** Betriebskapital nn **working conditions** Arbeitsbedingungen nfpl **working environment** Arbeitsumwelt nf **working hours** Arbeitszeit nf **working knowledge** Grundkenntnisse nfpl **working language** offizielle Sprache (-n) nf **working life** Berufsleben nn **working majority** ar-

beitsfähige Mehrheit nf **working model** Modell (-e) nn **working paper** Arbeitspapier (-e) nn **working party** Arbeitsgemeinschaft (-en) nf, Arbeitsgruppe (-n) nf **working population** arbeitende Bevölkerung nf **working week (GB)** Arbeitswoche (-n) nf
workload n Arbeit nf
workmate n Mitarbeiter (-) nm, Arbeitskollege (-n) nm
workplace n Arbeitsplatz nm
works n Betrieb nm **public works programme (GB)** öffentliches Bauprogramm (-e) nn **works committee** Betriebsausschuß (-üsse) nm **works council** Betriebsrat (-räte) nm **works manager** Werksleiter (-) nm
workshop n Werkstatt nf
workweek (US) n Arbeitswoche (-n) nf
world n Welt nf **the commercial world** Handelskreise nmpl **world consumption** Weltverbrauch nm **world exports** Weltexporte npl **world fair** Weltausstellung (-en) nf **World Bank** Weltbank nf **World Court** Weltgerichtshof (-höfe) nm
worldwide adj weltweit adj
worth adj wert adj **to be worth** wert sein vb
wpm (words per minute) abbr Anschläge pro Minute npl
wreck vb zerstören vb
writ n gerichtliche Verfügung (-en) nf **to issue a writ** eine Verfügung herausgeben vb
write down vb (depreciation) Wert herabsetzen vb
write off vb (debts) abschreiben vb (vehicle) zu Schrott fahren vb
write-off n Abschreibung nf, Totalschaden nm
wrongful adj unrechtmäßig adj **wrongful dismissal** unberechtigte Entlassung (-en) nf
xerox vb fotokopieren vb
Xerox (R) n (machine) Fotokopiermaschine (-n) nf
year n Jahr (-e) nn **year-end dividend** Sonderdividende am Schluß des Jahres (-n) nf **year-end inventory** Jahresschlußinventar (-e) nn **financial year** Geschäftsjahr (-e) nn **fiscal year** Steuerjahr (-e) nn **tax year** Steuerjahr (-e) nn
yearly adj jährlich adj **yearly income** Jahreseinkommen nn
yellow adj gelb adj **the Yellow pages (R) (GB)** Branchenverzeichnis (-isse) nn

yen *n* (currency) Yen *nm* **yen bond** Yen-Auslandsanleihe (-n) *nf*
yield 1. *adj* **yield curve** Renditekurve (-n) *nf* **2.** *n* Ertrag *nm* **yield on shares** Aktienrendite *nf* **3.** *vb* bringen *vb*
young *adj* jung *adj* **young economy** junge Wirtschaft (-en) *nf*
zenith *n* Höhepunkt (-e) *nm*
zero *n* Null *nf* **zero address** Adresse unbekannt **below zero** unter Null **zero defect** fehlerfrei *adj* **zero growth** Nullwachstum *nn* **zero hour** Stunde Null *nf* **zero rate/rating** abgabenfrei *adj* **zero-rate taxation** steuerfrei *adj* **to be zero-rated for VAT** mehrwertsteuerfrei *adj*
zip code (US) *n* Postleitzahl (-en) *nf*
zone 1. *n* Zone (-n) *nf* **currency zone** Währungsgebiet (-e) *nn* **enterprise zone** wirtschaftliches Fördergebiet (-e) *nn* **postal zone** Postbezirk (-e) *nm* **time zone** Zeitzone (-n) *nf* **wage zone** Tarifzone (-n) *nf* **2.** *vb* in Zonen einteilen *vb*
zoning *n* Einteilung in Zonen *nf*